Battle of Killiecrankie 1689

The Last Act *of the* Killing Times

Battle of Killiecrankie 1689

THE LAST ACT *of the* KILLING TIMES

STUART REID

Frontline Books

BATTLE OF KILLIECRANKIE 1689
The Last Act of the Killing Times

This edition published in 2018 by Frontline Books,
an imprint of Pen & Sword Books Ltd,
47 Church Street, Barnsley, S. Yorkshire, S70 2AS

ISBN: 978-1-52670-994-3

CIP data records for this title are available from the British Library

Pen & Sword Books Limited incorporates the imprints of Atlas,
Archaeology, Aviation, Discovery, Family History, Fiction, History, Maritime,
Military, Military Classics, Politics, Select, Transport, True Crime, Air World,
Frontline Publishing, Leo Cooper, Remember When, Seaforth Publishing,
The Praetorian Press, Wharncliffe Local History, Wharncliffe Transport,
Wharncliffe True Crime and White Owl.

For more information on our books, please visit
www.frontline-books.com
email info@frontline-books.com
or write to us at the above address.

Printed and bound by TJ International Ltd, Padstow, Cornwall

Typeset in 10.5/12.5 Palatino

Contents

Introduction

The battle of Killiecrankie, which was fought on 27 July 1689, probably ranks as one of the four most famous battles in Scottish history; following closely after Culloden, Bannockburn and Flodden. It was certainly a dramatic battle and arguably it was also probably the only occasion when the Highland clans really did roar down a mountainside in an avalanche of steel – the battle of Prestonpans in 1745 by contrast was fought on a flat Lothian cornfield bisected by an early railway line! However, for that very reason, the battle itself, unlike its background and its protagonists, has been a curiously neglected one. While the Highland war, and the Jacobite risings which followed have received no lack of attention, Killiecrankie, despite a well-known song, tends to be hurried over simply because of its apparent brevity and a belief that there is little to tell, and all of it uncontroversial. As the defeated General Mackay himself recalled, when the Highlanders crashed into his battle-line; 'he turned about to see how matters stood, and found that all his left had given way, and got down the hill which was behind our line, ranged a little above the brow thereof, so that in the twinkling of an eye in a manner, our men, as well as the ennemy, were out of sight, being got doun pall mall to the river where our baggage stood.'

In a matter of moments, it seemed, the clansmen charged down the hill and the redcoats ran away. Done – sorted. Yet, when we look at Killiecrankie more closely, there was rather more to it than that. The battle may indeed have been lost and won 'in the twinkling of an eye', but it was certainly not all over. After that first decisive clash, devastating though it was for both sides, the fighting continued until well after dark when the defeated army withdrew in relatively good order. Yet thereafter the battle was reduced in rhyme to all but a few lines before proceeding to elegies of lost leaders. This not only fails to explain what really happened during the battle, and why it turned out the way it did, but it does a disservice to those who fought and died there – on both sides.

Moreover, while the Highland War of 1689 is popularly accounted to be the first of the Jacobite risings which dominated Scottish history for fully half a century, it was actually very different in character from the eighteenth century risings which followed it. Indeed, the very term Jacobite would not be coined until sometime afterwards and while there is no dispute that the term is derived from the Latin *Jacobus*, signifying James, in writing this book the earliest instance of its use which I can find comes in General Mackay's memoires, written or dictated before his death in 1692, but probably no earlier than 1691. I cannot find a single use of the term in Scotland during 1689-90. Of itself this might be accounted mere semantics, but the fact of the matter is that the Highland War of 1689 was not a straightforward uprising in favour of an exiled rightful, lawful king. Instead, it was primarily the last act of a much more fundamental struggle which began in 1638 with the signing of the National Covenant. Killiecrankie and the Highland War was, in reality, the last act of the wars of the Covenant and the Killing Time that followed.[i]

In the popular imagination, those later risings of 1715 and 1745 pitted English Redcoats against Scottish Highlanders, in a proxy conflict between a German king in London and the 'rightful lawful king over the water'. But by then, after the Union of 1707, the Jacobites were more concerned with reasserting Scotland's independence than with upholding the pretentions of the old house of Stuart. By contrast that overt nationalist element was completely lacking in 1689. The overwhelming majority of the Redcoats at Killiecrankie were Scots Presbyterians, not Englishmen. Indeed, only one English regiment fought there and had its counterpart in an equally solitary Irish regiment on the other side. And if the majority of King James's soldiers were Highland clansman, King William's general, Hugh Mackay of Scourie, was himself a Highlander. In name and, in actuality, it was two *Scottish* armies which met at Killiecrankie.

Note on Terminology:
Cavalry will be found referred to as either Horse or Dragoons and in theory the two were quite different. The first were regarded as heavy cavalry, sometimes wearing armour and consequently requiring large strong horses. They were armed with broadswords, carbines and pistols. Dragoons on the other hand were intended to be mounted infantry albeit in practice they proved very reluctant to fight on foot

unless absolutely compelled to do so. They principally differed from Horse in carrying infantry firelocks instead of carbines and riding smaller and cheaper (but much sturdier) nags.

Infantry, more frequently referred to as Foot, were variously armed with muskets, firelocks and pikes, which will be properly discussed in due course, but for the present it should be noted that muskets were normally matchlocks (so called because the powder charge was ignited by a length of burning slow-match) and not therefore to be confused with fusils and firelocks, the contemporary term for what we generally recognise as flintlocks.

Spelling in the seventeenth century was an uncertain business and advantage has been taken of this to use common variations in order to distinguish between people and places. For example, Atholl is an area in Perthshire, which was largely in the hands of the Marquess of *Athole*, and likewise Argyll was dominated by the Earl of *Argyle*. Unfortunately, while Dundee was occasionally spelled *Dundie*, the latter spelling is more likely to confuse than enlighten.

List of Maps

Chapter 1

The Killing Time

The new century had opened promisingly enough with the happy accession of King James VI of Scotland to sit on the English throne in 1603. James himself unquestionably did well out of the move and smugly boasted that; 'Here I sit and govern it with my pen: I write and it is done: and by a Clerk of the Council I govern Scotland, which others could not do by the Sword.'[1] So he did, and no longer need he fear waking to find a ring of armed men standing in his bedchamber intent on abduction or worse, but with that security came a remoteness which was hardly calculated to bind King and people together as one, or to soften the blow when his son, Charles I, embarked upon a disastrous experiment in absolutism.

It was bad enough that for most of his reign Charles ruled Scotland without recourse to calling a Parliament and even neglected to venture north for his coronation until 1633, fully eight years after his accession. Unfortunately, at that point his benign neglect of his northern kingdom was replaced by a succession of moves aimed, amongst other things, at bringing the Scottish church into conformity with the controversial reforms being enacted in the Church of England. Two generations before, Scotland had firmly embraced the Protestant Reformation and, in particular, the teachings of John Calvin of Geneva. The Church of Scotland, familiarly known simply as the Kirk, became a Presbyterian one and this in turn saw a greater degree of democracy in both church and state. The Scots Parliament traditionally comprised three collegiate estates; the lords or tenants in chief, holding lands directly from the crown; the representatives of the royal burghs, and the Kirk. The latter had once been found from among the bishops, but after the reformation their seats were filled by ordinary ministers and lay representatives of their presbyteries. King James insisted on the return of bishops in 1610, (but only as presidents of their presbyteries and therefore still very much accountable to them) was otherwise content to let well alone, but Charles made the fatal mistake of insisting on overturning this pragmatic settlement by returning to a full-blown Episcopalian system with a Kirk firmly controlled by a hierarchy of bishops who were held directly accountable to the Crown as head of the church. At one and the same time, he also quite casually attempted to emasculate the great magnates or Lords of Parliament through the recovery of feus and other taxes attaching to church lands acquired by their families during the Reformation – monies which were now needed to support the ecclesiastical reformation. Not surprisingly, he soon found himself in trouble. In 1638, exactly fifty years before the Glorious Revolution, opposition to the King's autocratic reforms took concrete shape in the signing of the National Covenant, binding Scotland's people and Kirk together. Then came the Great Civil War, catastrophic defeat and the ten-year long Cromwellian occupation of Scotland which ended with the Restoration of King Charles II in 1660. Scotland's constitution, laws and religion were her own once again, but by then her once great magnates were dead or bankrupted by the wars and no longer able to influence politics as their fathers had done by simply raising their banners. Moreover, after a brief but humiliating reign as a Presbyterian client in 1650-51, Charles II pointedly declined to ever set foot in Scotland again and instead, just as his royal grandfather had done, he governed it distantly for the next twenty-five years by the pen and through a succession of expendable Royal Commissioners and a secret council appointed without reference to Parliament.

An 'Act Recissory', was passed in 1661 rendering null and void all legislation enacted since the coronation of Charles I in 1633 and a corresponding act of Indemnity and Oblivion also followed as a matter of course. Bygones were to be bygones and forgiveness offered to all but a token handful of individuals, but in reality, there was far too much unfinished business which was to dominate Scottish politics to the end of the century and beyond. Not unexpectedly, the greatest problems still centred around religion. While the Recission was confidently followed by another Act confirming the continuance of a Presbyterian Kirk; this was effectively nullified by the restoration of Episcopacy proclaimed on 6 September 1661 and in the following year all ministers of the Kirk were required to renounce the Covenant or lose their livings.

Upwards of 270 of them, perhaps a third of the total, stuck by the Covenant and refused to recognise the authority of the new bishops set over them. Having suffered the threatened consequences, they then took to preaching at outdoor services or conventicles. Naturally enough the authorities took a dim view of this defiance, but their resources for dealing with the problem were limited. Until then there had been no such thing as a Scottish Army, or at least not a regular standing army paid for out of the King's revenues. Instead, the government had relied time out of mind on levying out fencible men for 'the Scottish service' only as and when required, and almost invariably only in time of actual or threatened war, but in May 1662 Charles ordered the raising of six Scottish companies of foot, which were then regimented in 1664 under the Earl of Linlithgow, first as 'the King's Regiment' and afterwards 'His Majesty's Regiment of Guards'.[2] Three of the companies served as the garrisons of Edinburgh, Stirling and Dumbarton castles, but the rest went to Glasgow and the south-west to serve as an armed police force, under the command of Sir James Turner.

THE 'PENTLAND RISING' 1666

Like most of the regiment's officers, Turner was a veteran of the Civil War and the earlier wars on the Continent as well. Born in Dalkeith in about 1615, he was a good soldier, but a hard and totally unscrupulous one of flexible loyalties. Once a major general, by November 1666 he had been promoted to lieutenant colonel of the regiment and was busy levying fines on recalcitrant Covenanters and generally throwing his weight about in Dumfriesshire, when a rebellion quite unexpectedly broke out. His regime was not particularly harsh by the standards of the time as he had no great inclination to religion, but on 13 November, a small party of his soldiers arrested an old man at Dalry for non-payment of the fines due for his failing to attend the Kirk. Stirred up by a couple of fugitive Covenanters who were eating breakfast in a nearby inn, a mob rescued the old man and in the process shot and wounded the corporal in charge of the soldiers.[3] Without the shooting the incident might have been accounted of little consequence but the ringleaders were already wanted men with nothing to lose, so while the unfortunate Corporal Deane was put on the back of a horse and sent off to Dumfries for treatment, they invited others to join them and forestall the expected 'terrible reprisals'. As it happened, since March 1665 England had been at war with Holland and although Charles' other kingdom of Scotland was incidentally but peripherally involved in what was essentially a maritime conflict, most of Turner's troops had been recalled to man coastal fortifications such as the citadel at Leith. Consequently, he only had some seventy infantry at hand, and with most of them scattered in small parties up and down Annandale and Nithsdale, a third of them had been taken prisoner by the time the insurgents entered Dumfries early on the morning of 15 November. There

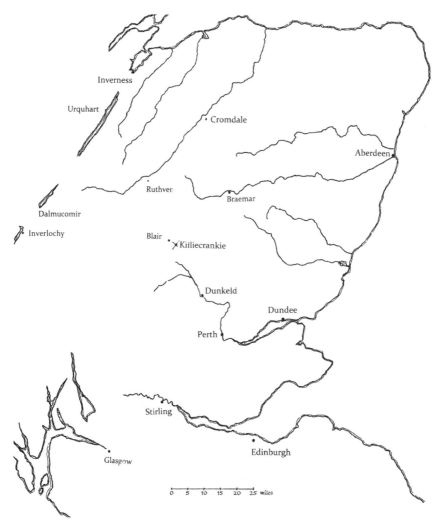

Above: Scotland in 1689. Most of Scotland was mountainous and devoid of proper roads. For all practical purposes, the only crossing point between southern Scotland and the rest of the country was by way of Stirling. From time to time the rebels attempted to by-pass Stirling to the west by way of Balquhidder and Mentieth but the small forces involved were easily blocked. Further north, the key to movement into the hills was by way of the numerous river valleys.

they seized Turner himself, still wearing only his nightshirt, drawers and socks, and, despite the cold, paraded him around for some time in that state before allowing him to get dressed.

4

Already they numbered some fifty horse 'provided with cloaks girded over their shoulder for fighting' (i.e. rolled tightly as a protection against sword-cuts) and perhaps as many as 200 foot. A little incongruously, having secured Turner, they then drank the King's health by way of declaring that their quarrel was only with the newly re-instated bishops, not with the Crown. There were suggestions afterwards that the outbreak may have anticipated a more serious insurrection proposed for the following Spring, but it seems unlikely. On the contrary, the unpremeditated nature of the rising grew painfully obvious over the next few days as the rebels wandered aimlessly around the south-west. Beyond Dumfriesshire there were no lack of recruits in Ayrshire and Clydesdale, despite constant heavy rain which ought to have kept honest men at home and although they declined to attack Glasgow on hearing that it was held by Major General Thomas Dalyell of The Binns, a terrifying veteran of the Russian service and ruthless servant of the Crown, a rendezvous at the Bridge of Doon on 21 November discovered them to be 700 strong.

There they were joined by another Civil War veteran, Colonel James Wallace of Auchans. It was Wallace who now started to turn the insurgents into a proper army by organising them into troops and companies, although he had great trouble in finding men able and willing to act as officers. He was also sensible enough to recognise that marching around in circles was a recipe for disaster, especially as the weather showed no sign of improving. Accordingly, the Covenanters marched eastwards, rather uncertainly heading for Edinburgh, and pursuing an illusory hope that the capitol would rise in the name of the Covenant. By the time they reached Lanark on 25 November, Turner, expressing admiration for their marching ability, estimated them to number 450 horse and something over 500 Foot. Of those, the former he said were said reasonably well equipped, with most having swords, or pistols or both, but the armament of the foot amounted to no more than a bucolic assortment of muskets, pikes, scythes, pitchforks and even simple wooden staves.

From Lanark it went downhill and eventually on 28 November the rebels were brought to bay standing on Rullion Green, in the Pentland Hills, some miles south of Edinburgh. Finding Dalyell coming up fast, Wallace (on Turner's advice) immediately moved off the low green and took up a strong position 'on the syd off the turnhous hill, which is the westmost, greatest and highest off the pentlanhills, and the tope off it doeth just resemble the tope off Arthur's seat.'[4] Once on the top, Wallace divided his little force into three bodies, facing eastwards; on the Covenanters' right was the Galloway horse under Robert MacClellan

5

of Barscobe – the man who shot Corporal Deanes – and on the left wing the main body of the horse under Major Joseph Learmonth of Newholm. Wallace himself took post in the centre with the foot and waited for Dalyell to close up; 'Now there was a great glen [the Glencorse Burn] betwixt us, so as neither of us could have access to other. There we stood brandishing our swords.' All of those involved, either in the fighting or as onlookers, agreed as to the formidable obstacle formed by the burn and the difficulty of getting up the fearsomely steep slope to the Covenanters' position, but it had to be done, as Dalyell's second-in-command, Lieutenant General William Drummond colourfully related:

> [the rebels] were at Collintoune 2 myles from Edenburgh, on Tuesday the 27th by midday to our admiration whatever their designe or invitacon was for soe desperate a march they found their plot p'vented; wee judged rightly they would get of to Bigger and betook us to fall in their way going over the Pentland Hills at Currie, our fore party of 100 horse discovered them on their march toewards Linton the Bigger way near a place called Glencorse Kirk and with great boldness sett upon them, and endured the danger to face all their strength, horse and foot, until our cavalry far behind came up and that spent near 2 houres, soe had God blinded these fooles to neglect their advantage, our party being in a ground whence they could not come off: some sharp charges past in this time, wch the rebells gave and received with desperate resolucon to our prejudice, at last our horse comes on and gave breathing to that weary party, but our foot was yet 4 miles from us, we found it convenient to draw from that ground very advantageous for their foot wch they after much consideracon began to employ agst us but we prevented them and got off a little to a better ground where they made a fashion to annoy us without any gaine; so soon as our foot came up we put ourselves in order and embattled in a faire plaine upon their noses; they upon the hill above did the like but gave us noe disturbance tho well they might. [5]

Once everyone was arrived and in place, Dalyell's army amounted to two troops of Horse Guards[6], and six other troops belonging to Drummond's Regiment of Horse. As to the infantry, there were two regiments of foot; a part of the King's Regiment, and Dalyell's own newly raised one. Estimates giving the General something in the region of 600 cavalry and 2,000 infantry seem optimistic, but there is no doubt that he outnumbered the rebels and in any case he was running out of time and had to fight at once, for as Drummond continues: [7]

> By this time the sun was sett, we must make haste and advanced a partie of horse and foot from our right hand to assault their left wing of horse wch instantly came doune and met them, and there the work began, wee fought obstinately a long time with swords until they mixed like chessmen in a bag; wee advanced our right wing and they their left to give reliefe; there again it was disputed toughly; then came a strong party of foot from their body and forced out right wing back to the foot in some disorder, but this was instantly rectified, their right wing of horse came from their ground foolishly and crosses their foot, apprehending their left wing to be in distresse, wherein they were mistaken and soe gave our left wing their slack, wch opportunity wee hold on and there went their cavalrie in disorder; our whole body then advanced and beat in their horse upon their foot; then confusion and flight followed; we pursued in the dark, killed all the foot and but for the night and steep hills had wholly destroyed them. Some prisoners there are fit for examples, I know not how many, but I conjecture not above 140, for there was sound payment. Our losse I cannot tell, but it is greater than many of their skins were worth.

The actual figure for the Covenanters' loss seems to have been in the region of about fifty killed and eighty wounded and captured. Wallace escaped to Holland and enjoyed a respectable old age in exile. Turner and his remaining guards pragmatically swore an oath to protect each other and having delivered him safely to his own people he ensured that they were well treated and set at liberty.

The rising was then followed by the appointment of a new Commissioner in the shape of John Maitland, Earl of Lauderdale, and the experiment of a more conciliatory policy. Letters of Indulgence allowed ousted ministers to return to their parishes in return for undertakings to eschew secular dissent. This approach met with some initial success but ultimately proved a failure. The policy was simultaneously rejected by Presbyterian extremists as an affront to God and to his Kirk, and resented by the loyalist or Cavalier party as being a dangerous concession. Unsurprisingly, the latter opinion prevailed and preaching at conventicles was made a capital offence. Not only was mere attendance penalised by threats of fines and imprisonment, but landholders were now held accountable for the good behaviour of their tenants and dependents. Predictably enough, repression bred resistance, which in turn escalated the government's attempts at suppression, culminating in the employment of what became known as the Highland Host in 1678.

No fewer than 3,000 Lowland militia and 6,000 Highlanders were levied out for the statutory forty days service and settled at free quarters in Glasgow and the south-west in a heavy-handed but bloodless exercise in intimidation. The Highlanders descended upon their involuntary hosts, hung about with all manner of outlandish weapons and archaic pieces of armour calculated to appear intimidating, while the less flamboyant lowland militia were primarily and more legitimately employed in disarming their counterparts in Ayrshire, Renfrew and the other suspect shires. The exercise failed in its purpose of course, for the Covenanters were unintimidated and tension escalated still further with the murder of the Archbishop of St. Andrews by Presbyterian terrorists in 1679.

In the wake of this incident the situation again deteriorated and a contributory factor in the widening gulf between the parties may have been the advent of a new generation of protagonists. It is striking just how many veterans of the Civil War, fought at Rullion Green.[8] They might now differ in their politics, but back in the day they had been comrades in arms and there still existed a degree of rough sympathy between the two; but now there was a new generation arising, on both sides, unrestrained by old friendships, and amongst this new breed was a professional soldier from Angus, named John Graham of Claverhouse.

He was more than likely the John Graham given a lieutenant's commission in Sir William Lockhart's Regiment of Foot on 13 March 1672, but at all events he was soon riding as a volunteer cavalryman in the Dutch service at the battle of Seneffe on 11 August 1674.[9] Whether, as legend would have it, he saved the life of Prince William of Orange there seems doubtful, but two years later he became a rittmeester or captain and after returning home at the end of 1677 received a commission as a captain of horse in King Charles' Scottish army on 23 September 1678[10]

DRUMCLOG AND BOTHWELL BRIDGE 1679

As such on 1 June 1679, while carrying out a routine sweep with his own troop and Captain John Inglis' Dragoons[11], John Graham of Claverhouse stumbled upon a field conventicle at Drumclog, in south Lanarkshire. Afterwards Claverhouse, clearly suffering from shock, described what happened next, explaining that the Covenanters:

> when we came in sight of them, we found them drawn up in batell, upon a most advantagious ground, to which there was no coming but through mosses and lakes. They were not preaching … They consisted of four battalions of foot, and all well armed with fusils and pitchforks, and three squadrons of horse.

Ordinarily a vigorous cavalry charge ought to have dispersed the rabble, but it quickly transpired that they were safely drawn up behind a wide stank or marshy ditch. Rather than search for a way around it, Claverhouse dismounted a few of his dragoons and some ineffectual volleys were being exchanged when the Covenanters, led by an eighteen-year-old student named William Cleland, decided to attack, outflanked the left of Claverhouse' battle line and proceeded to briskly roll it up.[12]:

> and imediately advanced with there foot, the horse folowing: they came throght the lotche … they recaived our fyr, and advanced to shok: the first they gave us broght down the Coronet Mr Crafford and Captain Bleith, besides that with a pitchfork they made such an opening in my rone horse's belly, that his guts hung out half an elle, and yet he caryed me aff an myl: which so discoraged our men, that they sustained not the shok, but fell into disorder.[13]

While there is no reason to doubt that Claverhouse was carried off involuntarily by his dying horse, the sight of their commander running from the battlefield was hardly calculated to encourage the rest of his men to stand their ground, and with those other officers going down as well, the whole lot fled after him. In a few minutes, some thirty-six of them were killed; mostly dragoons caught before they could regain their horses, and on meeting reinforcements coming down from Glasgow under Lord Ross of the Foot Guards, they all immediately fell back on the city.

Next day the insurgents, massively reinforced, attempted to storm the place, but plagued by factionalism they proved incapable of co-ordinating their efforts and were beaten off surprisingly easily. Nevertheless, that night the Earl of Linlithgow, having received reports of both Claverhouse' rout and the subsequent battle for Glasgow, hastily ordered every unit capable of marching to concentrate at Stirling. This meant abandoning Glasgow to the rebels and Ross was ordered to evacuate the place and join Livingstone at Larbert. With 1,800 men, the general then changed his mind about abandoning Glasgow, but only got the length of Kilsyth before hearing that the rebels had not only forestalled him, but were increased in number to all of 7,000 strong. In response, the Privy Council ordered the mobilisation of the militia on 5 June and no fewer than eight 'fencible' regiments would be present when the rebellion was crushed at the battle of Bothwell Bridge on the river Clyde on 22 June 1679.[14] The brunt of the fighting there was nevertheless borne by the Scots Army's regulars in the shape of the regiment of Guards and the Earl of Mar's Regiment of Foot together with a number of independent troops of horse and dragoons.[15]

Oddly enough, however, the army was commanded there not by Livingstone, but by the King's natural son, James Scott, Duke of Buccleuch[16], who was temporarily appointed Commander in Chief as a matter of political expediency – and just as hurriedly relieved of the post as soon as the emergency was over. At least while he did command, he was obeyed. This was rather more than could be said for his opponents, who were still at odds over points of doctrine and bitterly divided between those prepared to accept the Letters of Indulgence and those who rejected them! It was young William Cleland who won the fight at Drumclog, but at Glasgow and Bothwell Bridge command of the rebel host was nominally confided to a fanatic named Robert Hamilton of Preston. Whatever his qualifications for the post of commander in chief, they did not include the ability to unite the army's squabbling factions. Consequently, only a bare handful of Covenanters were actively engaged under David Hackston of Rathillet in defending the bridge itself, while the main body of insurgents, under Preston, remained half a mile further back, on Hamilton Moor.

Initially there were three troops of horse at the bridge, under Hackston of Rathillet, Henry Hall of Haughhead and Andrew Turnbull, and two companies of foot under John Fowler and Alexander Ross. Sometime during the night four more 'battalions' from Galloway, Glasgow, Lennox and Stirling were sent forward, together with the Galloway troop of horse and an artillery piece.[17] 'A little before day,' recalled a Covenanter named James Ure of Shirgarton, who had come up with 200 volunteers from Stirlingshire, 'we saw the enemy kindling their matches a great way off.' As soon as it was light to see he and his men deployed: 'hard upon the water-side against the west end of the bridge. Glasgow, when they came down, drew up on my right hand and Lennox on my left; there came also down about 200 Galloway foot: they had no other arms but pikes and halberts, with four pair of colours, and took ground on our right hand farthest from our enemy. There came one troop of their horse and drew up behind us, and then our cannon was drawn down, being a field piece and two muskets of found unmounted, so these were not made use of.'[18]

Up to what was literally the last minute, attempts were still being made to reach a peaceable settlement. The Duke of Buccleugh obviously stood outside the Scottish political establishment and was widely believed to have brought concessions from London, but as the insurgents could not bring themselves to trust each other it was inevitable that they could not trust Buccleuch or anyone else belonging to the King's army. The battle proper therefore began with an exchange or artillery, which much to the regulars' chagrin, was quickly won by the rebels for Buccleuch's gunners were a pretty scratch lot who ran away at the very outset[19], but then Lieutenant Creighton of the Greys took up the story:

> Now the bridge lay a short mile to the right of the King's Army, was narrow, and guarded with 3,000 of the Rebels, and strongly barricaded with great stones; but although the Officers were desirous to have passed the river, by easy fords, directly between them and the Rebels and to march to their main body on the moor, before those 3,000, who guarded the bridge, could come to assist them; yet the Duke was obstinate, and would pass no other way than that of the bridge. Pursuant to this preposterous and absurd resolution, he commanded Captain [Francis] Stuart (whose Lieutenant I was) with his troop of Dragoons, and 80 Musqueteers, together with four small Field-pieces, under cover of the Dragoons, to beat off the party at the bridge. The Duke himself, with David Lesly and Melvill, accompanyed us, and ordered the Field-pieces to be left at the Village of Bothwell, within a musquet-shot of the bridge. When the Duke and his men came near the bridge, the Rebels beat a parly, and sent over a Laird, accompanied with a Kirk Preacher… While this Parly lasted, the Field-pieces were brought down and planted over against the bridge, without being perceived by the Rebels. The messengers… they would not lay down their arms unless their conditions were granted them; whereupon the Dragoons and Musqueteers fired all at once upon those who guarded the bridge, and the Field-pieces played so warmly, that some hundreds of the Rebels were slain; the rest flying to the main body on the moor. The Duke, as soon as he had commanded to fire, retired into a hollow from the enemies' shot… and continued there till the action was over. Then Captain Stuart ordered the Musqueteers to make way for the Horse, to pass the bridge, by casting into the river the stones which had been placed there to obstruct the passage over it.[20]

11

Other accounts state that it was an English officer, Major Theophilus Oglethorpe, who went forward with his dismounted dragoons – and these were presumably the musketeers referred to by Creighton. At any rate, although the bridge was high and narrow, crowned with a barricaded gatehouse, after 'some short dispute' the dragoons carried it and debouched on to the open ground beyond, only to be counter-attacked and driven back to some houses clustered around the bridge-end. There they grimly clung on until Linlithgow's son, Lord Livingstone, came over the bridge with 300 of the Guards. Once Livingstone had secured the bridgehead, Buccleuch followed with the rest of the Guards and more cavalry and quickly pushed up on to the high ground beyond. There he could see the Covenanters' main body still standing back on Hamilton Moor and decided to halt at 'but two carabine's shot' distance and bring the rest of his army up.

Unfortunately, while Buccleuch was carelessly preoccupied with forming his second line, a rather haphazard counter-attack was launched against his right. A party of Highlanders belonging to the Marquess of Athole's militia regiment, which was posted in a 'hollow way' covering it, were driven back on to their supporting dragoons. However, the scratch collection of gunners had by now been rallied by the reproach, 'Would they fleg for country fellows?' and when the Royal artillery opened up at last, just a couple of rounds sufficed to throw the Covenanters into confusion. First their horse fled and finding themselves abandoned, the foot then turned and ran too. The collapse was as sudden as it was extraordinary, but Buccleuch lost no time in turning his cavalry loose.

Estimates of the casualties are tolerably vague and ranging upwards to as many as 800 of the Covenanters killed or wounded, mostly in the pursuit through the parks of Hamilton Palace, with a rather more reliable figure of some 1,200 rebels captured. Hackston of Rathillet escaped, though not for long, being executed in 1680 after his capture in the skirmish at Airds Moss. William Cleland lived to fight another day and was to be killed in action at Dunkeld in 1689, commanding the Earl of Angus' Regiment. As to John Graham of Claverhouse, Creighton records that he fought on the right, but otherwise there is nothing to record his part in the battle beyond apocryphal legend. All that can be said with any certainty is that he served there in no greater capacity than that of a captain of horse and if he was ruthless in his pursuit of the rebels, then that was only to be expected in the aftermath of the horror of Drumclog.

Afterwards it was business as usual. The surviving rebels turned terrorist once more and while the leaders of the Rullion Green affair had drunk the King's health, the Sanquhar Declaration by two of their leaders, Richard Cameron and Donald Cargill, renounced all allegiance to King Charles and promised reprisals against any who aided or supported his government and its servants. The Privy Council responded by authorising the army to shoot dissidents on sight and to prosecute and condemn them without recourse to the civil power during what became known as the Killing Time.

Richard Cameron himself was an early martyr, run down and killed in the skirmish at Airds Moss on 22 July 1680. Lieutenant Creighton was there and gives an intimate flavour of the fight, which cannot be equalled in its description of the brutality of hand-to-hand combat in the seventeenth century:

> The Moss is 4 miles long from east to west and 2 broad. The Rebels drew up at the east end, and consisted of 30 Horse and 120 Foot. I faced them upon a rising ground with my 30 Horse and 50 Dragoons. The reason why the Rebels chose this place to fight on rather than a plain field was for fear their Horse might desert the Foot, as they did on Hamilton Moor, near Bothwell Bridge: and likewise, that in case they lost the day they might save themselves by retreating into the Moss. I placed myself on the left, as judging that the best officer the Rebels had would command on the right. The action began about 5 in the afternoon, but lasted not long; for I ordered my men first to receive the enemy's fire, then to ride down the hill upon them and use their broad-swords. They did so, and before the enemy had time to draw theirs, cut many of them down in an instant. Whereupon they wheeled about, and Captain Fowler, who commanded the Rebels on the right, being then in the rear, advancing up to me, I gave him such a blow over the head with my broad-sword as would have cleaved his scul had it not been defended by a steel cap. Fowler turning about, aimed a blow at me, but I warded it off, and with a back stroke cut the upper part of his head clean off from the nose upwards. By this time the Rebells, leaving their horses, fled to the Moss; but the Royalists pursuing them killed about 60 and took 14 prisoners. Here Cameron, the famous Covenanter, lost his life…
>
> But this victory cost me very dear, for being then in the rear I rode into the Moss after the Rebels where I overtook a dozen of them hacking and hewing one of my men whose horse was bogged; his name was Elliot, a stout soldier and one of Claver's troop. He had received several wounds, and was at the point of being killed when I came to his relief. I shot one of the rogues dead with my carbine,

which obliged the rest to let the poor man and his horse creep out of the hole, but at the same time drew all their fury upon myself; for Elliot made a shift to crawl out of the Moss leading his horse in his hands, but was wholly disabled from assisting his deliverer, and was not regarded by his enemies who probably thought he was mortally wounded, or, indeed, rather that they had no time to mind him ; for I laid about me so fast that they judged it best to keep off and not to venture within my reach, till it unfortunately happened that my horse slipped into the same hole out of which Elliot and his horse had just got. When they had me at this advantage they began to show their courage and manfully dealt their blows with their broadswords, from some of which the carbine that hung down my back defended me a little. As I was paddling in the hole, the horse not able to get out, one of the rebels ran me through the small of the back with his broad-sword, and at the same instant two more wounded me under the ribs with their small ones. Then I threw myself over the head of my horse, taking the far pistol out of the holster in my left hand, and holding my broad-sword in my right; and as one of the villains was coming hastily up to me his foot slipped, and before he could recover himself I struck my sword into his skull; but the fellow, being big and heavy, snapped it asunder as he fell within a span of the hilt. The Rebels had me now at a great advantage. One of them made a stroak at me which I guarded off with the hilt of the sword that was left in my hand, but the force with which he struck the blow and I kept it off brought us both to the ground. However I got up before him, clapped my pistol to his side and shot him dead. As soon as this was done another came behind me, and with some weapon or other struck me such a blow on the head as laid me flat on my back, in which posture I remained a good while insensible, the rogues taking it for granted that I was dead, scoured off.

A little recovering my senses, I strove to lift up my head, which one of the rogues happening to see at some distance, immediately returned, and said in my hearing: 'God, the dog is no deid yet.' Then coming up to me, took his sword, and putting its hilt to his breast and guiding it with both his hands, made a thrust at my belly; but my senses were now so far recovered that I parried the thrust with the piece of the sword which remained still in my hand. The fellow, when he missed his aim, almost fell on his face, for the sword ran up to the hilt in the moss; and as he was recovering himself I gave him a dab in the mouth with my broken sword which very much hurt him, but he aiming a second thrust, which I had likewise the good fortune to put by, and having as before given him another dab in the mouth, he immediately went off for fear of the pursuers, whereof many were now returning. In this distress I made a shift, with much difficulty and pain, to get upon my feet, but my right leg being disabled by the wound I received from the broad-sword, I was forced to limp by the help of the carbine, which I made use of as a staff. I had lost my horse, for one of the rogues, when I had quitted him in the hole, led him away through the Moss. I recovered him about a year after from the man to whom the rebel had sold him.[21]

Creighton exaggerates the casualties, who actually amounted to five killed and nine captured. Although Richard Cameron was numbered among the slain he gained immediate immortality when Covenanters and *Cameronians* became synonymous. How many actually died or were imprisoned in the months that followed is obscured by contemporary propaganda and subsequent legend, but there is no doubting the escalation of casual violence, which saw the various independent troops of dragoons and horse augmented and then joined into full regiments; a Royal Regiment of Dragoons, which eventually became better known as the Scots Greys, and a Royal Regiment of Horse commanded by that loyal servant of the Crown, Colonel John Graham, of Claverhouse now otherwise known as "Bluidy Claverse".[22]

Then the game changed dramatically when King Charles died in 1685 and was succeeded by his openly Catholic brother James who almost immediately faced Protestant revolts in both kingdoms. In England, the public protagonist was his nephew, Charles' illegitimate son James Scott, Duke of Monmouth and Buccleuch, who was soon bloodily defeated at the battle of Sedgemoor in Somerset and afterwards executed as an embarrassment. Similarly, in Scotland, a complementary revolt was led by Archibald Campbell 9th Earl of Argyle.

Thus far, the Highlands have figured only peripherally in the story. One of the paradoxes of the Jacobite period is the dependency which the rebel leaders placed on the Highland clans, for historically they had little reason to follow the Stuarts. Contrary to popular legend, 'Jacobitism' among the Highlanders was not an instinctive expression of a patriarchal culture or of ancient loyalties, but in the west at least a pragmatic response to the long-term threat posed by the agents of central government and in particular the Argyle Campbells.

The background is summarised in a memorandum prepared in 1747 by the then Lord President, Duncan Forbes of Culloden, who wrote:

It has been for a great many years impractical (and hardly thought safe to try it) to give the Law its course among the mountains. It required no small degree of Courage, and a greater degree of power than men are generally possessed of, to arrest an offender or debtor in the midst of his Clan. And for this reason it was that the Crown in former times was obliged to put Sheriffships and other Jurisdictions in the hands of powerful families in the Highlands, who by their respective Clans and following could give execution to the Laws within their several territories, and frequently did so at the expense of considerable bloodshed.

It was a policy which enjoyed mixed success. The execution of it was accomplished not merely by the appointment of Sheriffs, but on a larger scale through the archaic granting of feudal superiorities over the western clans. In return those powerful families were to be held answerable to the Crown for the good behaviour of their vassals.

It was for that reason the Huntly Gordons gained the feudal superiority of Lochaber but much good it did them, for they failed entirely in their efforts to tame its clans. Far more successful in bridling the Macdonald mafias and at the same time advancing their own interests, were the Campbells of Argyle and Glenorchy. This might seem surprising given the fate of Archibald Campbell, 1st Marquis of Argyle, who dominated the Kirk Party to such good effect during the Civil War that he was widely regarded for a time as the *de facto* ruler of Scotland. Whether or not his ambitions really extended to the Crown, he was one of the individuals specifically excepted from the act of Indemnity and Oblivion when King Charles II enjoyed his own again. However, his son Lord Lorne, had commanded Charles' Lifeguard of Foot at Worcester in 1651, and was therefore allowed to succeed his executed father as 9th Earl of Argyle, not least because the Crown recognised he was probably the only man capable of keeping the wild men of the west in check. At the same time, he was also confirmed as Justice-General of Argyllshire and the Isles and eventually the threat to law and order from a defiant confederation of rebellious MacDonalds and Macleans was sufficiently great to justify the raising of two Highland Companies on the regular establishment. Authorised by King Charles on 4 September 1678, the two companies, commanded by John, Earl of Caithness[23] and Colonel James Menzies of Culdares respectively, were 'to be raised for securing the peace of the Highlands', a term which has misled some historians into thinking that they were a forerunner of the Highland Watch or police companies raised in the eighteenth century. In fact, they were specifically intended to serve in military operations against the Macleans and MacDonalds, and therefore as regulars (of a sort) they were ordered south when the Covenanters rose in 1679, albeit the battle of Bothwell Bridge was fought and won before the summons reached Argyle.

There is no denying that a formidable degree of private interest was involved in this six-year-long quasi-war being fought out in the Highlands and eventually Argyle overreached himself. By 1681, with the loyalists of the Cavalier party in the ascendant and Argyle's usefulness no longer as necessary as once it was, Charles decided that he was become overmighty. That might be debateable but Argyle was certainly upsetting far too many people, or more accurately perhaps he had too few friends, and in a dramatic reversal of fortune soon found himself *forfaulted*, his estates seized and, worst of all, his creditors were moving in. On 19 December, he was tried and found guilty in a trumped-up charge of high treason, but then escaped (or was allowed to escape) from Edinburgh Castle two days later. In his absence anarchy returned to the Highlands as Athole and Gordon vied ineffectually for supremacy over the west and the MacDonalds and MacLeans thumbed their collective noses at both of them.

Then, in May 1685, Argyle dramatically returned from exile in Holland aiming to raise a rebellion in concert with that being launched in England by the Duke of Monmouth (and Buccleugh). Many of those who accompanied him on the ill-fated expedition were fugitive Covenanters who promised to be able to bring out the south-west once again. Instead the *soi-disant* Earl insisted on landing in his native Argyllshire with the understandable intention of first levying his own people. From the very beginning it was a complete fiasco. Not only had he launched the uprising prematurely, rather than wait to co-ordinate it with Monmouth's rising in England, but the area was already heavily policed by loyalist levies largely drawn from the western clans under the Marquess of Athole, and in any case his former tenants in Kintyre largely refused to rise at all. For a time, anarchy reigned and by the middle of June Athole could neither feed nor control his Highlanders, who were plundering the countryside unmercifully. Argyle, for his part, was everywhere unsuccessful and when two English frigates captured his ships, he reluctantly agreed to try and raise the south-west after all. By this time, however, it was too late and after avoiding a fight near Dumbarton, in a last desperate throw the rebels straggled towards Glasgow, haemorrhaging men at every step. By 18 June they were dispersed entirely and Argyle got across the Clyde at Inchinnan with a single companion only to run into a small party of militia. Game to the last he drew his pistols only to find the powder wet and having quite literally been knocked on the head he was taken first to Glasgow and then to Edinburgh. He had already been sentenced to death back in 1681 so there was no need to embarrass anyone by putting him on trial again for his present rebellion. Accordingly, and without more ado he made his tryst with the Maiden on 30 June 1685.

His son, inevitably named Archibald, took no part in the rising (although prudently lodged in the Tower of London for its duration) but with no prospect of recovering his father's forfeited estates he went to Holland and attached himself to Prince William of Orange. His subsequent return to Scotland in late 1688 with all his lands and his justiciary powers restored by Dutch William would therefore be greeted with utter dismay in the West Highlands; not least amongst those Camerons, MacDonalds and MacLeans who had ravaged Argyllshire with impunity three years earlier. In the wars to come, fear of Argyle and the renewed ascendency of Clan Campbell was to be a far more immediate motivator in those clans rallying to King James' standard, rather than a supposed mystical loyalty to an ungrateful Royal house which for generations had harried and, at best, despised them.[24]

NOTES

[1] Quoted in C.V. Wedgewood, '*Anglo Scottish Relations 1603-1640*', Transactions of the Royal Historical Society 4th Series vol. xxxii (1950), p.31.

[2] Dalton, C., *The Scots Army 1661-1688* (William Brown, Edinburgh, 1909), pp.13-17. The earliest references to it as the regiment of Guards do not appear until 1668. Notwithstanding regimental legend it had no connection whatever with the Marquis of Argyle's Regiment, raised for Charles I's service in Ireland in 1642. The 'Irish Companies' subsequently assigned as a guard for Charles II in 1650 served as such in the capacity of jailers and likewise had no connection with the regiment formed by Lord Lorne as a Lifeguard of Foot in the following year. It in turn was completely destroyed at the battle of Worcester and had no connection with the six companies raised a decade later in 1662.

[3] The unfortunate Corporal George Deane of Sir Alexander Thomson's Company later petitioned the Privy Council that he was 'barbarouslie shot in the bodie with a great many pieces of tobacco pipe, ten whereof afterward were by the surgeon's care taken out.' Quoted in Terry, C.S., *The Pentland Rising and Rullion Green* (Maclehose & Son, Glasgow, 1905), p.7.

[4] Quoted in Terry, ibid, p.66.

[5] Dalton, pp.24-25. Another eyewitness commented that the hillside was so steep that anyone riding pillion would inevitably slide off backwards!

[6] The two lifeguard troops were commanded by the Earl of Newburgh and Earl of Rothes, although it is unlikely that either of them did so in person. Just a few years later Newburgh's corpulence would provide the necessary excuse for passing command of his troop to Athole. Notwithstanding, they were not ceremonial units, but were clad in heavy buff leather coats and armed with carbines as well as sword and pistols. Dalton, p.11.

[7] The order of battle provided by Terry (pp.76-77) is entirely erroneous and includes a number of units not raised until the following year.

[8] It is interesting to note that not only did Sir William Drummond's cavalry regiment have veteran officers, but a great many of the ordinary troopers were unemployed former officers,

(including at least one Civil War major general, Colin Pitscottie) riding in the ranks, as the contemporary expression went, 'for bread'.

9 Dalton, pp.95-96 & 100. There is a possible difficulty in this identification in that the Lieutenant John Graham of Lockhart's Regiment, apparently transferred with a number of others to Sir George Monro's Regiment of Foot with commission date of 1 September 1674. It seems likely however that Claverhouse was indeed named to a lieutenant's commission in Monro's newly raised regiment but did not in the end take it up.

10 Dalton, p. 110.

11 One of three troops which were later to be regimented as the Royal Regiment of Dragoons – the Scots Greys – in 1681. At this time dragoons differed from other cavalry or Horse in that they were really mounted infantry and expected to fight on foot if so required.

12 Oddly enough the lieutenant of Captain Inglis' Dragoons was also named William Cleland, although the two men were certainly not related. Both, as it happens, would later be killed in action; the loyalist William Cleland in a skirmish with Argyle's rebels at Muirdyke in 1685 and the Covenanter at Dunkeld four years later.

13 The narrative is sadly confused here by a lack of punctuation. The cornet, who was shot dead, was actually named Robert Graham (though he was not so far as is known a kinsman of Claverhouse), while Mr Crafford was not the cornet but a corporal of horse (sergeant) named Crawford. Captain Blythe is unidentified and so was probably riding in the ranks as a volunteer rather than holding a command.

14 The militia regiments concerned were those listed below. In addition, Lauderdale's Midlothian regiment was assigned to guard Edinburgh, while the Earl of Mar's Stirling Regiment, together with the combined Linlithgow and Peebles militia, were assigned to hold Stirling and the Forth crossing. The Earl of Mar was ordered to join the army with his Highlanders from Aberdeenshire, but both they and the Aberdeenshire Militia under the Earl Marischal, George Keith, were still on the march when the battle was fought.

Edinburgh Regiment	Lieutenant Colonel James Douglas
East Lothian Regiment	Sir James Hay of Linplum
Berwickshire Regiment	Sir Archibald Cockburn of Langton
Perth [Earl of Athole]	Major Murray
Perth [Marquis of Montrose]	Lieutenant Colonel Patrick Graham
Fife [Earl of Rothes]	Colonel Brymer
Fife [Earl of Wemyss]	David, Earl of Wemyss
Forfar Regiment	Patrick Lyon, Earl of Strathmore and Kinghorn

15 The Earl of Mar's Regiment eventually became the Royal Scots Fusiliers. Cavalry units present included:

Lifeguard Troop

James, Earl of Airlie's Troop [horse]

James, Earl of Home's Troop [horse]

Captain John Graham of Claverhouse' Troop [horse]

Captain John Strachan's Troop [dragoons]

Captain John Inglis' Troop [dragoons]

Captain Francis Stuart's Troop [dragoons]

Major Edmund Mayne's Troop [English unit - Monmouth's Horse]

Major Theophilus Oglethorpe's Troop [English unit – King's own Dragoons]

Captain Henry Cornwall's Troop [English unit]

In addition, there may have been two other English troops, although they cannot be identified.

16 Better known in England as the Duke of Monmouth, he had assumed both the surname Scott and the style of Buccleuch in 1663 on marrying Anne Scott, the child-heiress to the title.

[17] Terry, C.S. *John Graham of Claverhouse, Viscount Dundee* (London, 1905), p.72.

[18] Terry, C.S. *John Graham of Claverhouse,* p.74. The curiously named 'muskets of found' (?) were probably similar to some light cannon captured by Cromwell's men at Dunbar, firing half-pound balls 'which were handled like muskets'.

[19] See the plaintive statement by John Slezer, reproduced in Dalton, C. *The Scots Army 1661-1688* (William Brown, Edinburgh, 1909), p.56: 'The Establishment of the Artillery attenders within the Kingdome of Scotland consists only of four gunners to serve in his Majesty's Castles. I am honoured indeed with a Lieutenant's place of the Ordnance for that Kingdome. But I have neither Gunner nor no living soul to dispose on nor do I know where to find out one single man fit for that purpose when there shall be occasion for it, as did appear in the last Rebellion at Bodwell Bridge when every Governor thought to find use for his own Gunners, and that with much adoe I obtained only one Gunner to go along with four pieces of Canon besides three men that were pressed from Leith who proved very unfit for that service.'

[20] Creighton, J., *The Memoirs of Captain John Creighton* quoted in Almack, Edward, *The history of the Second dragoons: 'Royal Scots greys'* (London, 1908), pp.7-8.

[21] ibid, pp.11-13.

[22] While he was certainly so designated in later histories of the Killing Time, it is not at all clear whether the sobriquet was actually applied in his lifetime.

[23] Caithness was actually John Campbell of Glenorchy, who claimed the Caithness title in 1676 by virtue of being the estate's mortgagee in possession on the death of the 6th Earl. Subsequently this was successfully challenged in the courts and the title recovered by George Sinclair of Keiss, but by way of compensation Glenorchy obtained the title Earl of Breadalbane in 1681.

[24] Hopkins, Paul, *Glencoe and the End of the Highland War* (John Donald, Edinburgh 1986), pp.95-103.

Chapter 2

Revolution

The so-called Glorious Revolution of 1688 which toppled King James was not quite the spontaneous defence of Protestant liberties which generations of Whig historians afterwards proclaimed it to be. The King's personal popularity might be a matter of debate. His open Catholicism certainly aroused what was sometimes a near-hysterical reaction amongst some politicians, who regarded his countervailing robust toleration of Protestant dissenters with almost as much outrage as his adherence to Rome! Arguably, however, the real issue was still the same fundamental dispute over the Royal prerogatives and the primacy or otherwise of Parliament which had brought about the Great Civil War half a century before. Unlike his father, however, James was in a surprisingly strong position. The swift crushing of the twin rebellions which greeted his accession in 1685 not only served as a salutary warning to others minded to challenge royal authority, but provided plausible justification for expanding his army. Given the broad lack of appetite for turning political opposition into a renewed civil war his position should therefore have been unassailable when after fifteen years of marriage, the Queen presented James with a healthy son on 10 June 1688. Instead, according to popular legend, the implied prospect of a Catholic dynasty brought King James tumbling down in a near bloodless coup which assured the Protestant ascendancy for all time to come. In reality, whilst the importance of religion in the seventeenth century should never be underestimated, it is also important to appreciate that the revolution was actually engineered by a combination of European and dynastic politics.

Up until the moment of the child's birth, the acknowledged heir to the three kingdoms of Britain was King James's impeccably Protestant elder daughter, Mary, born of his first wife Anne Hyde. The advent of another daughter in 1688 would not have mattered, but the arrival of a son blasted Mary's claim and more importantly the associated claim of her Dutch husband, Prince William of Orange. Ironically, as it happens, Mary would eventually predecease her father in 1694 and so neither she nor her husband would ever have sat on the British thrones but for the birth of Prince James Edward and the coup which followed.

Be that as it may, ever since the Queen so unexpectedly fell pregnant, Dutch William had been plotting that coup and in June engineered an invitation from seven prominent public figures, calling upon him to come to the defence of Parliament and the Protestant religion and place his wife, Mary upon the English throne. James was stubborn and autocratic, but he was neither a fool nor blind to the danger. For over a century, ever since the beginning of the revolt in the Netherlands which created the Republic, Scots and English mercenaries (along with Germans and Frenchmen) had served with some distinction in the Dutch Army, formed into discrete national regiments and brigades. They were not part of the British Crown's forces but were nevertheless considered to be technically on loan to Holland.[1] Both Charles II and his brother had accordingly asserted their right to recall their 'natural born' subjects in time of crisis. Thus, when faced by that rebellion in the West Country in 1685, King James had appealed to his Dutch son-in-law for the return of the British regiments. William, whose own claim to the throne would have been knocked aside had the Duke of Monmouth succeeded in seizing it, readily complied with the request, although the affair was all over before the regiments could be employed. In 1688 it was a very different matter, and in a vain attempt to draw William's teeth, James again attempted to recall the Scots and English Brigades as early as 17 January 1688. On this occasion the Dutch naturally prevaricated, but by the time his son was actually born in June, James had not only mustered and augmented his English forces but summoned his Scottish army as well.

Crossing the border on 1 October, under the command of Lieutenant General the Hon. James Douglas and Major General John Graham of Claverhouse, it was quartered in the London area by the end of the month. It might be described as small but perfectly formed. Aside from the Lifeguards, at this point in time it comprised two regiments of cavalry; Claverhouse' Royal Regiment of Horse and the Earl of Dunmore's Royal Regiment of Dragoons, together with the two battalions of Footguards under James Douglas, Colonel Thomas Buchan's Regiment (the Scots Fusiliers) and Colonel John Wauchope's Regiment. All in all, the little army mustered a fairly respectable total of

3,763 officers and men. There was also a small artillery train under Captain John Slezar.[2]

On 5 November 1688, the blow fell and in flat contradiction of all naval advice concerning sea-borne operations so late in the year, His Mightiness, William, Prince of Orange landed with a Dutch army at Brixham in Devon. Once the landing was confirmed, all of King James' forces, both Scots and English, were ordered forward to concentrate at Salisbury. Unfortunately, no sooner had they done so than James suffered an uncharacteristic and quite catastrophic loss of nerve as some of his most trusted commanders deserted him. Instead of fighting the invaders with every chance of the success, he fled back to London and gave orders for the army to follow. This it did in a fairly uncertain manner, haemorrhaging yet more officers and men as it went. One of them was the Honourable James Douglas, who very promptly went over to William with his Scottish regiment of Footguards at Maidenhead and urged Claverhouse to do the same. Instead, Claverhouse, by now made Viscount Dundee, asserted his continued loyalty to James by taking command of a brigade comprising the Royal Horse Guards (Blues) and both of the Scottish Regiments of cavalry. The King appeared for a time to have gotten a grip of himself but on 10 December Dundee, as we must now call him, was at Reading, preparing his brigade for action, when word came that James had once again fled; all the way to France!

It was time, the Scots recognised, to be gone. Dundee was no longer in contact with Buchan's and Wauchope's infantry regiments at this point, although it could be assumed that all of them would soon follow Douglas' example, but the cavalry officers were at first unanimous in deciding to make their escape to Scotland while they still could. Wasting no time, the two regiments parted company with the Blues and reached Watford by nightfall. Next morning a report that the Dutch were approaching saw them drawn up outside the town and ready to fight, but instead came a letter from William, requesting Dundee to remain there until he should receive further orders. For obvious reasons, a fighting retreat all the way to Scotland held little appeal and so they returned to their quarters until instructions came for their dispersal. The dragoons were ordered to Islip and the surrounding villages in Oxfordshire, while the Royal Regiment of Horse was ordered to Abingdon in Berkshire. That was effectively the end of them. Dundee had no desire to transfer his allegiance to William and so abandoning his regiment to eventual disbandment, he rode hard for Scotland after all.

Escorted by a number of other officers and troopers, including the Earl of Balcarres, he returned there safely enough, but soon found the

King's party badly outnumbered. Back in September James had not only summoned his Scots army, but had also sent down word to his Secret Committee of Council – the Scottish equivalent of the Privy Council – of which Balcarres was one, warning that a Dutch invasion was imminent and ordering the shire fencibles to be called out in the traditional manner; the royal castles were to be 'well furnished' with supplies, the gentry modelled into troops of horse and the Highland clans ordered to have their men in readiness. It would, as Balcarres commented, 'have made a very considerable army' but unfortunately the dissident Presbyterians in the south-west used the mustering of the militia as cover for assembling the thousands of men who now descended on Edinburgh in a dramatic replay of the infamous Whiggamore Raid of 1648.[3]

After the defeat of Charles I in what is known as the First Civil War, of 1642-1646, a pro-Royalist Scottish government entered into an agreement or Engagement with the King committing the Scots to place him back on the English throne, in return for the establishment of Presbyterianism in both kingdoms. Violently opposed to such an accommodation with the very man whose actions provoked the National Covenant only ten years earlier, large numbers of Covenanters from the south-west marched on Edinburgh and toppled the government in favour of one properly subservient to the Kirk. Now they were determined to do it again, and when a newly elected Convention of Estates[4] met in Edinburgh on 14 March, thousands of douce Covenanters from Glasgow and the south-west were incongruously joined on the capital's streets by the wild clansmen of the newly returned Earl of Argyle, all loudly urging that the Convention join with their English counterparts in recognising Dutch William as King of Scots in place of the fugitive James.

Not that the Convention took much persuading. The political manoeuvring need not detain us greatly. It is sufficient to say that just as in England there was considerable opposition to the King as both a man and as a ruler, and support for him was rapidly evaporating. The Secret Committee was itself split, partly on partisan and partly on personal grounds. The Marquis of Athole for one, far from taking the lead in rallying the old Cavalier party, as might have been expected, was more concerned to ensure that whatever happened he himself remained on the winning side. He was therefore one of a number of members of the Council who hastened to London and William in December. The King's remaining supporters generally found it prudent to keep their heads down. In fact, some of the more prominent of them, including the Earl of Melfort, James' Secretary of State for Scotland, had already accompanied him to France and then to Ireland. and thereby completely lost touch with what was actually happening in Scotland. This had serious repercussions when a letter from King James eventually arrived in Edinburgh on 16 March. Whether originating directly from James himself or whether it was drafted by the Earl of Melfort, it was an unmitigated disaster. Predicated on the mistaken belief that the Cavalier party (the term Jacobite was not yet in use) was in far stronger position than was actually the case, it made no concessions to popular feeling beyond offering the possibility of a parliament and a promise of pardon to all who returned to their duty by 31 March 1689. Otherwise, instead of adopting the optimistic tone which the crisis demanded, it hectoringly threatened 'infamy and disgrace... in this world and the Condemnation due to the Rebellious in the nixt.'[5]

It was hardly civil, let alone conciliatory, and not surprisingly, on 4 April, with the Presbyterian mob still howling outside their windows, the Convention responded to this intemperate bluster by unambiguously declaring that King James VII had 'forfaultit [forfeited] the Croun'. A week later they underlined the statement by formally adopting the *Claim of Right*, asserting that by attempting to transform a limited monarchy into an arbitrary and despotic power, James had violated the ancient Scottish constitution. His grandfather's absolutist conceit that there was such a thing as the Divine Right of Kings was uncompromisingly rejected and having thus justified themselves to the world, the Convention then proceeded without further ado to offer the throne to William on 11 April.

Up above them, the Castle was still held in King James' name by the Duke of Gordon but while he kept the gates barred, fired the occasional cannon and periodically flew King James' standard from the ramparts, that was pretty much all that he was prepared to do. Earlier he had already demonstrated a willingness to give up his charge and at one point a horrified Dundee had physically prevented him moving his furniture out. The Castle was then formally summoned to surrender as early 13 March and a little flexibility by the leaders of the Convention in granting the terms proposed by Gordon could have seen the place promptly delivered up without much difficulty. Instead, the Castle would continue to be held in King James's name for exactly three more months. It was not a particularly vigorous defence; and as an anonymous journal reveals, was pretty much conducted on a shoestring. At the outset, Gordon had just 120 officers and men (none of whom were trained gunners) who proved both mutinous and prone to desertion, and he was also short of supplies and above all short of ammunition. Most of the latter, and the arms traditionally stockpiled in the Castle, had already been removed to Stirling where it would soon be used to equip the new regiments being raised by the Convention, but nevertheless over time the Castle's guns would inflict significant casualties and visit occasional damage upon the burgh. Latterly, however, some heavy mortars shipped north from England would quite literally batter the place to pieces around Gordon's head and together with the failing of his supplies, this would eventually see the Castle surrender on14 June, and on terms not so very different from the ones originally proposed.

That lay in the future and outside the Castle, in the meantime, the King's most prominent supporter in Scotland was John Graham of Claverhouse, Viscount Dundee, but he was in trouble. Not only were he and his colleagues outnumbered by the Presbyterians, but as 'Bluidy Claverse' he had made far too many enemies among them when he was earlier serving in the south-west. Consequently, in addition to his political troubles, he was soon becoming increasingly concerned for his own personal safety and the very real prospect of being arrested on capital charges which might now be laid against him relating to that period. In the circumstances, talk amongst the Cavaliers, turned to their withdrawing from Edinburgh to a safer location and establishing a rival Convention at Stirling, which was to be protected by some of the Highland clans under Cameron of Locheil and MacDonald of Keppoch. It would also, as everyone recognised, be tantamount to starting another civil war, but that was increasingly recognised as inevitable. Most of neighbouring Ireland was already held in the name of King James (who himself landed there on 12 March) and the King's viceroy, Richard Talbot, Earl of Tyrconnell was supposedly preparing to send thousands of men to Scotland.

Accordingly, on the evening of 18 March, Viscount Dundee led the last remaining sixty-odd officers and troopers of his Royal Regiment of Horse out through Edinburgh's West Port (gate) and took the road for Stirling. As a coup, it was a curiously lackadaisical affair. Not only was his departure from Edinburgh delayed by a last-minute conference with Gordon, which required him to scramble up the side of the Castle rock in his boots and speak to the Duke by a postern, while his troopers waited fully accoutred and conspicuous below, but having won clear of the gates without hindrance he and his party proceeded at a leisurely pace and stopped for the night at Linlithgow. Afterwards they claimed to have been expecting a rendezvous there with other prospective supporters, but while they slept the government moved swiftly. The Parliament House was secured and orders given to organise a regiment from amongst the unruly mobs of Cameronians and other presbyterian enthusiasts roaming the capital's streets. Within the space of just two hours the next day Earl of Leven enlisted no fewer than 780 of the Westland Covenanters into what would become a splendid regiment of foot, while by hard riding, and eschewing the comforts of a feather bed, old Sir Charles Erskine of Alva got to Stirling ahead of Dundee's party. The Erskine family effectively owned Stirling at this time and when the Cavaliers eventually turned up they found the burgh's gates firmly shut against them.

Frustrated, Dundee may have considered making for Ireland, but eventually he determined to remain in Scotland and await both his King's instructions and just as importantly the necessary legal authority to act in his name. For the present, there was no real alternative but for him to go home to Glen Ogilvy and make unconvincing protestations of his peaceful intentions. In his absence, Leven's new regiment was set to blockading Edinburgh Castle and on 25 March the immediate crisis evaporated with the landing at Leith of three veteran regiments of foot belonging to the Dutch Army's celebrated Scots Brigade. They were commanded by Colonel Hugh Mackay of Scourie, a Scottish soldier of fortune originally from the far north, but so long domiciled in Holland as to consider himself Dutch.

Nevertheless, the Convention looked upon him as the answer to the maiden's prayer and 'immediately upon his landing, conferred upon him the General command of all the forces of the kingdom, raised and to be raised, which he made no difficulty to accept of, tho he had no particular instruction for it from the King, being sure his Majestie would be well satisfied.' He therefore lost no time in securing control of both Edinburgh, and more crucially, Stirling and its precious magazine, as he explained, speaking pedantically and in the third person:

> The General, immediately upon his landing, distributed money to the three Scots regiments, which we shall henceforth, for distinction, call Dutch, to make them up each to 1200, as also to the Earle of Levin, to levie of 780 men, according to his Majestys order: and finding the disposition of that kingdom tending to a civil war by the retreat of the Lord Dundee, with several other noblemen and members of the Convention … as well as by the combination of severals of the Highland clans for their mutual defence, being afraid of the rising fortune and apparent favour of the Earle of Argyle, under the present government, who had considerable pretensions upon their estates, besides, that some of them had part of his estate in possession, by a gift of the late King, under whose reign the Earls

father had been forfeited; judging, I say, that those dispositions would tend to a rebellion, and not questioning but what was at the root, self-interest and preservation, as well in Dundee, with the other offended members of the Convention, as in the combined Highlanders, would be pretended King James's interest: to make their party the more formidable, dispatched an express to Sir Thomas Livingstone to hasten his march to Scotland, as also to the Lord Colchesters regiment of horse.

But this latter, being countermanded, after the revolted battalion of Dumbartons regiment[6], came not doun till the matter of a month thereafter. Upon Sir Thomas Livingstones arrival, the General commanded him to Stirling and adjacents, both to secure that pass with the foot they had sent thither at his disbarkment under Lieutenant-Colonel Lauder, and to be so much nearer the province of Angus, where Dundee lay with the matter of 60 or 70 horse of his former regiment; the General, at his arrival, had ordered a trench to be made about that part of the Castle of Edinburgh, which lies towards the country, to hinder the communication of intelligence and provisions, with the Duke of Gordon, after he had discovered his intentions to hold it out, and placed guards and the entries towards the city to the fame purpose ; it being impossible and vain to undertake anything else, both by reason of the small number of the forces, with the want of cannon, bombs, and other ingredients, for an attack, and the natural strength of the Castle rendering it very difficult to be attacked with prospect of good and speedy success.

For the moment, there was no alternative but to blockade rather than besiege the Castle while he waited for those heavy mortars to arrive. In any case as Gordon was reluctant to visit any unnecessary death and destruction on the capital, there was no great urgency to press the matter, beyond the obvious embarrassment to the government of his sitting there. Dundee, on the other hand, did present a real and present threat. On 30 March, he was formally declared a rebel by the Convention almost as a matter of course, but at first no action was taken against him. However, two weeks later, a rather inept agent named Brady was picked up in Greenock and was found to be carrying a whole bag of un-ciphered letters and instructions from King James, calling upon or rather ordering his followers to rise up in arms and form regiments under Dundee, the Earl of Balcarres and other leaders. Up until now the Convention, only too aware of the shakiness of their position had been reluctant to act too aggressively, precisely in order to try and avoid provoking a fight. In the wake of Brady's capture, there was no alternative but to act; their scruples evaporated and a wave of arrests followed. The Earl of Balcarres was taken at once, but forewarned, Johnnie Graham of Claverhouse hastily raised King James' standard on the top of Dundee Law sometime between 12 and 15 April and then rode north, just a day ahead of the dragoons sent to secure him.[7] He was already in close touch with Sir Ewen Cameron of Locheil and other Highland leaders anent raising their men in James's name, and now he essayed to try his luck in the north east of Scotland as well, encouraged by the knowledge that the area had been the nearest thing to a Royalist heartland during the Great Civil War fifty years before.

As the crisis deepened by the day, the Estates responded by calling out the horse militia on 18 April and authorised the raising of no fewer than ten new volunteer regiments of Foot and a regiment of dragoons. If King James and his supporters wanted a war, they could have one. Strictly speaking, only nine additional regiments were raised, since Leven's were seemingly included in the total, but one of the new ones, the Earl of Angus' Regiment, had two battalions. Rather more significantly they and indeed all but three of the regiments were recruited wholly or at least substantially in the Covenanting south-west, or at least had strong Presbyterian connections. The Army of the Covenant was come again and Bothwell Bridge and the Killing Time were going to be avenged.

Nevertheless, it was obviously going to take a little time to recruit, muster, equip and train these Covenanting levies, so in the meantime: 'The General engaged the Earle of Mar also, to cause observe Dundee with 3 or 400 Highlanders about the braes or height of the province of Marr, where he was very likely to pass; for about this time Mar began to change in favour of their Majesties interest and service; and likewaies he ordered the Laird of Grant, a person of a considerable estate and Highland interest, and following, to make all diligence to the north, and not only to hinder the passage of his own country, called Strathspey, from the Lord Dundee, but also to cause guard all the foords of Spey, which he might easily have done, had he used diligence, and followed his directions; but instead of that, Grant stayed some days after the General at Edinburgh, while he believed him before him to the north: which wrong step of his was certainly without any design of prejudice to the service, tho' highly punishable, had he been a man of service.'

As it happens, Mar, Grant (who was attending the Convention) and the Earl of Strathnaver were the three commanders who were not accounted Covenanters, but the first was dying, and the other two not yet impressed with the urgency of the situation. Matters were not improved by continuing rumours of an imminent invasion from

Ireland, which meant that most of his men were going to have to remain in and around the capital for the moment, under his second in command, Brigadier Bartholomew Balfour. Precious few were actually available to him. Of the old army only the Royal Regiment of Dragoons, now commanded by Sir Thomas Livingstone, had returned to Scotland and although he had sent 'reiterat orders' to Lord Colchester's Horse to join him, when they finally arrived Mackay was dismayed to find them exhausted, and their horses 'spoyled in their backs'. As a result, only 120 of them were adjudged fit for duty under the Major and two captains[8], but on 20 April they were despatched with Livingstone's Regiment to the burgh of Dundee, 'whither he sent also 200 chosen firelocks of the three Dutch regiments, judging he would spare no more for that expedition'.[9]

Mackay himself, determined to 'frustrate the practices of Dundee', followed hard on their heels and;

> Having joyned his party at Dundee, composed of 120 English horse, of the Lord Colchesters regiment four troops of Sir Thomas Livingstones regiment of dragoons, leaving the other [two] troops at Dundee, with Lieutenant-Colonel Livingstone, to keep the province of Angus in awe, which was very disaffected, and 200 of the three Dutch regiments, in all not exceeding 450 men, he marched to Brechin, where he halted that night, making a detachement of 50 foot, and as many dragoons, under command of his nepheu, Major [Aeneas] Mackay, to Livingstone, ordering him to seize upon the Northwater bridge, the ordinary passage to Fettercairn, where he was to halt till nixt morning, taking special care he permitted none to pass before him, and to fall into the village a little before or at the break of day, keeping the half of his party in body, and ranging the houses with the rest, in case, as the General had some intelligence, that Dundee with his party, might be lodged there that night, knowing nothing as yet of his motion northward, which had certainly fallen out, if a certain officer, as was suspected, going to levie a company in the north, and had seen the General pass the ferrie at Dundee, had not advertised the Lord Dundee thereof, as he was within eight miles to Fettercairn, where he designed to lodge that same night that the General sent out Major Mackay to surprise his quarters, if he hapned to be there.
>
> The second day the General finding among the party of English horse but 40 that could pass the hills, left the Major, who was sickly, with 80 horse at Brechin, all sore backed and in disorder, and marched with the rest of his party to Fettercairn, where, having

understood from Major Mackay how Dundee, being advanced within 7 or 8 miles to that place, had turned another way, upon the news of his being abroad, but no certainty whether back again to the north, or whether he had taken the way up Strathdee, Brae-mar, and so into Glenshee, by which way he could enter into the province of Angus again behind the General, which obliged him (notwithstanding he was very impatient to be near him before he fortified his party) to make an halt at Fettercairn at the foot of the hills which separate the southern from the northern provinces of Scotland, called in history the Grampian Hills, till he should have certain notice what way Dundee had taken, and for that end dispatched several poor countrymen, with money in hand, (and a promise of more at their return, with sure intelligence), upon country horses after him towards both the ways which he might have taken, who brought notice that Dundee, having understood the Generals motion, made a feint as if he passed by Braemar towards the south into Angus, but that after some miles march he had turned doun towards Strathdone and Strathbogy, being the Duke of Gordons lands, which he, with the Earle of Dumfermling, married to the Dukes sister, laboured to raise in rebellion.

Upon which advice the General marched over the hills, pursuing his way the whole night till he had past the river Dee at Kincardin, where he had certain news of the ennemy, (as we may henceforth call him), by an express from the Master of Forbes, who nixt day met him with the matter of 40 gentlemen of his name on horse, and about 5 or 600 country foot, who were so ill armed, and appeared so little like the work, that the General, thanking the Master for his appearance for their Majesties service, ordered him to dismiss those countrymen, with orders to be ready to come together whenever any ennemy party threat'ned their oun province, desiring the said Master to bestir himself as much as he could, and make as many friends for the government, with assurance of his effectuall recommendations to the King in his favour, which the Master also did observe very zealously, contributing all along, together with Sir George Gordon of Edinglassie, to keep two considerable and very disaffected provinces in awe, under the obedience of their Majesties government.

The fact that the Duke of Gordon was supposedly a committed supporter of King James might have counted for much when Dundee arrived to raise the north-east. Instead, the Duke was all-too conveniently shut up in Edinburgh Castle and thereby happily spared from making dangerous decisions. Notwithstanding the area's reputation then and afterwards as an Episcopalian stronghold, there were Presbyterians enough to make a mockery of that boast and bitter memories too of the Civil War. Without strong local leadership by the Duke or anyone else there was a general consensus to sit tight and wait out the storm. The Earl of Dunfermline had supposedly been given the Duke's letter of authority to make use of his horses and to raise his people, and thanks to his efforts (or more likely his wife's) about 300 of his brother-in-law's men were mustered at Strathbogie, but he himself was not a Gordon and notwithstanding his wife and that letter of authority they stubbornly refused to follow him or anybody else for that matter. Similarly, the Duke's Strathavon and Glenlivet men were even less co-operative; first protesting that they had few arms and then flatly refusing to come out at all as it was now the planting season. In the end only about forty men under John Grant of Ballindalloch and Sir Alexander Innes of Coxton actually joined Dundee at Castle Gordon, near Speymouth, on 1 May. Uncomfortably aware that Mackay was closing in fast, Dundee gave up at that point and hastily moved off towards Inverness and the promised rendezvous with the Highland clans, but as Mackay rather smugly explained afterwards, even that turned out to be difficult:

> The General, being advanced the length of Strathbogy, got notice that Dundee had past Spey 12 miles from Strathbogy, whom, tho his party was much weakned, he resolved to pursue hotly, to give him no time, either to draw to his party, by his cunning, such as had not declared themselves, or draw to those plain countries the combined Highlanders, and to force those that had no mind to it to take arms with them: nixt day then, being on his march towards the river of Spey, a gentleman brought him a letter, writ by the Lord Dundee, from besides Inverness, signifying to the Magistrates of Elgin in Murray, a country open toun, six miles on the other side Spey, that he had met accidentally with one Colonel Macdonald[10], with 900 or 1000 brisk Highlanders, with whom he intended to meet Mackay, or return the chase upon him ; and therefor desired to make quarters for that number of foot besides his horse, for that he intended to be with them nixt day, that is to say, the same day the General got it, which letter, the Magistrates hearing of his approach, sent him, being unwilling to receive a visit from such hungry guests, who kept at that time Inverness blockt up, to force them to a composition, to which, being but an open country toun, they agreed, buying off the hazard of ane attack at the loss of a little money.

As we saw in the previous chapter, the Highlanders' supposed attachment to the House of Stuart was something of a myth, albeit it was a carefully nurtured myth. The lead on this occasion was supposedly being given by Sir Ewan Cameron of Locheil and a notorious young robber-baron named Coll MacDonald of Keppoch, although neither man was actuated by loyalty to King James *per se* but rather by a well-founded fear of the consequences of the new Earl of Argyle's return. However, whilst John Drummond of Balhaldie hopefully insisted throughout his narrative in referring to Dutch William's supporters as being the rebels, rather than those about to rise up against the Convention government, it was a touch more complicated than that. To his dismay, Dundee arrived at Inverness to find the unscrupulous Keppoch besieging, or rather blockading the burgh with about 1,000 of his own people and some of his Cameron friends in pursuance of a quite unrelated local feud, which had nothing to do with kings and princes. Dundee's hasty intervention brokered a composition by which Keppoch lifted the siege in return for a payment of 4,000 merks[11], but doing so effectively cost him everything. On the one hand, the realisation that King James's general was prepared to ally himself with the wild clans of Lochaber alienated influential local leaders such as Rose of Kilravock, who might otherwise have been persuaded to declare for James, while on the other hand Keppoch disappointed him and Mackay called his bluff:

> The news of this unexpected junction of such a party of Highlanders with Dundee, put the General at first to some nonplus what resolution to take, for he considered that it would be matter of the last consequence for their Majesties service, considering the small number of forces at that time in the kingdom, if he should happen to be beat. Of which advantage the ennemy would not fail to profit, because the whole north, by fair or foul means, would declare for him, there being nothing, particularly in the north, to oppose them, if that small handfull were routed : and on the other hand, the retiring southward, yea, the halting at Spey would give time and occasion to Dundee to render himself master of Inverness, as well as of Elgin, with the provinces of Murray, Ross and Caithness, which were mostly affected to that party, beside the affront and disadvantage it would be to the government to be so early upon the defensive.
>
> Those considerations then thus weighed, and the General relying upon some succours out of the province of Sutherland, which he knew to be well affected to their Majesties and the Protestant

interest, as well as from the Lairds of Balnagown, chief of the Rosses, and the Laird of Grant, both gentlemen of a considerable command of men, and well affected, resolved to push forward, and instead of lodgeing, as he had determined before he had received the foresaid letter at Spey, to take his quarter that night at Elgin, where the inhabitants expected Dundee with his Highlanders, dispatching an express with orders to the English horse, which he left at Brechin, to pass the hills, and follow him in all possible diligence, being very well satisfied to see his small party so desirous of action, that the 200 old foot he had with him kept the horse and dragoons at the trott for seven miles betwixt Spey and Elgin, where he arrived with so much day, that he had time to view the ground, and post his guards in advantageous places, resolving to halt there till the rest of the horse would join him, dispatching presently well affected persons of the country towards Inverness, both to encourage the inhabitants to stand firm to the government, with assurance of speedy relief, and to get news of the ennemy, sending at the same time messengers to advertise the Earle of Sutherlands men, with those of the Lord Rae, Balnagown and Grant, to be in readiness to march with their best arms upon his first orders.

Finding that Mackay was unintimidated and had already secured Elgin, Keppoch suddenly discovered a pressing need to return home with all his men in order to secure his booty, as did his Cameron allies. Dundee was left on his own and had to evacuate Inverness on 8 May and retire up Loch Ness. Without a shot being fired, Mackay rode into the Highland capital as a liberator and set about ensuring that it would be held in the name of the Convention for the rest of the campaign:

The General having got up his fourscore English horse, marched straight towards Inverness, dispatching the Laird of Grant, who had joined him at Elgin, after he had been two days there, to his own country to have the men thereof in arms, in case he might have occasion to call for him, and ordered the Lord Raes tutor (he himself being a child) to send under two principall gentlemen thereof, 200 chosen men, and the Laird of Balnagown, and 100 to Inverness provisionally, till he saw how matters would dispose themselves : being then arrived at Forres, he got news that Dundee was retired into the Highlands from before Inverness, not willing to hazard in action, so he continued his way thither, where he met Balnagown with great protestations of his affection to the Protestant cause and their Majesties government, which he also made appear thereafter, by his readiness to comply with such as commanded in those northern parts their Majesties forces, having then got into Inverness, together with his own party, some 4 or 500 men of the forementioned families, which were only those he could make state upon. He ordered the palisading of all the avenues and entries with the principal streets of the toun, and made a review of the inhabitants, which he found to be about 300 well armed and resolved men for the defence of their toun.

Dundee, meanwhile, having briefly spoken with Alexander McDonnell of Glengarry and extracted a promise from him and from the other chiefs that the clans would hold a general muster on 18 May, he decided to emulate the Marquis of Montrose' tactics of half a century earlier and pushed south with his cavalry alone, hoping to profit by Mackay's temporary isolation. Two days later he emerged from the hills to first surprise an outpost at Dunkeld and then early on the morning of Saturday 11 May, he and his men rode into Perth, and scattered a newly formed troop of Militia Horse being organised there by Captain William Blair, the Laird of Blair.[12] A good account of the affair is provided by one of the rebel volunteers, James Phillip of Almerieclose, who tells how the rebels initially halted outside the city, while Dundee slipped forward with just twenty men and quietly secured the gates and market place. Once that was accomplished the rest of the party stormed in at 02.00 hours and quite literally caught Blair and his troopers sound asleep. No-one appears to have been hurt, far less killed in the affair but a number of prisoners were taken, including Blair and his lieutenant, Robert Pollock, as well as a couple of infantry subalterns from Mackay's Regiment, who had been looking for recruits. Perhaps more importantly the rebels also seized about forty horses, and a quantity of money and ammunition. They also, obviously, secured the arms and accoutrements of the unfortunate troopers and presumably even stripped them of their new red coats, for Almerieclose smugly relates that he and his comrades were 'clothed with the spoils'.[13] By any accounting it was a neat little victory, but a yet more enticing prospect still lay ahead.

Having sorted themselves out again, the raiders now pushed eastwards, while Dundee insouciantly stopped at Scone Palace to dine with an acutely embarrassed Lord Stormont. Marching by way of Stobhall, Cupar Angus and Meigle to Glamis, they collected dozens of eager recruits on the way from amongst various Angus lairds, including David Haliburton of Pitcurr. Then from Glamis, on 13 May the rebels marched on the burgh of Dundee itself, where Almerieclose fondly visualised a fearful panic as the streets were hastily barricaded with wagons and anything else that came to hand.[14] News of the raiders' approach also saw a desperate scramble by all the other troops in the area to reach the safety of the burgh before they too could be snapped up by the rebels. For some of them it was a near run thing; Lord Rollo's troop of militia horse got in safely, but while Lieutenant Colonel Sir David Erskine of Dun managed to hurry at least one company of the Earl of Mar's new regiment within the walls, he lost his baggage and some of his drums.[15] Nevertheless, badly frightened though some of them might have been, there were in the end enough soldiers to defend the burgh and raise a red banner by way of defiance.

Of themselves, what by now must have been well over 100 rebel cavalrymen were no real threat in themselves to the walled burgh, but included amongst its defenders were two troops of the Royal Regiment of Scots Dragoons. The regiment's new colonel, Sir Thomas Livingstone, had until recently been lieutenant colonel of Balfour's Regiment in the Dutch service before displacing the Earl of Dunmore on 31 December 1688 and his loyalty to Dutch William was therefore unquestioned. Not so his kinsman, William Livingstone of Kilsyth, who continued serving as the regiment's lieutenant colonel. Kilsyth and a number of the other officers, including most of the captains, secretly remained loyal to King James. It could hardly be otherwise. The regiment was originally raised for the express purpose of harrying the Covenanters of the south-west. Some of them had fought under Claverhouse at Drumclog and alongside him at Bothwell Bridge. Just half a year ago he had been their brigadier and whatever their feelings towards the new King, it was expecting rather too much of them to readily serve alongside their erstwhile foes (and victims) in a new army of the Covenant.

When they were sent to arrest Dundee in Glen Ogilvy in April not only did the dragoons fumble his capture by very conveniently knocking on his door the day after he had gone, but it was quietly intimated to his lady wife that should the right circumstances arise they intended to change sides. Now an opportunity had arrived.

The plan was a simple one. The rebels ostentatiously displayed themselves outside the burgh and Kilsyth immediately proposed to accept the challenge and sally out with his dragoons, supported by 300 of the militia. Once they were safely outside the burgh, of course they had no intention of fighting the rebels but intended instead to defect to them. Alas for the rebels' hopes, sallying out was flatly vetoed by Erskine of Dun and the other loyalist officers. The dragoons remained inside the walls and after some inconsequential skirmishing which saw just one raider get himself shot, Dundee reluctantly drew off and retired into the hills.

Ironically, even long afterwards, Mackay would still excoriate Kilsyth for his supposed cowardice in *not* sallying out, but the conspiracy to bring the dragoons over to King James was not yet dead and would shortly give the General a nasty surprise.

NOTES

[1] This had certainly been the case since Queen Elizabeth I sent an army under the Earl of Leicester to Holland in 1585, although Scots mercenaries had already been serving there for over a decade.

[2] Cannon, Richard, *Historical Record of the Royal Regiment of Scots Dragoons* (Longman, Orme & C. London, 1840), pp.19-20.

An undated return provides the following numbers:

Troop of Life Guards	Lord Livingstonee	132
Royal Regiment of Horse	Major General Graham	352
Royal Regiment of Dragoons	Earl of Dunmore	357
Regiment of Foot Guards	Lieutenant General Douglas	1251
Regiment of Foot	Colonel Buchan	744
Ditto	Colonel John Wauchop	927
Total		3,763

Colonel Buchan's Regiment subsequently became better known as the Royal Scots Fusiliers, while Wauchope's Regiment had been formed as recently as March [with the aid of a French subsidy] in order to provide proper employment for those all-too few officers of the Dutch Army's Scots Brigade who did obey James' call to return home. Ironically it was itself transferred to the Dutch service in 1701 and disbanded in Holland three years later.

[3] Balcarres, Colin, Earl of, *Memoirs touching the Revolution in Scotland*, ed. Lord Lindsay (Bannatyne Club, Edinburgh, 1841), p.7.

[4] A Convention of Estates differed from a full Parliament in that it was not presided over by the King or his appointed Commissioner and therefore supposedly lacked the authority to enact legislation. Once William accepted the Scottish crown, authorisation was given to conduct business in his name as a full parliament.

[5] *Acts of the Parliament of Scotland* 6, p.5.

[6] Dumbarton's Regiment, the Royal Scots, was actually carried on the English Establishment at this time and was therefore not part of the Scots Army. Dumbarton had commanded the regiment since 1655 and it was the appointment of the Duke of Schomberg to be colonel in his place which provoked the mutiny, rather than loyalty to King James. They were still very much mercenaries at this period and the affair was therefore soon settled and the regiment sent to Flanders.

[7] Dundee Law is a very prominent flat-topped hill rising up some 500 feet immediately at the back of the burgh. While the location is suitably dramatic it is unlikely that anyone in Dundee itself will actually have been able to see much of what was going on. As to the standard, it was evidently the old red Lyon Rampant, for James Phillip of Almerieclose, who was present, describes it as the *Signa Caledoniis pro Rege* – standard of the Scottish kings and later refers even more explicitly to 'the tawny lion'. *The Graemid*, ed. Rev, A.D. Murdoch (Scottish History Society, Edinburgh 1888), pp.46 & 166.

[8] Lord Colchester's Horse was an English regiment, eventually becoming the 3rd Dragoon Guards. A list of the regiment's officers serving in September 1689 includes a lieutenant

colonel, but no major. (Dalton, C., *English Army Lists and Commission Registers* 3, p.22). In 1688 the major had been Lionel Walden. As a firm supporter of King James, he may have left at the revolution but it is quite possible he was still serving with the regiment at this time his being sick was a diplomatic prelude to his departure.

9 Mackay refers to this provisional battalion as *fusiliers*. Originally, the term distinguished men armed with fusils (pronounced *fusees*) or firelocks rather than with muskets or common matchlocks. By this period, however, the matchlock musket had been entirely superseded by the fusil in the Dutch service, so the general's usage of the term simply denotes that none of them were encumbered with pikes. In fact, the detachment, commanded at this time by Lieutenant Colonel John Buchan were, according to Mackay 'most of them grenadiers', so it presumably comprised the three regimental grenadier companies plus as many volunteers as would make them up to the 200.

10 This gentleman was not a military officer at all, but Coll MacDonald of Keppoch; his first name was constantly being mistaken by outsiders as a contraction of Colonel.

11 A merk was a silver coin, worth fourteen shillings. Keppoch was therefore demanding £2,800 sterling.

12 Notwithstanding the troop being levied in Perthshire, this gentleman derived his name and title from the Barony of Blair, near Irvine in Ayrshire, which should not by any means be confused with Blair Atholl just a few miles to the north of Perth. His troop eventually passed to Sir George Gordon of Edinglassie.

13 *The Graemeid*, pp.59-62. In an obscure passage, Almerieclose also speaks of plucking the golden apples from the captured standards, which was probably a dog Latin rendering of oranges. For lack of anywhere to secure them, the captives were carried around with the rebels for some time before being hustled off to the Hebrides. There Blair eventually died of 'hard usage' at Duart Castle, although Pollock was eventually exchanged after some nine months.

14 *The Graemeid*, pp.66-68. Almerieclose adds the fascinating detail that Dundee donned his armour in honour of the occasion: 'breast-plate and back-piece of strength, and a helmet under a covering of black fur'. This was presumably the same armour he wore at Killiecrankie. The helmet was most likely of a style favoured by some German cavalry; a conventional Cromwellian-style lobster-tailed pot distinguished by a Tartar style fur band or turban encircling the skull. This idiosyncratic affectation was probably intended to render him more easily recognisable to his troopers in action.

15 Sir David Erskine of Dun was in command of the regiment by virtue of the fact that the Earl of Mar himself was terminally ill and indeed would die just ten days later. It was raised in part in Aberdeenshire, where Mar had considerable estates, but seven of the companies were quartered in Fife and in the Stirling area at this time, so presumably Dun was bringing the other three down south to join them when the crisis broke.

Chapter 3

Highland Summer

From the burgh of Dundee, the rebels retired westwards again and returned back into the hills with the sense of a job well done. Behind them, in the Lowlands, they left consternation and even at times something approaching blind panic. With General Mackay still far in the north and the new regiments still in the process of forming, there was reckoned to be no alternative but to hasten Sir John Lanier up from Berwick. There was already one English cavalry regiment, Lord Colchester's Horse, serving in Scotland and now a reluctant Lanier crossed the border with his own regiment of horse and the Hon. John Berkeley's Dragoons, and two regiments of infantry besides, those of Colonel Ferdinando Hastings' Foot and most of Colonel James Leslie's Foot[1]. Regarding Scotland as barbarous and uncomfortable, Lanier himself quickly decided that Edinburgh was quite far enough, but the dragoons and the infantry were perforce pushed forward into lower Perthshire and Angus to guard against another raid. For the moment, however, the rebels were wholly pre-occupied with events in the Highlands.

The first night was spent by the raiders at their leader's home in Glen Ogilvy, and from there they quickly passed unmolested by way of Cupar Angus and Dunkeld and then followed 'rugged paths' to Loch Rannoch. That was the easy part of the journey. As Almerieclose recounted with considerable feeling, Dundee then led his troopers, 'through the mountains, forcing his way by plain and rock and cliff, by sweltering bog and gully. Now many of the wearied horses sink into the marsh, and are lost in its depth. Failing to raise them, the riders place the saddles on their own shoulders, and pursue their way on foot. I myself, having lost my horse, have to tramp by rugged path and hill, by rock and river. At length, by stream, by marsh, and quaking bog, by forest blocked with uprooted trees, by precipice and mountain height, we reach Loch Treig, and there fix our lofty camp.'[2] As if that were not bad enough, they awoke next morning to a hard frost, 'our hair and beards stiff with ice', but notwithstanding the late snows of this unwelcome cold snap (which also deposited two feet – 60cm – of snow on Edinburgh Castle in the early hours of 20 May) the worst of the journey was now over and they soon descended into Glen Roy and headed for the rendezvous with the clans.

In the meantime, in March, Alexander Maclean of Otter[3] and Donald MacDonald, younger of Sleat, had gone to Ireland to seek assistance from King James's viceroy, Richard Talbot, Earl of Tyrconnell.

Rather to their surprise, on arriving in Dublin on 6 April, Maclean and young Sleat instead met with King James himself and quickly convinced him that if given 2,000 regulars and an adequate supply of arms, upwards of 5-6,000 clansmen could be raised at once; more than sufficient to secure Scotland. In grateful anticipation, James bestowed knighthoods and colonels' commissions on them both and, echoing the events of 1644, duly promised a brigade of Irish regulars under Major General Thomas Buchan; which was to comprise the Earl of Antrim's, Colonel Cormac O'Neill's and Brigadier General Robert Ramsay's regiments. So far so good, and in the meantime Sir Alexander thoughtfully raised two regular companies to serve as a disciplined cadre for his own projected regiment. Unfortunately, there was a fly in the ointment in the shape of the city of Londonderry, which had declared for Dutch William and stubbornly refused to open its gates. Having laid siege to the place, James, perhaps not unreasonably, was only prepared to release the three regiments once the city fell and they were no longer required. As it turned out of course, Londonderry famously held out and Ramsay, who had once been King James' Adjutant General, was killed in a major sortie by the garrison on 6 May.

By that time, however, the two highlanders – together with Maclean's cousin, Sir John Maclean of Duart – had already decided to go it alone, without waiting for the promised Irish brigade. Sleat landed in Kintyre on 2 May and the two Macleans followed a couple of days later. Wasting no time, Sir Alexander appointed a man from the Isle of Gigha, Donald MacNeil of Gallachallie, to be his lieutenant colonel, and having ordered him to gather in as many recruits as possible, then headed for Mull with his Irish cadre. At first all seemed to be going well, but as soon as word of the landing reached Edinburgh the Convention acted with commendable swiftness.

On 7 May, a scratch force of eight more or less complete companies were hastily put together under a Captain Young of Lord Blantyre's Regiment – there is some uncertainty as to whether he was William Young or the Alexander Young who later became lieutenant colonel of Lord Strathnavar's Regiment. The ad hoc battalion was formed by taking the most complete companies from the regiments then raising in the south-west and so comprised four companies of Lord Bargany's Regiment, and two each of Lord Glencairn's and Lord Blantyre's regiments, making some 500 men in all. Within a week, Young had them assembled, marched them to Troon and there loaded them aboard twelve boats which lifted them directly across the water to Tarbert on 15 May. The swift amphibious operation took the Kintyre men completely by surprise and next day Young went looking for them. Just beyond the Loup the rebels attempted an ambush. Some 300 of them under Gallachallie, young Sleat and another Gigha laird named Archibald MacDonald of Lairgie, took up a strong position on the steep hill overlooking the road to Kilchalmanel. However, they had no broadswords so instead of essaying a wild charge down the slope in the approved style, they simply opened a heavy but ineffective fire with their Irish muskets. Young's men, marching below, were themselves no more than raw recruits of course, not yet uniformed and barely trained, but they were at least more or less properly equipped. Unintimidated, the gallant captain quickly formed a battle-line and went straight up the 'precipices'. His audacity reaped its due reward; for without losing a man he killed two of the insurgents, captured a couple more and entirely dispersed the rest.[4]

Some of the Jacobites quite literally headed for the hills, but most of them, after abandoning Skipness Castle, took refuge on nearby Gigha, where it looked for a time as though they might be persuaded to surrender. Anxious to clear the decks quickly, the Convention authorised Young to offer them good terms and in the meantime reinforced him to a strength of 1,200 men with a company of Argyle's Regiment and some local volunteers.

Meanwhile, alerted to Gallachie's plight, Sir Alexander Maclean decided to mount a daring rescue. At this stage, he still only had his two companies of Irish regulars, but Duart readily lent him another 100 men and the necessary vessels – traditional Hebridean birlinns or longboats. Fortunately, the two frigates which constituted the entirety of the Scots navy were off the Ulster coast at the time, and although a small flotilla of English ships, commanded by Captain George Rooke, was known to be somewhere in the area, Maclean reached Gigha safely and had all the survivors gathered in by 26 May. At this point, Captain

Rooke turned up, manned his own boats and attempted to cut out Maclean's birlinns sitting in the shallows, only to be driven off by a heavy small arms fire. Baffled, at about 20.00 hours, Rooke drew off to pick up Young's battalion from the mainland, whereupon Maclean moved quickly to seize this brief window of opportunity, embarked his own men from the north end of Gigha, and ran up the Kintyre coast.

All that night he was closely pursued by Rooke, but his birlinns could keep closer inshore than the warships and eventually got away and returned safely to Mull on 31 May. As many as seven of Maclean's boats and a few men were lost *en route* but in the end, he brought off about 200 men who were formed into a unique regiment. Unable to return home whenever the fancy took them, in the usual Highland fashion, they to all intents and purposes turned into properly trained regulars. That was on the plus side for the rebels, but by securing undisputed control of Kintyre, Captain Young had then made it extremely difficult for King James to land the Irish army being promised by Dundee.

In the immediate term, the debacle also prevented the Hebrideans from attending the celebrated great mustering of the clans on 18 May on Dalmucomir, a meadow lying at the southern end of Loch Lochy, just a few miles from Locheil's home at Achnacarry.[5] Proving the truth of the old adage that the pen is mightier than the sword, Philip of Almerieclose's account of the mustering creates a glorious vision of an Ossianic host which probably never existed, or at least neither on the scale nor in the extravagant form he described.[6] Some of the chieftains whose presence is celebrated in his epic poem were in fact nowhere near Dalmucomir that day! Sir Alexander Maclean, for one was busy mounting that dramatic rescue of MacNeill of Gallachallie and McAlister of the Loup, yet in Almerieclose's version all three of them somehow contrived to appear with their men on the roll call of the clans, alongside some other notable absentees.

What was more, in rendering good Scots into Latin, Almerieclose (aided and abetted by his later translator) indulged in some very curious flights of fancy. Belted plaids sometimes became flowing togas; there are an abundance of shining helmets, of flowing plumes and other archaic pieces of armour. Sir Ewen Cameron of Locheil, it seems had a breastplate of leather, 'harder than adamant' which in reality will not, alas, have been the classical muscled cuirass conjured by that description, but was more likely a more utilitarian buff leather coat or jerkin. It is the description of the clans' weaponry, however, which is most revealing when all the classical fancies are stripped away.

With the exception of some brass-stocked hunting pieces carried by one contingent, no firearms are mentioned[7]. Swords, as might be expected, do figure highly, but the frequency of the references to them may be misleading, for it is unlikely that most of them were the basket-hilted broadswords popularly associated with Highland clansmen. Fortunately, as it happens, a number of Highland wapinschaw or weapon-showing returns, survive from the mid-eighteenth century (see Appendix 2).[8] These are extremely detailed lists setting out exactly what weapons each individual in five Atholl parishes actually possessed or had access to. What they reveal is that by and large the full panoply of broadsword, targe and other ancillary weapons such as muskets and occasional pistols normally associated with Highland warriors was largely confined to tacksmen and the like; heads of households and their sons, amounting in all to about 25 per cent of the total. What the returns also show, however, is that while many of the ordinary clansmen, the labourers, farm servants and other ghillies who would have filled out the three ranks standing behind the well-armed front rank, did indeed have 'swords', they lacked targes to go with them. There were in total 451 swords recorded in the Atholl returns, including three archaic 'tua handit' ones, but they were accompanied by only 125 targes. This means that rather than the basket-hilted broadswords of legend, most of those swords would actually have been dirks or 'short skeans and long knives (such as the Irish use)'. Instead, their primary weapons according to Almerieclose were battle-axes (presumably Lochaber axes) and *hastilia* or *framea* which were loosely rendered by his nineteenth century translator as spears, but were most likely the pikes which represented the easiest way of arming those kerns unable to source firearms, whether in Scotland or in Ireland.

This of course broadly confirms Lieutenant General Henry Hawley's infamous observation before the battle of Falkirk in 1746 that the Clans: 'Commonly form their Front rank of what they call their best men, or True Highlanders, the number of which being alleyways but few, when they form in Battalions they commonly form four deep, & these Highlanders form the front of the four, the rest being lowlanders & arrant scum.'[9]

In reality, the Clans were as poorly armed as most insurgents and seeing them thus arrayed before him, Dundee, as a professional soldier, quite naturally proposed to have then 'disciplined' or properly trained. Initially the chiefs, surprisingly many of them being brash young men swaggering around in the military red coats appropriate to the newly granted commissions from King James, were all for the notion of turning their men into proper soldiers. However, Sir Ewen Cameron of Locheil, speaking with all the hoary authority of his sixty-three years which had included fighting Cromwell's men in the hills three decades before, demurred and patronisingly declared: 'That to pretend to alter anything in their old customes, whereof they are exceedingly tenatious, would intirely ruin them and make them no better than new-raised troops.'[10] Strictly speaking this was bombastic nonsense. The clansmen were perfectly capable of being disciplined, but there was no point in training them in conventional tactics when they lacked the necessary weapons and equipment. Better to simply hurl themselves as enthusiastically as possible at the enemy and hope for the best. It would indeed work, and in spectacular fashion, at Killiecrankie but it would be at a terrible cost.

Not that it probably mattered at this stage in the game, for by now General Mackay was again on the move. Notwithstanding all the steps he had ordered to be taken to ensure that Inverness was properly fortified and defended, the general was decidedly uneasy at the uncertain loyalties of some of the local clans, and was consequently reluctant to simply march away and leave them to it. Accordingly:

> He dispatched an express to Colonel Balfour, commanding in chief, the forces in the south, ordering him to dispatch Colonel Ramsay[11] with 600 chosen men of the three Dutch regiments, (supposing them by that time pretty far advanced in their recruits) with officers conform, and for his more speedy junction, ordered him to come the shortest cutt over Athole and Badenoch, in which latter country the General was to meet him, to secure his march in case Dundee, with the Lochaber men, would form a design upon him in his march. Balfour having received the General's orders, made the detachment under Colonel Ramsay, dispatching him presently forward, but by misfortune, or rather providence, whose directions are above our reach, a fleet of Hollands herring busses appeared upon the coast at the mouth of the Frith, the same day Ramsay was bussie to pass his detachment over from Leith to Bruntisland, which the government supposing to be a French invasion, being greatly alarmed, countermanded Ramsay, till they had discovered the truth of the matter, which hindred him two or three days, and proved the occasion of all the difficulties and hazard for the service, wherewith the General had to wrestle with a small handfull of men for two or three months thereafter.

However unlikely it was, a landing by the French would obviously have completely transformed the situation and the Duke of Gordon, still sitting defiantly in Edinburgh Castle, smugly recorded a report 'that the great leaders in the Reformation, upon appearance of the Dutch doggers, got together horses, attendants, arms, &c., and made vast preparations, as if they had been to fly to, or for the King's host'. General Mackay for his part had in the meantime convinced himself:

> That Athole play'd foul play, and falsified his engagement at their parting to him: Therefor considering his country henceforeward as ennemys, he dispatched several expresses to meet Ramsay with direction how to order his march, according as he would be informed of Dundees motion, judging, according to his intelligence, that if Ramsay should follow his orders, so as to have marched immediately after Balfour had received command to detach him, he might easily pass all hazard of being intercepted by Dundee, before he could have assembled a sufficient party to dare undertake it: and for the men of Athole, besides that they had not openly declared themselves as yet, the Marquis with his eldest son being at Edinburgh. The General judged Ramsays party, such as he had ordered it, sufficient to secure their passage through that country.

Unfortunately, not only was Colonel Ramsay delayed for about three days by the false alarm raised by those wretched fishing boats, but most of Mackay's 'expresses' or messengers, trying to reach him were turned back by armed bands of Athollmen. Worse still, in one case the messenger was actually seized by Athole's baillie or estate manager, Patrick Stewart of Ballechin, and the despatches he carried forwarded on to Dundee. Notwithstanding his reservations about moving into the hills, Mackay decided he had no alternative but go out and to meet Ramsay on the road.[12] In the event, however, to the general's palpable disgust, it did not work out as planned, for:

> Ramsay, after he had advanced within twelve miles of the place where the General had promised to meet him with his party to secure their junction, seeing the men of Athole in arms as he marched through their country, tho they attempted nothing upon him, who magnified extremely Dundees Highland forces, which they affirmed, tho falsly, were betwixt him and the General, from whom he received no late advertisement ; withall being altogether a stranger to the Highlanders and their numbers, believed them to be really so formidable, that it would be no prudence in him, and as little safety to the service to hazard that party, and so returned with all diligence again to Perth. But the morning before his resolution of returning, he dispatched an express to the General, giving account of his being advanced so far, and his intention to lodge at Ruthven

in Badenoch, where the General had placed a garison of countrymen.

The following night which express coming to Inverness, on Saturday night at even, the General having ordered provisions only for two days for his party, and leaving some three or four hundred country men, under command of [David Ross of] Balnagown, whose men they were mostly, for the guard of Inverness, marched out Sunday morning early with about 100 English horse, 140 dragoons, at most 200 old foot, and 200 Highlanders of the Lord Reays and Balnagowns men, in all about 640 men, having sent orders to the Lord Strathnaver to repair speedily to Inverness with all the ready men he had, as well as to the gentlemen of the Lord Reays family, to bring thither 200 men more of their best armed, which was punctually and speedily obeyed, and so after he had taken care for the security of Inverness, which he judged of great importance for the service, as much as his present bad enough circumstances would allow, he pursued his way with all diligence to meet with Ramsay, and secure their junction at all hazards, notwithstanding he had dayly intelligence out of Lochaber, and could not learn as yet that Dundee had got any considerable number besides his horse together, not willing to spare any pains or neglect the reasonable methods of securing the service, as well as, because he could not make use for intelligence but of such as knew the Highlanders, and who might appear among them without suspicion.

That lack of reliable intelligence was beginning to cause some real problems for both sides. Dundee, at this point, was still waiting for the arrival of the MacLeans with the Hebridean contingents, but judging the opportunity too good to pass up, he marched swiftly to intercept Ramsay with the 1,800 men immediately available, only to discover him gone and Mackay coming down fast from the north. This, obviously, was rather more than he had bargained for but, after a hasty consultation with his officers, Dundee decided to fight anyway. As a result, the two armies first came in sight of each other in upper Strathspey on 28 May, but a lack of supplies was already forcing the rebels to move in dispersed bodies in order to find enough food, and then a misunderstanding by Locheil resulted in the clans coming together again several miles to the south of where Dundee had intended. For his part, the premature concentration alerted Mackay to the proximity of the rebels' main body and he thereupon turned cautious and hastily retired to Culnakyle. Equally wary, Dundee sat where he was for a time. A sixty-strong company of the Laird of Grant's newly raised regiment, under Captain John Forbes[13], had been thrust into Ruthven Castle and he was content to sit blockading the place while he waited for young Sleat and the Macleans to turn up.

In the meantime, he secretly re-established contact with some of his old colleagues in Livingstone's Dragoons, still hoping that they would now find the opportunity to bring the regiment over to him. Unfortunately, by now the plot was turning sour. Kilsyth was getting cold feet and Mackay was dramatically alerted to what was going by the arrival of two purported deserters from Dundee's forces:

> Two days after the arrival of Lieutenant Colonel Livingstone by the party, two deserters came into our quarter from Dundee, who being brought to the General, he examined them, demanding why they had left Dundee, for one of them had been a serjant in Wachop's regiment in England, and deserted after Sir David Collier was made Colonel of it, carrying three more with him, which made the General suspect him the more, telling him he lookt on him as sent from Dundee to spy his camp, and that he would be treated accordingly, if he would not give a better account of himself. Whereat the fellow desired to speak with him alone; so all officers being commanded out of the room, except Sir Thomas Livingstone, he told the General that he was betrayed by his own men, and being asked who they were, he named Lieutenant-Colonel Livingstone, Captain Murray, Livingstone, Crighton, and several others, few excepted, (but the Colonel, the Major, and Captain Balfour) of all the dragoon officers, who were not actually in the plott, or had less or more communication of it. And being further enquired what proofs he had of these assertions ; he answered, (as did also his comrade) that beside that Dundee usually assured his Highland Chiefs of Clans, that he was sure of the dragoons, but that it was not yet time to call them, being more useful to him where they were ; that he saw him read letters from his Lady to the same purpose, naming particularly the forementioned officers, together with one Lieutenant Murray of the same regiment, a young debauched fellow, but one of the liveliest instruments in that plot.

Clearly, given the level of detail divulged to the General, these men were no ordinary 'deserters' but double agents and, in response to this unsettling intelligence, Sir Thomas Livingstone made sufficient discreet enquiries to establish that whilst many of his officers were indeed acting suspiciously, the ordinary troopers did not appear to be actively involved. For the moment then, Mackay resolved to keep them close and have them watched, but otherwise do nothing. Then, confirmation came a couple of days later, when a shortage of supplies compelled young Forbes to surrender Ruthven, though he 'capitulated for his own and his garrison's liberty'. Afterwards, on his way to re-join Mackay, he passed through Dundee's camp and noted obvious preparations being made for an advance, Fortuitously, this amateurish security lapse was then followed by a strange encounter with 'two men on horseback, the one clothed in blue, and the other in red', who passed themselves off to him as Mackay's scouts.

Forbes duly reported both encounters to the General, who shrewdly realised that the supposed scouts must in fact have been go-betweens. Mackay's supposed superiority in cavalry was now not such a comfort as it had once been, and when Dundee resumed his advance on 2 June, the General decided to retreat.

He had, as he explains, three options. He might of course fall back directly on Inverness, but he quickly rejected that action as being too obvious. A march of some twelve miles down Strathavan and Glenlivet, on the other hand, could bring him to a rendezvous with some reinforcements coming up from Edinburgh, but again he judged this too risky because, 'if Dundee had understood the country and his trade to have informed himself exactly thereof, he might have gained betwixt our party and the regiments which we expected from the South, and put the General to a hard pull'. Instead therefore, he took the third option and left a garrison in Ballachastell (now Castle Grant) before marching his hungry army down the Spey to Balvenie. where he was joined by Sir George Gordon of Edinglassie and the Master of Forbes, with some local levies. At this point, Mackay's immediate priority was still to link up with the hoped-for reinforcements, and so the following day he continued retreating eastwards, rather than north to Inverness.

Pursuing hopefully, Dundee nearly caught up with him at the foot of Glenlivet and the clansmen even stripped off their heavy plaids in readiness for action. Mackay countered by deploying all his cavalry (including perforce the dragoons) as a rearguard and successfully fell back first to Edinglassie and then to Suie Foot, where he was at last joined on 4 June by Berkeley's Dragoons, and Sir James Leslie's Foot.

At about the same time Dundee had the misfortune to contract a nasty bout of dysentery and it was now an increasingly confident Mackay's turn to pursue the rebels. With the arrival of the reinforcements he could safely arrest the suspect dragoon officers (eventually they were deprived of their commissions, but no other action was taken against them) and local loyalists, such as the Laird of Grant and Gordon of Edinglassie, exacted a bitter revenge on those rebel stragglers they rounded up; hanging them out of hand as common criminals in their civil capacities as Sheriffs of Inverness-shire and Banffshire respectively. Unsurprisingly, these summary executions were bitterly resented and would lead to reprisals by Cameron of Locheil and his people, but in the meantime the first of the MacLeans finally arrived under Duart's lieutenant colonel, Hector Maclaine of Lochbuie.

Once again there was something of a shambles. Dundee was evidently too debilitated to exercise effective control of his forces, let alone try anything clever. The Macleans turned up near Boat of Garten on or about 7 June, but Locheil, deputising for Dundee, had arranged a rendezvous under cover of darkness to try and conceal their arrival from Mackay. Instead, the two parties missed each other completely. Daybreak discovered the Macleans friendless and alone, and worse, while they waited for MacIain of Glencoe to turn up and guide them into Dundee's camp, they whiled away the time by plundering everyone in sight. Predictably enough, by the time he found them, Sir Thomas Livingstone had turned up like the devil at prayers with 200 dragoons, anxious to demonstrate their loyalty. This they did in fine style, cutting down stragglers and recapturing a quantity of plunder as they herded the clansmen like sheep. Eventually Lochbuie managed to rally about 100 of his men on a steep hill called Knockbrecht and when the dragoons shook out into a dismounted cordon around them, the highlanders charged back down the hill in a tight wedge, broke through and escaped in the gathering darkness. Less fortunately, about forty of Lochbuie's men who had already been rounded up were once again executed out of hand, while on the other side an unnamed captain of Berkeley's Dragoons was killed along with about twelve troopers from both regiments.

With his army melting away through straggling or because men were simply returning home to secure their booty, Dundee rapidly gave over any hopes of remaining even in Rannoch and took what remained of the clans back to Lochaber. They were all determined on heading that way anyway, but leading them there retained at least the illusion of control and might make it easier to call them out again later.

Nor was the latest news from Ireland encouraging. Londonderry remained defiant and consequently the promised assistance from Ireland still proved illusory. Dundee had vainly written to King James, proposing that the convenient but hostile south-west of Scotland be by-passed in favour of a major landing by the Irish army at Inverlochy, but this required a level of assistance from the French Navy which was simply not forthcoming. It was not until early July that it was possible for King James to ship even a single regiment of infantry from Carrickfergus under Colonel James Purcell.[14] Poorly trained and perhaps worse equipped, Purcell's Regiment was accompanied by the nucleus of a badly needed dragoon regiment, intended to be raised by a seasoned professional named Colonel Alexander Cannon, together with a shoal of other officers to serve with these regiments and to 'discipline' the clans.

At first all went well, and convoyed by three French warships they accidentally ran into and captured both of the Scottish Navy's only two warships, the *Pelican* and the *Janet* on 10 July.[15] The subsequent landing, however, went a little awry. Colonel Purcell's Regiment was safely landed on Mull, but the boat carrying most of the dragoon cadre – thirty men with twenty horses – was taken prisoner by a party of Argyle's Regiment under Campbell of Auchinbrec.[16]

Mackay meanwhile, satisfied that the rebels had dispersed for the present, took his weary army back to Inverness, where he re-organised the garrison, and then, to the undisguised relief of the Convention, at last set off back to Edinburgh on 20 June. The Royal Regiment of Dragoons had demonstrated their willingness to fight the clans but he was sensible enough not to strain their loyalty too far by requiring them to serve alongside their old Covenanting foes in the new regiments being organised in the south. Behind him therefore, he left Sir Thomas Livingstone in charge of the Highland capital, with a substantial garrison comprising his own regiment, with Sir James Leslies Foot, and a further 300 regulars brought north by Ramsey. Originally, they were to have reinforced Mackay, but as Leslie's Regiment was still three companies short, he resolved to leave the 200-strong detachment of Leven's Regiment and another 100 men of Colonel Ferdinando Hastings' Regiment at Inverness – a decision he was later to regret. In addition, there were two locally raised regiments; the Laird of Grant's and Lord Strathnavar's. Both were regular units, commissioned like the others on 19 April, but although they were as yet still very poorly equipped, they were reckoned to be keen enough. Then, if the worst came to the worst, Livingtone was assured he could call upon another 200 men under Ross of Balnagowan and other levies from Sutherland and the far north. Inverness was therefore as secure as Mackay could make it.[17]

A similar concern was displayed by the General for other communities of strategic and political importance. Marching round by way of Aberdeen, Mackay decided that Berkeley's Dragoons, (another English unit) with the assistance of local leaders such as the Master of Forbes, would suffice to look after the north-east. As a first step to ensuring this he sent an expedition under Forbes up Deeside to establish a garrison in Braemar Castle, and as a secondary objective tasked him with arresting a prominent local rebel; the notorious Black Colonel, John Farquharson of Inverey. Accordingly, Forbes set off with, '50 horse, 50 dragoons of Barcklays, with 60 foot, and some provisions, to take possession thereof, [Braemar Castle] with a written order to the captain of dragoons to push forward with the horse and dragoons, leaving the foot to follow with the provisions: and having put 20 of his dragoons in the house in passing, marched forward without halt, and before day, to the house of Inverey, three miles further, with all the diligence and secrecy possible, whereby he might readily surprize them, with several other gentlemen of note, who, upon the separation of Dundees party, retired that way. But instead of following his order when he had got into the house, he stayed till he had refreshed his horses, whereby day surprised him before he had got the length of his prey, which escaped him nevertheless so narrowly, that he got sight of them running in their shirts to a wood near the house where they were.'[18] The Black Colonel promptly retaliated with a surprise attack which chased Forbes out of Braemar, which he then burned in retaliation for the destruction of his own home. Understandably annoyed, Mackay settled the nonsense by wearily turning back and establishing a garrison comprising seventy-six of his elite 'Dutch' fusiliers under Captain Alexander Gordon,[19] a little further downriver at Abergeldie Castle, and then eventually got himself safely back to Edinburgh by 12 July.

There he found little had changed. While Mackay was at Inverness, King William had taken the coronation oath and authorised the Convention to recast itself as a full Parliament on 5 June 1689, (James was unimpressed and declared that all who sat after that date were to be accounted traitors!) but this made very little if any difference to the conduct of the war. True, Edinburgh Castle had finally surrendered a week later, on 13 June, but that reflected no credit on the government. The Duke of Gordon has received little recognition for his achievement in holding out for three long months, latterly under heavy bombardment, and despite critical shortages of food and ammunition and a near mutinous garrison. Yet aside from the sheer embarrassment which he caused for the government by sitting defiantly just a few hundred metres up the hill from the Parliament House, and the general inconvenience and occasional suffering visited on the ordinary life of the capitol, Gordon had tied down a considerable quantity of men and resources which ought to have been properly employed in the field. Moreover, even in the month that followed his surrender, little or nothing was done to prepare for Mackay's latest plan; a projected march on Inverlochy.

Before leaving Inverness, the General had written to the Duke of Hamilton, King William's Commissioner in the newly-erected Parliament explaining that: 'he saw no way to subdue the Highlanders, considering their country was full of mountains, bogs, woods and difficult passes with inaccessible retiring places, where it was impossible to hunt them out, as well as to subsist a forthnight in such barren and desart countries, but by placing a formidable garrison at Innerlochy, with other smaller ones in their places; therefore wished that his Grace, with the Parliament and Council, would take it to consideration speedily before the season were further spent, to provide the necessary materials for such a design against his arrival in the south.'

In outline, the intention was to carry out a pincer movement. At Inverary, the Earl of Argyle had already assembled a force comprising his own, the Earl of Glencairn's and the Earl of Angus's Regiment, mustering four battalions in all, plus Young's little provisional battalion from Kintyre and four troops of horse, all of whom were to be ready to move north in concert with the General. For his part Mackay's intention was, 'to carry only six battalions of foot, making at most 3000 men, with four troops of horse, and as many dragoons, new levies with him for that expedition, with intention to join Argyle with what forces he commanded in his country, if the service so required, ordered the rendezvous of the said forces, the foot consisting of a battalion of each of the three Dutch regiments, with the Viscount Kenmores, Earle of Levins and Hastings regiments, the two latter not compleat, because of detachments they had in the north at Perth, taking his way thither over Stirling, both to see the castle and some regiments of foot with troops of horse and dragoons of the new levies which lay that way.'

Unfortunately, on his arriving in Edinburgh, he; 'found not the least dispositions made for the design he proposed, viz. the placing of a garrison at Innerlochy, as the only means appearing to his judgment capable to subdue the rebells, to which there must needs a Fort be built.' His instincts were sound and, when it was eventually built, Fort William as it became would place a considerable bridle on the western clans for years to come. The problem was the logistics.

Soldiers and supplies aside, the practicalities of actually building the fort; not least the number of workmen who would have to be recruited (estimated at 2,000) and convoyed to the spot, and even the picks and spades required were problematic. Consequently, he was in no mood to deal sympathetically with Lord Murray over another, and yet more urgent matter, which suddenly spiralled into a crisis.

In December 1688, John Murray, Marquess of Athole, sometime prominent supporter of King James and president of the Privy Council, hastened to London and attached himself to Dutch William. Yet, beyond registering his new-found loyalty, he did nothing. Effectively side-lined by his rivals in James' regime he made no real attempt to assert himself under the new regime and soon retired to take the waters at Bath. That left his eldest son, Lord Murray, in charge of the family estates. Despite the earnest solicitations of King James' party, including Dundee himself, Murray, who happened to be married to the Duke of Hamilton's daughter, was resolved to remain loyal to the new government. Unfortunately, he had a serious problem. Simply put, the supposedly immense power of the Murray family was an illusion. Athole was not a Highland chieftain in the accepted sense and, while his 'people' were conventionally accounted as highlanders, they belonged to a disparate variety of small clans and were in reality no more than his tenants. His hold over them was feudal rather than absolute, and defiance of him was common both then and in the following century. Worse still, much of that present defiance proceeded from or rather found its leadership in Patrick Stewart of Ballechin, Athole's own baillie or estate manager – who allegedly had designs on becoming made the next Marquess of Athole by a grateful King James!

Mackay explained it all thus:

> Some few days before his departure from Edinburgh, he (Mackay) was advertised by the Lord Murray, eldest son to the Marquis of Athole, that his father's steuard Balleachan, with fome gentlemen of the county of Angus, adherents of Dundee's party, were fortifying themselves in the house of Blair Athole to secure that country the better for King James's interest, resolving to defend it against the Lord Murrays order, the Marquis being at this time in England. Murray being Duke Hamiltons son-in-law, the General desired to speak with him of those matters, in presence of the Duke, where he declared that he had no hopes of perswading the men of Athole to join with the Kings forces against Dundee, their inclination being more for King James than their Majesties government, but engaged to do his best to render himself master of the castle of Blair before Dundee could be there ; to which end, and to hinder them from joyning Dundee, he was to go to Athole and gather all his father's vassals together, believing that Balleachan and the tenents he had with him durst not deny him entry in his own house ; to which the General answered, that he desired no more of my Lord Murray, than to keep his men from joyning against him, promising to make all possible haste to prevent Dundee, being resolved to take the country of Athole in his way to Lochaber; but by the delays of government

in the furnishing of meal, as well as of horses for the transport thereof, he was detained at Edinburgh eight or ten days after the Lord Murray went to Athole, who advertised him of having the men of his country together, as also of Balleachans refusal to deliver the castle of Blair into his hands, and that on the contrary he had dispatched messengers to Dundee to hasten him up to his succour, as well as that of his other friends, who seemed to be blockt up in the castle of the Lord Murray.

Mackay was already unhappy with the deteriorating situation in Atholl, which had frustrated Ramsay's attempt to reinforce him at Inverness. Consequently, he proposed to march directly through that area on his way to Inverlochy. The latest news from Murray only confirmed that resolution and when he next received another letter from Murray, assuring him that he had collected sufficient of his people to deal with Ballechin all by himself, he briskly dismissed any implication that there was no need to go by Atholl and treat it as hostile territory. So long as Ballechin held Blair Castle, he declared, it was his duty to deal with him – and 'cause hang him too'.[20]

In Lochaber, meanwhile, most of the chiefs, with the exception of Locheil (who still wanted revenge for the hanging of his clansmen by the Laird of Grant) favoured moving south into Argyllshire, to face the threat head-on and clear the way for further Irish reinforcements. Such a course, however, would achieve little in the short term and, worse still, with no immediate prospect of an Irish army, risked turning the Highland war into an introverted and ultimately futile diversion. Half a century earlier, during the Great Civil War, the celebrated Alasdair MacCholla doomed the Marquis of Montrose's attempt to seize Scotland by turning aside to conquer Kintyre. Dundee had no intention of repeating that particular mistake and while he retained hopes of raising the north-east, Atholl offered a readier objective. It was not just that Ballechin had risen, for Dundee was buoyed up by 'a deliberate and well founded desyne... of the E. of B. [John Campbell, Earl of Breadalbane] his joyning him with 1600 of his men. To which also he had prepared Argyleshire and a Good part of Perthshire who were all ready to ryse with him.'[21]

This, at last, was the opening Dundee had been hoping for. Breadalbane had apparently committed himself at last; his character was an equivocal one, marked at every turn both before and afterwards by naked self-interest, but there was no doubting his power and his influence if he would openly declare for King James. Moreover, by the very nature of things, it is likely that Dundee had some word of

Mackay's proposed expedition – the protracted preparations were hardly secret – and quite apart from the prospect of raising all of the hill country north of the Forth, the necessity of quite literally heading Mackay off at the pass explains why Dundee now came southwards without waiting to re-assemble his army or secure any supplies for it.[22] First, on 10 July, he wrote to the gentry of Atholl ordering them to rise in the name of King James and at the same time sent a detachment of Sir Alexander Maclean's Regiment to reinforce Ballechin. Then, as soon as the Sleat MacDonalds landed, he marched on 23 July, and the race to secure Atholl was on.

NOTES

1 Notwithstanding its Scottish colonel, Leslie's was an English regiment and would later become the 15th Foot. Three of its companies remained in England as a garrison for Berwick-upon-Tweed.

2 *Grameid*, pp.74-78.

3 Maclean had been granted Otter (a parish in Cowal) by way of reward for his services during Argyle's rebellion in 1685, but he was rarely referred to by that designation and he simply appears in most accounts of the Killiecrankie campaign and its aftermath, as Sir Alexander Maclean. A professional soldier, he afterwards went into the French service.

4 Dr Paul Hopkins, 'Loup Hill, 16th May 1689: The First 'Battle' of Dundee's Jacobite War', *Kintyre Antiquarian and Natural History Magazine*, no.18 June 1998 and no.19 July 1998.

5 The site of the muster was effectively destroyed in 1813, first by the creation of the Mucomir Cut, which diverted the River Lochy as part of the Caledonian Canal works, and also by the subsequent raising of the water level in the loch by some twelve feet.

6 James MacPherson's publication of the Gaelic epic *Ossian* still lay in the future when Almerieclose wrote his *Grameid*, and its authenticity remains a matter of debate, but it is remarkable how Almerieclose foreshadows him in his account of the Dalmucomir muster. In fairness, Almerieclose's 1888 translator, the Rev. Alexander Murdoch, probably bears more than his fair share of the responsibility for this romanticised vision. In choosing to translate *hastilia/hastilibus* and *framea* as spears, rather than as pikes, it is hard to avoid the impression that Murdoch's own classical education was his primary guiding influence.

7 Significantly that one reference is to brass firearms, identifying them as expensive hunting weapons. No doubt there were other, less expensive, ones but there is an exact parallel with the early days of the American Civil War when volunteers from rural areas of the Midwest and Deep South turned out with all manner of privately owned shotguns and small calibre hunting rifles but then scrambled to replace them as soon as possible with sturdier military calibre weapons.

8 Atholl, John, Duke of, *Chronicles of the Atholl and Tullibardine Families* (Edinburgh, 1908) 1 (App): x-xx provides an accounting of the 523 men (equating as it happens to a good-sized infantry regiment) in five Atholl parishes in 1638 on the eve of the Civil war. Innes, M.[ed.] *The Black Book of Taymouth* (Bannatyne Club, Edinburgh, 1855), pp. 398-404, includes a similar return for Glenorchy at the same date.

9 Quoted in Tomasson and Buist, *Battles of the '45* (Batsford, London, 1962), pp. 61-62.

10 Balhaldie, J. Drummond of, *Memoirs of Sir Ewen Cameron of Locheil* (1842), pp: 250-251.

[11] This was Colonel George Ramsay, commander of one of the Scots Brigade regiments and not to be confused with his kinsman, Robert Ramsay lately killed at the siege of Londonderry.

[12] There was only one road and while shifted in places, built up, tinkered with and otherwise improved by generations of highway engineers from George Wade onwards it is still recognisable as the modern A9.

[13] A younger son of Forbes of Culloden and not by any means to be confused with the Master of Forbes in Aberdeenshire.

[14] Lieutenant Colonel of Henry Cornwall's Regiment (later 9th Foot) at the revolution, but went to Ireland with King James. Dalton, Charles *English Army Lists and Commission Registers*, vol.2, p.30.

[15] Both frigates, frigates *Pelican* (18 guns) and *Janet* (12 guns) were converted merchantmen, although the former at least had two decks. Grant, James *The Old Scots Navy from 1689 to 1710* (Navy Records Society, London 1914), pp.26-46.

[16] Grant, James *The Old Scots Navy from 1689 to 1710* (Navy Records Society, London 1914), pp.29-30.

[17] Mackay to Melville 13 June 1689, in Mackay H., *Memoirs of the War carried on in Scotland and Ireland 1689-1691* (1833), p.227.

[18] The Horse belonged to Forbes' own Troop. The identity of the Foot is less certain. Again, they may have been Forbes' local levies but it is possible that they included a detachment of the Earl of Mar's Regiment, which had been partly recruited in the Aberdeen area.

[19] Captain Gordon belonged to Balfour's Regiment. His ensign, Charles Gordon of Pitchaise obviously made an impression during his stay, for ten years later he obtained Abergeldie by marriage to its heiress, Rachel Gordon of Abergeldie.

[20] Atholl, John, Duke of, *Chronicles of the Atholl and Tullibardine Families* (Edinburgh 1908), Vol.1, p.296.

[21] Quoted in Hopkins *Glencoe and the end of the Highland War*, pp.152, 173 and 166n.

[22] A desperate lack of supplies meant that the Jacobites had to support themselves by plundering, and stealing cattle as they went. Coll MacDonald of Keppoch had been the principal protagonist, but a raid on Glen Urquhart on 28 June by some Camerons, resulting in the deaths of James and Patrick Grant of Shewglie, proved problematic. The Raid of Inchbrine is traditionally dated to sometime in 1691 or 1692, long after the Shewglie brothers supposedly fought at Killiecrankie, (see Mackay's *Urquhart and Glenmoriston*, pp.199-202) but Hopkins (*Glencoe and the end of the Highland War*: pp.150, 172 and 157n] on the other hand cites evidence that James and Patrick Grant of Shewglie may have been killed early in 1689 and Balhaldie likewise admits that one Glengarry's own people was killed at this time along with some un-named Grants. (Balhaldie, pp. 252-55). It is possible that two quite separate incidents may have been conflated over time, and that the Shewglie brothers did indeed die in a later affray, but be that as it may, there seems no doubt that Glen Urquhart was raided by the Camerons sometime shortly before Killiecrankie, partly in mistaken retaliation for the hanging of some of their number by the Laird of Grant, and that Glengarry had a furious falling out with both Locheil and Dundee over it. Balhaldie claimed it was soon smoothed over but how far that really was the case is open to doubt.

Chapter 4

The Battle of Killiecrankie: Armies with Banners

Delayed in getting away from Edinburgh, both by a shortage of oatmeal and the horses necessary to carry it, General Mackay finally left Stirling on 25 July and headed north to Perth, which was designated as the jumping off point for the expedition. There he assembled six understrength regiments of foot 'making at most 3000 men'. That was still, nevertheless, a respectable force, but instead of the eight troops of Horse and Dragoons he anticipated, there were only two militia troops ready to march, Colchester's worn-out mounts were still in no condition to go anywhere. The other cavalry he had been promised were on their way, but the latest news from the north meant he could delay no longer but needed to march at once, without waiting for them. The Earl of Annandale's and Lord Belhaven's little troops, mustering no more than fifty men apiece, (assuming they were fully recruited) ought to be sufficient for scouting purposes, but without the others, and particularly lacking Colchester's regulars, it did mean that Mackay was going into battle without what he and everyone else regarded as his most powerful weapon against the Highlanders.

As expected, Lord Murray had been rebuffed from his own front door. Lacking even a petard (an early form of shaped charge) to blow it in, all he could do was stand back and blockade the castle, but now, suddenly, he was warned that Dundee himself was imminently expected at Blair. Should he arrive there before the general, Murray confessed he would be unable to prevent the rest of his father's people from joining the rebels, and their doing so would in turn encourage others to come out as well; not just in Atholl, but further afield in Badenoch, in Balquhidder, and even in Menteith. As yet, Mackay was blithely unaware of the strong possibility that the Earl of Breadalbane

might join the rebels, but even without that particular complication, the General was utterly convinced of the necessity of securing Blair in order to forestall a general uprising. Next day he hurried on to Dunkeld, 'where by 12 of the clock at night he received a letter from the Lord Murray signifying Dundee's entry into Athole, and his own retreat from the castle of Blair, (which till then he made the fashion to keep blockt) and his passing a strait and difficult pass two miles below the said house, leaving it betwixt him and the ennemy, the farther side whereof he affirmed to have left guarded, for our free passage to the Blair where he supposed Dundee to be already.'[1]

The situation was rapidly becoming critical and Mackay immediately responded by ordering Murray to hold on to the Pass of Killiecrankie 'till I be with you, which God willing, shall be tomorrow in the forenoon'. In the meantime, by way of insurance, Lieutenant Colonel George Lauder of Balfour's Regiment, who for some reason had replaced Buchan in command of the elite fusilier battalion, was sent off that night to make sure that Murray did as he was told. Mackay himself then followed shortly before daybreak, and 10.00 hours found him at the southern end of the Pass. As his men had covered all of eleven miles since leaving their camp, they were allowed to rest there for two hours while he took stock of the situation, but it was worsening by the hour. Word now came back from Lauder that he had safely marched all the way through the Pass but found it completely unguarded! A further 200 men under Lieutenant Colonel William Arnot of Leven's Regiment were hastily despatched to back him up and, in the meantime, Mackay, on meeting Murray, quizzed him as to what had happened to his men. Abashed, his lordship gloomily confessed that, 'most of them were gone to the hills to put their cattle out of the way, so that he had at present but two or three hundred of them by him'. Even those men were nowhere to be seen in the Pass or anywhere else for that matter, but Mackay afterwards diplomatically professed himself sympathetic to Lord Murray's plight and forbore to condemn him. Nevertheless, it was obviously high time to get moving again, and so the Redcoats set off into the deep gorge, a narrow, gloomy passage where in places it was sometimes necessary for horsemen to move in single file. 'Balfour's, Ramsay's and Kenmore's battalions first, then Belhaven's troop of horse, followed by Levin's regiment, with a battalion of the Generals; after those followed the baggage horses being odds of 1200, and last of all the Earle of Annandales troop of horse with Hasting's regiment,

Opposite: Battle of Killiecrankie, 27 July 1689

which were left behind the baggage, lest the ennemy might detach men about the hill to attack it, or that the country men, [ie; Murray's people!] seeing it without sufficient guard, might not fall a plundering of it.'

According to legend, only a single marksman named Ian Ban Beg MacCraa, opposed Mackay's passage; shooting an officer mounted on a white horse at a spot now variously known as The Trooper's Den or the Horseman's Well. Otherwise, the passage of the defile was without incident. At about 16.00 hours on the afternoon of 27 July 1689, General Mackay emerged from the northern end of the Pass of Killiecrankie into the sunlight, and then halted on a flat riverside cornfield to let the long column close up behind him.

At Blair Castle, meanwhile, according to Balhaldie, some of Dundee's 'old officers' (i.e. the experienced ones who had actually seen some active service abroad) argued in a noisy council of war, that after the dash into Atholl the army was not yet ready to fight a major battle with an enemy correctly assumed to be superior in numbers. In rushing forward so precipitately, they had not only left substantial numbers of men behind, but those they had brought were fatigued and short of supplies. Instead, the professionals advocated relinquishing Blair for the present, and retiring northwards to rendezvous with the rest of the army. Once safely united, a battle might then be accepted on more equal terms and fought on ground of their own choosing.

Others, however, sagely opined that such a retreat could just as easily see the existing forces disintegrate and fresh men hesitate to join a lost cause. Instead Alasdair Dubh McDonnell, younger of Glengarry, spoke up in rebuttal and argued strongly in favour of fighting at once. Swayed by Glengarry's ebullient confidence, the other chieftains, many of them still young men like himself, vocally fell in behind him, swearing that their men were full of spirit, eager for the fray and that consequently falling back now would be fatal to their morale. Whether Dundee was swayed by these boasts or, as seems more likely he had already decided to fight, it was according to Balhaldie at least, the intervention of the highly respected (and much older) Locheil which proved decisive in the end. Pressed by Dundee for his opinion he responded by agreeing with Glengarry that the only acceptable course was:

> To fight immediately, 'for our men,' said he, 'are in heart; they are so far from being afraid of their enemy, that they are eager and keen to engage them, least they escape their hands, as they have so often done. Though we have few men, they are good, and I can venture to assure your Lordship that not one of them will faill yow. It is better to fight at the disadvantage of even one to three, than to delay it till

Mackay's dragoons and cavalry have time to joyn him. To pretend to stop them in the Pass is a vain project, for they have undoubtedly gott through it ere now, and to march up to them and not immediatyely to fight, is to expose ourselves to the want of provisions, seeing we can spare no men for forageing; besides we will discover that, even in our oun oppinion, we are unequall to the enemy, which would be of dangerous consequence among Highlanders.'[2]

There was rather more in that vein, and the story was no doubt considerably improved over the years to Locheil's advantage, for it is worth emphasising that the decision was no mere triumph of bombast over military logic, far less a dramatic intervention to reverse a counsel of despair. There were very sound practical reasons for fighting, which cannot have escaped Dundee and his military colleagues. In the first place, fighting a battle without delay was both a political and a military imperative. General Mackay represented the legitimate Scottish Government and all that the government needed to do was to sit tight and hold its nerve. Dundee, on the other hand, needed to fight and win a battle to assert both his own, and King James' continued legitimacy – and he had to win that battle soon. The preceding campaign in Badenoch and Strathspey, had been frustratingly indecisive and ultimately futile, and there was no reason to suppose that another round of the same dodging about might not have the same outcome. The difference was that, unless he was stopped, this time Mackay would march into the rebel heartland of Lochaber and plant a fort there which would simultaneously hold the clans in check and prevent the establishment of an Irish bridgehead.

Now was the opportunity to pin Mackay down and initiate a battle which this time he could not evade. No matter the apparent discrepancy in numbers and the rawness of Dundee's highland levies, the Braes of Killiecrankie were exactly the right place to fight that battle. Blocking the Pass entirely, or even ambushing Mackay as he made his way through it, would not actually produce the decisive result Dundee needed. Paradoxically, such was the narrowness of the Pass that even if an ambush was prepared and successfully sprung, Mackay's passage might be blocked but the actual physical destruction of his army would be problematic to say the least. What was more, afterwards the position might be reversed with Mackay blocking the southern end and so preventing the rebels from coming out of the hills by the most direct route. Just beyond the northern end of the Pass, however, was that rarest of all things; the perfect battlefield, a clear slope overlooking the road, where Mackay would have no room to manoeuvre and no means to retreat down that awful gorge; a battlefield where he could not attack and could do little to oppose a Highland charge. Far from trying to prevent Mackay from coming through the Pass it was in Dundee's interest to draw him through it, and Locheil's real role was not in persuading Dundee to fight, but to back him up by animating everyone else to fight.

In the meantime, Lauder's intrepid little battalion, now accompanied by Belhaven's troop of horse, was sent forward again by Mackay, this time tasked with exploring along the road towards Blair. They did not get very far. After little more than a few hundred yards they took post on a low hillock, covered in silver birch trees, just short of Aldclune. From there they could see some scattered parties of armed men equally cautiously advancing towards them and Lauder promptly sent back word to Mackay who galloped up to have a look for himself. Naturally enough, both officers assumed that they were looking at the advance guard of Dundee's army coming down the strath from Blair Castle and that a head-on clash was imminent. However, no sooner had Mackay ordered Brigadier Balfour to bring up the rest of the army as quickly as possible, than the General became uncomfortably aware that the rebels immediately to his front were not the ones he needed to be worrying about. The main body of the Highland army was actually closing in on him from a different direction entirely.

Leaving Stewart of Ballechin's Athollmen to 'amuse' the redcoats and mask his real movements, Dundee had earlier set off from Blair at a cracking pace, in what was at first, almost the opposite direction entirely. The rebels began by marching due north up the Water of Tilt, and then fetched a broad compass round about the north side of the Hill of Lude before eventually emerging on to the lower slopes of Creag Eallaich (509m), a mountain overlooking the mouth of the Pass. Coming from the direction and height which they did, the rebels most likely then formed their battle line by following a narrow terrace still to be found just above the 200-metre contour, marked by the steadings at Orchil and Lettoch, and by a track connecting the two with a third steading at Orchilmore a little to the south-east. Their intention, or at least their hope, may still have been to fall upon the soldiers as they debouched from the Pass, but by the time the Highlanders so unexpectedly came in view on the hillside above them, the bulk of Mackay's army was already safely through the defile and properly formed up again in the cornfield. Some of them, claimed Balhaldie, were even sitting down in rank and file as they waited, but others were taking on extra ammunition, while the last of the rear elements closed up. Surveying what was about to become the battlefield, Mackay very quickly decided that the cornfield was no place to make his stand, for:

> I discover'd the Highlanders approaching and gaining the heights, and pretty near before I could get my men to the ground which I judged by their motion they wold be at; so changing ye march and facing with every battalion as it stood by a *quart de conversion* to the right, having viewed the ground where I judged a propos to range them, I made every regiment march straight before its face up a steep bray, above which there was a plaine capable to containe more troupes than I had, and above that plaine the mater of a musket shot, a rising of a hill above which and betwixt it and a great hill at his back Dundie had place enough to range his men; I could not have rang'd myn but upon one line, both because I wold not be outwinged nor obliged to draw so neare the enemy having the advantage of the hill above us, by which he should force us to attack him against the height or be incommodate with his too neare fire. The enemy seeing me ranged sooner than he thought, (having, as I believe, designed to cum down upon the same ground before I could get possession of it, in which case he should have forced me over a river with his fire, which could not be without manyfast hazard of great disorder) he halted upon the height the space of more than two hours, wherin nothing past but som light skirmishing. [3]

So far so good, but having occupied what is now known as the Urrard plateau, Mackay explained in his later memoires exactly how he ranged his men to prevent their being outflanked on the broad 'plaine':

> The General having got upon the ground which he had remarked, he began to even his line, leaving a little distance betwixt every little battalion, having made two of each [regiment], because he was to fight three deep ; only, in the midst of the line, he left a greater opening where he placed the two troops of horse (the other being come up just as he had taken his ground with Hastings battalion) of a design when the Highlanders approached, and that the fire of the line should be spent, to make them fall out by the larger intervall, to flank the ennemy on either side, as occasion should offer, not daring to expose them to the ennemy's horse, which was composed all of gentlemen, reformed officers, or such as had deserted of Dundee''s regiment out of England, which was the reason he placed them behind the foot till all the fire were over on both sides.

General Mackay's Army

The extreme left of the Government's battle-line was firmly anchored by Colonel Lauder's fusiliers still ensconced in their birch wood. Next to them, deployed in two small battalions, or rather wings, stood Brigadier General Bartholomew Balfour's Regiment of the Scots Brigade. With both Balfour and his lieutenant colonel otherwise employed, and Major Patrick Balfour left behind with the second battalion at Stirling, the regiment must have led on this occasion by Captain James Fergusson of Balmakelly, an active officer who would survive the battle and later go on to command the Cameronians. On the right of Balfour's Regiment was another 'Dutch' unit, Colonel George Ramsay's Regiment, again formed in two small wings. While he had recently appeared to be a little out of his depth in exercising an independent command, George Ramsay of Carriden, near Linlithgow, was later described as 'a gentleman of a great deal of fire and very brave; of a sanguine complexion, well shaped, a thorough soldier.'[4] He would also prove to be one of the few officers to emerge from the coming debacle with any credit. All the units on this flank were perforce placed under the overall command of Brigadier Balfour, for the left wing was effectively separated from the rest of the army by what Mackay rather obscurely described as 'a boggy ground, which on a sudden could not, without hazard of bogging, be galloped.'[5]

On the other side of this morass stood Viscount Kenmure's Regiment. One of those commissioned on 19 April 1689, it was raised partly in his native Kirkcudbrightshire, and partly from amongst Protestant refugees from Ulster. While it is easily dismissed as raw and ill-trained, Mackay presumably selected it as being the best of the available new regiments. There was no question of Mackay keeping it in the rear out of harm's way, but he proceeded to make what proved to be a fatal error in deliberately creating another 'opening' in the battle line between Kenmure's Regiment and the Earl of Leven's Regiment off to its right. In effect, the regiment was left standing all on its own in the very centre of Mackay's battle-line with nothing but fresh air on both its flanks and in its rear.

Instead, within the gap, but by no means filling it, Mackay placed his artillery, which comprised three pack-mounted 'leather guns' under Captain James Smith, and the two troops of militia horse, mustering about fifty officers and men apiece, both under the overall command of Lord Belhaven. On the right was the Earl of Annandale's troop, commanded by Lieutenant William Lockhart of Cleghorn, and on the left Belhaven's own troop under Lieutenant William Hamilton, younger of Raploch.[6] The intention was not to try and hold the gap with a handful of mounted men but rather to use it as a gate and to counter-attack through it as soon as the Highlanders came within range.

Be that as it may, on the other side of the open space, the battle-line then continued south-eastwards along the plateau or shelf with the two battalions of the Earl of Leven's Regiment. Although earlier employed in the blockade of Edinburgh Castle, it was otherwise untried and had lost 200 men detached to reinforce the Inverness garrison. Standing immediately on Leven's right was General Mackay's own veteran regiment from the Dutch service, standing in two wings commanded by his brother, Lieutenant Colonel James Mackay. At first, as was only fit and proper, being the senior regiment present, it had occupied the traditional post of honour on the right wing, but then Mackay, still overly sensitive about his flanks, soon decided that he was going to need to extend his battle line a little further, for: 'The ennemys being upon their ground much about the same time with us, seemed to extend their order beyond our right wing; which the General observing made his line move to the right by the flank, least their design might be to flank, get betwixt him and the pass.'

Whether this was actually the case is unclear. As we shall see, Mackay may in fact have been mistaken in his interpretation of the rebel movements, but he responded by extending his own line. With the existing battle line already stretched, this could only be done, however, by bringing up Colonel Ferdinando Hastings' Regiment from the baggage train, and rather than use it to plug the wide gap between Kenmure's and Leven's regiments as he might more sensibly have done, he placed it on the right of his line. Nevertheless, the general did so reluctantly. The regiment was, as it happens, an English one, and indeed confounding traditional stereotypes, it was actually the *only* English unit to fight at Killiecrankie. Unfortunately, it is evident that the regiment had not fully recovered from the upheavals attendant on the revolution, when its previous commanding officer and a number of captains were arrested, and it was already low in numbers even before 100 men were detached to the Inverness garrison. That weakness is why Mackay had assigned it to guard the baggage in the first place and consequently, with a fight coming on, he now felt compelled to order a 'detachment of firelocks of each battalion to the right hand to fortify Hastings regiment'. Although he does not explicitly say so, it seems likely that by itself the regiment was only strong enough to form a single wing and that these detachments may have provided a second, *ad hoc* one, thus complicating yet further the organisation and cohesion of his battle line.

All in all, aside from the cavalry, and a Highland Independent Company, commanded by Robert Menzies, younger of Weem, which took post somewhere beyond Hastings's right, Mackay's reckoning that he had no more than 3,000 regular infantry in total, broadly implies that his six regiments mustered an average of about 500 men apiece; but it was not as simple as that.

At the best of times all military units suffer from surprising levels of wastage on active service and although in this case there had been very little real fighting thus far in the campaign, numbers were inevitably whittled down on a daily basis by sickness, by straggling and of course the absence of various detachments, which although often small in themselves were all-too significant in aggregate.

At the core of Mackay's army were his three veteran 'Dutch' regiments of the Scots Brigade. Each of the regiments had originally comprised ten companies of fifty-five men when they sailed from Holland seven months earlier, but they had since been ordered to double their establishment to 1,200 men apiece, in two battalions.[7] Although it is clear from Mackay's narrative that he took only one battalion from each of the regiments up to Killiecrankie and left the new ones at Stirling, his narrative confusingly refers to the tactical wings as battalions.[8]

Conversely, as part of the process of rebuilding what had once been King James's army, a fair number of officers and men were transferred out from his regiments to stiffen older units and provide cadres for new ones. Consequently, Mackay attempted to excuse their poor performance at Killiecrankie by grumbling that, all appearances to the contrary, his three Scots Brigade regiments were no longer the hardened veterans they appeared to be but were now 'mostly new levied men'.

Whatever their origin and level of experience, all six of Mackay's infantry regiments were comprised of both musketeers and pikemen. An *Act concerning the Militia* ratified by the Scots Parliament as long ago as 16 November 1668, stipulated that all pikemen were to be 'armed with pikes 15 foot long' (4.5 metres), which was only very slightly shorter than those carried during the Civil War, and this specification does not appear to have been amended by any subsequent legislation, although on active service pikemen were in any case notoriously prone to shortening their pikes unofficially. Armour did not feature in the Act and there is no suggestion that any armour was issued to Leven's and Kenmure's pikemen in 1689, but it is possible that both regiments included a small detachment of armoured halberdiers, for the Jacobite assault on Dunkeld a month later would be headed by men wearing armour which could only have been scavenged from Killiecrankie.[9]

As to the musketeers; although all the 'Dutch' musketeers carried modern firelocks, King William was understandably dismayed to find that the English regiments he inherited from King James had only half of their musketeers equipped with firelocks, while the other half still had to make do with the older matchlock muskets, which had a slightly lower rate of fire. This was probably still the case with Ferdinando Hastings' Regiment at Killiecrankie, but in the two newly raised Scots regiments, Leven's and Kenmure's, the proportion of matchlocks may perforce have been higher and surviving records of equipment issues also show that obsolete collars of bandoliers for matchlocks were still being issued in place of the cartridge boxes associated with firelocks in some units. Certainly, in the case of Kenmure's Regiment, at their first raising only the corporals were given patronashes or cartridge boxes, while the ordinary musketeers had bandoliers – sling belts from which were suspended a number of individual wooden or tin powder chargers, suggesting that firelocks may have been confined to NCOs and the grenadiers.[10] As to those bandoliers, in theory, the number of powder chargers equated to the number of rounds made up from the standard one pound (454g) of gunpowder issued to each man, i.e. at this time fourteen rounds, but the individual chargers, loosely hung from the bandolier by cords, were easily lost.

Included amongst the musketeers was a company of elite grenadiers, armed with firelocks. Notwithstanding popular legend, these were not comprised of the tallest men in a regiment (who at this time will have been assigned as pikemen) but were assault troops trained to attack or defend fortifications and undertake any other tasks demanding intrepidity and initiative. While hand grenades were obviously useful in attacking or defending fixed positions, they were not generally used on the battlefield, although fragments of an exploded one have been excavated at Killiecrankie.

Frustratingly, however, we cannot be entirely certain as to the relative proportions of pikes to muskets, which sometimes varied from regiment to regiment, especially when both officers and men took the view that real soldiers carried muskets, and often took unilateral action to exchange pikes for muskets whenever the opportunity arose.

At the time, the official ratio in the Dutch Army was one pikeman to three musketeers, and surviving muster rolls show that the English regiments at Sedgemoor four years earlier had the same ratio.[11] In the Scots Army, however, the proportion of muskets to pikes could fluctuate quite dramatically from regiment to regiment according to what was actually available from the magazines when it was first raised and equipped, but the Killiecrankie regiments ought to have been unexceptional in this regard. No figures appear to be available for Leven's Regiment at this time, but as it was the first unit to be raised, and therefore had first call on the Stirling magazine, we can reasonably expect the proper ratio to have prevailed. Kenmure's Regiment similarly received an issue of 450 bayonets on an establishment of 600 men – which confirms an intended ratio of three musketeers for each pikeman, and indeed given that some other units are known to have been worse equipped, this would suggest that Kenmure's was taken north by Mackay precisely because it was fully recruited and properly equipped and so fit for service.[12] Overall, therefore, probably no more than 25 per cent of Mackay's 3,000 infantry were armed with pikes rather than with muskets, and perhaps less.

Paradoxically, however, in terms of those men actually standing in the battle-line, the 'Dutch' regiments had a much lower ratio of musketeers to pikemen at Killiecrankie. Lieutenant Colonel Lauder's 200 strong fusilier battalion was created by taking detachments of sixty to seventy musketeers from each of the three regiments in the brigade[13]. Ordinarily, such a loss might be absorbed without too much inconvenience, but then, reacting to the Jacobites' apparent extension of their left, Mackay, as we saw, brought Hastings' Regiment up into the battle-line, and in doing so was forced to reinforce it. He tells us that, once again, this had to be done by assigning detachments of firelocks from each of the other battalions. We are not told just how many men were in each detachment, or whether Kenmure's and Leven's regiments contributed contingents, but there can hardly have been less than fifty men in each detachment, and perhaps, if they were once again drawn only from the 'Dutch' regiments, sixty to seventy men, which means that not only were the parent regiments weakened accordingly but the overall proportion of musketeers to pikemen in Mackay's centre could have slipped from 3:1 to 2:1. Of itself this may not necessarily have been critical, for lower ratios of muskets to pikes were certainly common in the past, but the reduction in firepower must have been a significant factor in weakening the centre of Mackay's line.

Furthermore, at Killiecrankie, Mackay tells us that he chose to deploy his men not in the traditional six ranks but in just three. Not surprisingly, there were more than a few who rushed to judgement afterwards, although Bishop Burnet, summed the question up best by remarking that: 'Many blamed Mackay for drawing up his army as he did; others justified him; but success failed him.' It is probably as fair a judgement as any defeated general has a right to expect, but there were two good reasons for drawing his men up in only three ranks.

In the first place, Mackay was concerned about the danger of being outflanked if he adopted a more compact formation and, in particular, he feared the possibility that the rebels might try to get between him and the Pass, hence the need to stretch his battle-line.

Conversely, thinning the line to three ranks optimised his available firepower in order to employ the Dutch Army's platoon firing system. In a six deep-formation not all of his musketeers could fire at once, but rather had to fire by successive ranks, while a three-rank-deep firing line allowed all of them to discharge their weapons at the same time. Far from being the worst possible formation in which to receive a Highland charge, as some historians have blithely charged, Mackay's three-deep line was probably the best one he could have adopted in the circumstances, and this would of course be triumphantly demonstrated by the Duke of Cumberland at Culloden fifty years later. All of the British regiments there were likewise drawn up in a three-rank deep firing line and that battle was decisively won by infantry firepower rather than by artillery or by cold steel.

Nevertheless, there were other, unforeseen flaws in Mackay's deployment.

Naturally enough, the pikemen were not scattered along the line, company by company, but were consolidated and brought together in large bodies or 'stands' in the centre of each wing, calculated to form a potent attacking formation, or conversely, a rallying point when attacked themselves. In practice, the dwindling numbers of pikemen compromised their effectiveness while at the same time the blocks of pikes created 'blind' spots in the firing line and relied on the musketeers on either flank to provide them with fire support in attack or defence.

Frustratingly, Mackay tells us very little about his pikemen at Killiecrankie and how they performed, beyond passing approving remarks on the brave stand made by some veterans belonging to his own regiment and recording a successful counter-attack by Hastings' pikemen. Otherwise we know nothing of their role or deployment and, particularly, we do not know whether it was only the musketeers who were deployed in just three ranks, or whether the pikemen were similarly reduced as some accounts suggest. Whilst a three-rank deep formation to facilitate platoon firing made very considerable tactical sense, similarly reducing the depth of the stands of pikemen did not. Not only would the necessary solidity of the pike formation be compromised yet further, but doubling the frontage obviously increased the 'blind' areas in Mackay's line, which would be inadequately covered by fire. For that reason, although thinning the musketeers, Mackay probably kept his pikemen in six ranks, and while we cannot be absolutely certain that he did so, a Gaelic poem about the doings of Glengarry's people implies that Kenmure's Regiment at least was standing in the old six ranks rather than three. If true, that would be applicable to the pikemen rather than to the regiment as a whole, and was more than likely duplicated across the rest of Mackay's battle-line.[14]

As to the rest of the army; having decided to bring Hastings' Regiment up into the front line, Mackay had no second line. In the event that the rebels broke through his overstretched front line, all that he had available to contain the breach were the two troops of militia horse, standing behind the guns. Even they, however, were intended to intervene proactively by charging against the oncoming clansmen, rather than merely reacting to a crisis. The fact of the matter was that Mackay had left no reserve of any kind, but at least he could comfort himself that the rebels were equally deficient in that regard, 'and so we lookt upon one another for at least two hours.'

Dundee's Highland Army

While Mackay's army was undoubtedly stretched to occupy its chosen position, the same was even more true of his opponents assembling on the hillside above him. In the first place, the Jacobites were a good deal weaker in numbers than Mackay's men. All in all, Dundee appears to have been able to pull together no more than about 2,000 Highlanders, and another 3-400 Irish, against Mackay's 3,000-odd regulars. Consequently, in all conscience, it is doubtful whether the Jacobites could truly be described as forming a proper battle-line at all. As Balhaldie noted, on observing the extent of Mackay's battle-line, Dundee was in turn obliged to 'inlarge his intervals' in order to try and match it, so that eventually his men were drawn up not in a continuous battle line but in three quite distinct and surprisingly widely separated bodies.

The rebel right wing, standing high above Balfour's command and ranged between the steadings of Orchil and Lettoch, comprised just a single regiment, albeit a large one, comprising two battalions of Highlanders from the Western Isles. This was commanded by young Sir John Maclean of Duart and his lieutenant colonel, Hector Maclaine of Lochbuie. How strong the regiment actually was we are not informed. As we saw in the previous chapter, Almerieclose grandiloquently declared them to be all of 1,000 strong at Dalmucomir, as they marched past Dundee with battle-axes on their shoulders. This would be remarkable if true, for they were not actually present at the muster! Writing somewhat more soberly half a century later, Duncan Forbes of Culloden carefully reckoned that in 1747 the total fighting strength of the Clan Maclean was then in the region of a much-more-realistic 500 men, and this is probably what they turned out at Killiecrankie.[15]

Mirroring that first boggy gap in Mackay's line by standing at least 150 metres away from the Macleans' left, was an Irish regiment commanded by Colonel James Purcell. Balhaldie sourly recorded that just days before the battle; 'Major-General Cannon overtook him [Dundee] with three hundred new-raised, naked, undisciplined Irishmen; which had this bad effect, that the Clans, who had been made to believe they were to be supported by a powerfull army from Ireland, with arms, ammunition, and all other provisions, saw themselves miserably disappointed: but they were still further discouraged, when they heard that the ships that King James had sent over with great plenty of meale, beefe, butter, cheese, and other necessarys, were taken by English ships in the Isle of Mull, where Generall Cannon had loitered so long, that the enemy had information of their arrival.' As regulars, Purcell's men ought to have been armed with pikes and matchlock muskets, but may well have been sadly deficient in both. In Ireland itself, a number of King James's newly levied regiments actually had more pikemen than musketeers and there is no good reason to suppose that Purcell's men were any better provided.[16] Immediately next to the Irish were two Highland regiments; the first led by the Captain of Clanranald and the other by Alasdair McDonnell of Glengarry. There were supposedly some 4-500 of Clanranald's people on parade at Dalmucomir in May, but given the known exaggerations in that account there were more realistically perhaps as few as 200 of them at Killiecrankie where they were under the effective command of Donald MacDonald of Benbecula.[17]

The numbers of Glengarry's men are even more problematic. Traditionally, his followers were not confined to his own immediate McDonnell clansmen but included a great many others who were neither his immediate kin nor his tenants. Dalmucomir supposedly saw 300 of them turn out, dressed in triple-striped tartan, with another 100 pikemen, distinguished by a red stripe in their plaids, marching behind Alasdair's younger brother, Angus McDonnell of Scotus. At least one estimate credits the regiment with as many as 600 men at Killiecrankie, albeit this erroneously claimed the Glencoe Macdonalds, and the Appin Stewarts were included as well as the Grants of Glenmoriston and Glen Urquhart. Of those supposed contingents, however, neither the Appin nor Glencoe men actually joined the army until 30 July, a full three days after the battle. Similarly, the presence of at least some of the Grants at this time may also be doubtful. While young John Grant of Glenmoriston was recorded as being present at Dalcomera and probably at Killiecrankie as well, it may have been a different matter with the Grants of Shewglie. That raid into Glen Urquhart by a predatory band of Camerons a month before the battle may well have dampened Jacobite enthusiasm in the glen whether the two Shewglie brothers were killed then or later. The estimate of 500 or 600 men, is more likely therefore to represent the combined total for *both* Glengarry's *and* Clanranald's regiments.

Also standing in the rebel centre, and perhaps eyeing the MacDonalds and their friends a little uneasily, were some of Sir Ewen Cameron of Locheil's clansmen, although their exact position is a touch uncertain. Balhaldie claims that they were separated from Glengarry's people by another gap in the line, filled by Dundee's cavalry, but this assertion was probably either a device to mask Locheil's later veering across the front of Leven's Regiment, or perhaps more likely reflected a shifting of position to put a little distance between the two regiments. Indeed, seeing such a move to the left by Locheil and consequent outward shuffling of Maclean's and Sleat's regiments, may have been what encouraged Mackay to extend his right wing by bringing up Hastings' Regiment.[18] As to their number, a large body of Camerons had been present (perhaps as many as 600 of them) at Dalmucomir, under Locheil and his lieutenant colonel, John Cameron of Glendessary. That muster, however, was held very much in the Camerons' home territory and the clan regiment was no doubt bulked out there with local men who came along to the grand day out but were not otherwise capable of marching off to war. In any case, Balhaldie very explicitly states that Lochiel had only some 240 of his Lochaber people with him at Killiecrankie, while the rest of his clansmen, raised in the further reaches of Morven, Sunart and Ardnamurchan, were still on the march under his eldest son John, and would not join the army until a few days afterwards.[19]

At all events, another substantial gap then separated Lochiel's Regiment from the Jacobite left wing. Standing directly above Mackay's and Hastings' regiments, this was itself comprised of two regiments. One of them, commanded by Sir Alexander Maclean, was of course something of an oddity for the rebel army in that they were to all intents and purposes Highland regulars. Built up around a cadre of two Irish companies, it was largely comprised of the Kintyre men he had rescued from near certain capture on Gigha. Since then they had largely served as Dundee's personal escort battalion, while Sir Alexander proceeded to prove Locheil to be wrong by properly disciplining or training them up into what was reputed to be the toughest regiment in the army.

Immediately before Killiecrankie, his lieutenant colonel, Donald MacNeil of Gallachallie, was sent on a detour to assist Farquharson of

Inverey in the Braemar area and when he re-joined the army soon afterwards, Inverey came too with a little contingent of about sixty men.

The other regiment on the left was a much more typical Highland unit commanded by Sir Donald MacDonald, younger of Sleat. Balhaldie reckoned it to be 700 strong, which seems more than a little optimistic unless, as seems possible, it also included a stray contingent of Keppoch Macdonalds and also perhaps Inverey's men, who lacked the discipline instilled in Maclean's Regiment.

As a Highlander himself, Mackay was more than familiar with his opponents' fighting methods and described how they:

> Never fight against regular forces upon anything of equal terms, without a sure retreat at their back, particularly if their ennemies be provided of horse ; and to be sure of their escape, in case of a repulse, they attack bare footed, without any cloathing but their shirts, and a little Highland dowblet, whereby they are certain to outrun any foot, and will not readily engage where horse can follow the chase any distance. Their way of fighting is to divide themselves by clans, the chief or principal man being at their heads, with some distance to distinguish betwixt them. They come on slowly till they be within distance of firing, which, because they keep no rank or file, doth ordinarly little harm. When their fire is over, they throw away their firelocks, and every one drawing a long broad sword, with his targe (such as have them) on his left hand, they fall a running toward the ennemy, who, if he stand firm, they never fail of running with much more speed back again to the hills.

Some recent historians have essayed to represent this 'Highland Charge' as a unique tactical doctrine devised by the celebrated Alasdair MacColla, during the Great Civil War of the 1640s.[20] In reality, similar shock tactics were common throughout Europe both at the time and in the following century as officers strove to overcome the deficiencies of muzzle-loading firearms. King Charles' Cavalier army for one, was prone to marching up to its foes, firing a single volley and then falling on happy go lucky (charging in a disorderly manner) with swords and the butt-ends of their military-issue muskets. Other armies would later do the same, albeit usually in a less disorderly fashion, in what were termed volley and bayonet tactics. All that was unique about Highland clansmen was that, as Mackay remarks, a shortage of muskets meant that the initiating volley was not particularly effective.

In addition to the clans and Purcell's Regiment, Dundee also had a small body of about forty cavalrymen; being the last remnants of his regular Royal Regiment of Horse, together with a number of reformado officers[21] and other volunteers; albeit there were far fewer of the latter than at the outset of the adventure when they mustered two troops. They were comprised of minor Angus lairds for the most part, but they also included James Seton, the 4th Earl of Dunfermline. Aside from his brother-in-law, the Duke of Gordon, the latter was still the only Scottish nobleman of rank to have rallied to King James thus far, and he perhaps, not unnaturally, thought his elevated social status to be sufficient justification for his taking command of the cavalry. However, Sir William Wallace of Craigie, one of Dundee's original officers, trumped him by flourishing King James' commission. Whether this was an entirely new commission supposedly signed by the Earl of Melfort on the King's behalf, or whether it was actually Craigie's original commission as a troop commander in the Royal Regiment of Horse does not appear, but there was no denying its being the King's commission and in the face of it Dunfermline stiffly gave way.

Now, as an earlier Sir William Wallace had once pithily declared, it was time to 'hop', but both sides at first seemed curiously reluctant to enter the ring.

NOTES

[1] Mackay, p.49.

[2] Balhaldie, pp.258-264.

[3] 'A Short relation as far as I can remember, or what passed before, in and after the late defaite in Athole, of a parte of their Majesties forces under my command.' Strathbogie 17 August 1689, in Mackay, p.264.

A *quart de conversion* was literally a quarter turn. In this case, rather than wheel from column of march into line, they may simply have faced to the right exactly as they stood before marching up the hill.

[4] Fergusson, J. *Papers Illustrating the History of the Scots Brigade in the Service of the United Netherlands* (Scottish History Society, Edinburgh, 1898), vol., p.508.

[5] Mackay, p.53. As usual the general's language might be a touch tortured, but the present author retains fond memories of the major re-enactment of the battle by the Sealed Knot society in May 1973, during which he saw an unwary cavalry trooper quite literally sink up to his horse's belly in that same bog!

[6] National Archives of Scotland (NAS), PA2/33, f.56-56v *Commissions to the lieutenants of horse*. Annandale, whose support for the new regime was equivocal, had remained behind in Edinburgh, sitting as a member of the Parliament. With Belhaven in overall command both troops were therefore commanded by their lieutenants. Annandale's troop was recruited in his native Dumfriesshire and Wigton and might justly be accounted Covenanters, while Belhaven's men may have hailed from Lanark, Stirling and Clackmannan, rather than East Lothian, but still no doubt also had a fair few committed Presbyterians in their ranks, (see Appendix 1).

[7] Fergusson, J. *The Scots Brigade in Holland* (1899), vol.1, pp.516-518.

8 Technically there was some justification for this in that earlier in the century infantry regiments were temporarily divided for tactical purposes into two battalions. Over time battalions became more permanent units and when they in turn needed to be split, the two halves were designated as wings rather than battalions, precisely in order to avoid the terminological confusion evident in Mackay's narrative.

   In all three cases, the incomplete second battalions left at Stirling were commanded by the majors; John Buchan of Mackay's, Patrick Balfour of Balfour's and William Murray of Ramsay's.

9 See discussion of this practice, unique to the Scots army in Chapter 6.

10 *Register of the Privy Council of Scotland* (1689), P.152.

11 Scott, C.L., *The Armies and Uniforms of the Monmouth Rebellion* (Partizan Press, Leigh on Sea, 2008), p. 34.

12 *Register of the Privy Council of Scotland*, pp.152, 542-3. Unfortunately, when it came to equipping the reconstituted regiment in September of that year, a plea to the government for 'what snapwarks [firelocks] muskets, bandoleers they wanted', together with pikes and bayonets, was answered by warrants for 200 obsolete matchlock muskets and 100 pikes!

13 It will be recalled that a detachment from the fusilier battalion, under Captain Gordon, comprising three officers and seventy-six men had earlier been left behind as a garrison for Abergeldie Castle and they, as was customary, will then have been replaced by a further subvention from their parent units.

14 Hopkins, Paul, *Glencoe and the end of the Highland War* (1986), p.157.

15 Stewart, of Garth, David, *Sketches of the Highlanders of Scotland* (1822), vol, pp.26-27. Almerieclose *The Grameid*, p.140.

16 Balhaldie, p.257. Describing them as 'naked' obviously suggests that they had no uniforms, but most of King James' Irish regiments at this time were dressed in undyed white coats which may not have been recognised by onlookers as military uniforms, especially if coats were the only garments issued.

17 Allan MacDonald, the Captain of Clanranald (a traditional title for the chief which by this period was peculiar to that clan) was only 16 at the time and while he was very properly present at the head of the clan, actual oversight of the regiment was exercised by his Tutor or guardian, Colonel Donald MacDonald of Benbecula.

18 Balhaldie, p.266. In so doing Balhaldie also contrived for some reason to omit any mention at all of Sir Alexander Maclean's Regiment and to replace it with Locheil's Regiment on the left wing.

19 ibid, p.266.

20 Most notably: Stevenson, Dr. David, *Alasdair MacColla and the Highland Problem in the Seventeenth Century* (John Donald, Edinburgh 1980). Stevenson provides a splendid and indispensable discussion of the 'Highland Problem' and Alasdair MacColla's place in Scottish history, but unfortunately his excursion into military matters is seriously flawed.

21 'Reformadoes' were officers who volunteered to temporarily serve in the ranks as ordinary troopers, for want of any men to command. The term derives from their being the left-overs after weak regiments were *reformed* or combined together to form viable units.

Chapter 5

The Battle of Killiecrankie: An Avalanche of Steel

In all the circumstances, it is probably not surprising that once the two armies were drawn up neither side showed much enthusiasm for actually starting the fight. Both had, in effect, rushed into the encounter without fully thinking through what was going to happen next. Mackay, for his part, was presently occupying as good a position as the circumstances allowed and while the intrepid Captain Young had successfully essayed a frontal attack straight up a steep hillside a couple of months earlier, the General instead rather prudently; 'resolved to make the best of that ground, and rather receive the check there in good order, than to put his men out of breath and in disorder, by attacking the enemy against an hill'. As he could neither manoeuvre nor retreat, all he could really do was await the rebels' next move and hope that it came in daylight.

The Highlanders' reluctance to advance, on the other hand, he initially ascribed to irresolution, and in that, he may not have been too far wrong for, skirmishing aside, this was the first time they had come to a pitched battle with regular troops. If nothing else, from their elevated vantage point, it will have been all-too obvious to the rebels that although Mackay did not have as many cavalry as they had originally feared, they were still badly outnumbered by the Redcoats. Balhaldie also offers the traditional explanation that, although the Highlanders were eager and impatient for action, the sun was shining full in their faces and Dundee would not allow them to engage 'till it was nearer its decline' and had gone below the crest of the hills opposite.[1] That seems unlikely, since the sun would have disappeared as soon as they descended, and instead Mackay eventually came to the conclusion that the Highlanders were simply playing a waiting game in order to try to intimidate his men:

> The General not willing to attack, for the reasons already alledged, and the Highlanders apparently out of irresolution, which he apprehended to be of design to expect the night, wherein they might happily hope to frighten our men by a sudden motion doun the hill with a loud shout, after their manner, very likely to put new men unaccustomed with an ennemy in a fright and disorder, tho' they could be kept more allert and ready then he could hope for during the whole night ; neither durst he venture to pass the river in their presence and so near them, both by reason of the hazard, the souldiers, ordinarily taking such a motion for a subject of apprehension, and the imputation which he had to expect, if he were beat in retiring. He resolved then to stand it out, tho' with great impatience, to see the ennemy come to a resolution, either of attacking or retiring, whereof they had more choice than he.

It was to be a matter of waiting then, and in the meantime, he was irritated by constant sniping as he passed to and fro along his battle-line, trying to encourage his men with turgid exhortations to defend their King, their country and the Protestant religion. This sniping, he claimed, was no random harassing fire, but was deliberately targeted at himself, for 'he always in action giving his ground to every one, they distinguished him, which drew their papping shot over all where he moved, whereby severals were wounded before the engagement.' In retaliation for this ungentlemanly conduct, and also in the hope of provoking an attack before the light failed, 'he ordered the firing of three little leather field-pieces, which he caused carry on horse-back with their carriages, which proved of little use, because the carriages being made too high to be more conveniently carried, broke with the third firing'.

This apparent fiasco was unfortunate, but perhaps not entirely unexpected. Bishop Burnett explained that the leather guns in question were, 'of white iron, tinned and done with leather, and corded: so they would serve for two or three discharges. These were light, and were carried on horses'. Made as long ago as 1650 by James Wemyss, the then master gunner of Scotland, they were indeed quite remarkable weapons. The barrels were quite literally simple tubes rolled from sheet iron and welded ('tinned') along the seam. A series of reinforcing rings were then shrunk on and the whole lot tightly bound around with cord, and covered with a leather skin. As originally constructed, most of the guns were also double barrelled and this may still have been the case at Killiecrankie.[2]

As lightweight anti-personnel weapons they were handy and highly mobile, but they were only ever intended to discharge small shot; a handful or more of musket balls or similar sized pieces of scrap metal bursting out of a canvas bag or tin canister, just like a large shotgun. Cannonballs were a different matter entirely since they required a much heavier charge of gunpowder and reducing that charge for safety's sake would have severely limited their effectiveness, especially at a range of 400 metres. This is graphically illustrated by the story of how one of Glengarry's men – said to have been James Grant of Shewglie – was allegedly knocked over by a cannonball which struck full on his targe, no doubt leaving him a little shocked but otherwise unhurt, while on the other hand overcharging the guns to cast a cannonball so far might account for their collapse.[3]

Be that as it may, Captain James Smith and his gunners were still at their posts when the Highland charge rolled over them, but whether they ever had the chance to use their guns at close range as they were intended is not revealed.

At any rate, rather more effective in bringing on the engagement, was a sharp skirmish aimed at dislodging a party of some sixty of the Camerons, who rather too boldly came forward to occupy one of the hillside steadings. From there they were bringing down a harassing fire on the troops below and still, rather unsportingly, trying to assassinate Mackay himself.[4] Goaded into action, he sent a captain with a detachment of his own regiment scrambling up the hill to evict them, 'judging withall that that skirmish might draw on a general engagement, which he earnestly longed for before the night approached'.

In this, at least, Mackay was absolutely correct in his judgement, for as a later Jacobite commander, Lord George Murray, commented following a very similar incident in 1745; Highlanders had 'a freit (superstition) not to turn their backs upon the first sight of the enemy'.[5] The un-named captain duly rushed the buildings, sending the Camerons running back to their main body and almost at once – at about 20.00 hours, or half an hour before sunset, the whole Highland army riposted by coming forward, down the steep slope and into a storm of musketry that must have confirmed some of the worst fears of their leaders. On Mackay's left, however, the immediate result was nothing if not dramatic:

> At last towards sun setting [wrote Mackay] they began to descend, and having made a ragged fire threw away their snaphans[6] and ran

down the hill with drawn broadswords and targes; the battalion of Hastings which was ranged upon the right hand, because the rest were drawn up in order before it had past the defile; that of my regemet, my Lord Leven's, and Kenmore with the half of Ramsay's battalion made pretty good fire, the other half of Ramsay's, with Balfour's whole battaillon, and Lauder's detachment of 200 men, gave ground, or rather fled without any firing.[7]

That bald summary might serve for all too many histories of the campaign, but the rout was not quite so straightforward and the battle was far from over. Nevertheless, it was the critical moment which Mackay had anticipated, and in which the battle could be lost or won in just a few minutes. Now was the time to launch his cavalry through the gap in his front line. Lord Belhaven's Troop was ordered to ride forward, wheel to its left and sweep Balfour's front, while Annandale's was to swing to the right and plunge into the flank of the Highlanders attacking Leven's Regiment. Instead, to his utter chagrin, the counter-attack collapsed at the very outset, for; 'notwithstanding I brought them up myself, and that the Lord Balhaven who commanded them did behave very honestly; after a little confused firing they reversed upon the Lord Kenmore's right wing and so began the first breach so neare as I could remarque.'[8]

Given a little breathing space, the hapless Covenanters might yet have recovered from being ridden over by their own cavalry, but of course, hard on the horsemen's heels, came the howling mob of MacDonalds of Clanranald and Purcell's Irishmen.[9] Worse still, the indications are that instead of simply braving that 'pretty good fire' and boldly attacking Lord Kenmure's men head on, most of the Highlanders very sensibly poured into the yawning gap in the battle-line, overrunning Smith and his gunners and clawing away at the exposed flanks of the infantry to send the entirety of Kenmure's Regiment and the left hand battalion of Leven's Regiment tumbling back in a panic-stricken rout.

As Mackay had earlier predicted, once they broke, the hapless infantrymen were swiftly overtaken and cut down by the lightly equipped clansmen, for, as he had warned; 'if they happened to give way… before that rabble of the Highlanders, they might freely conclude few or none of them should escape those naked pursuers far speedier of foot than they'. For some, possession of a horse may have been critical to their survival. Contemporary practice required only the major and adjutant of an infantry regiment to be mounted in battle, while the other officers from the colonel on down were expected to stand on foot with their men, and if necessary to die with them too. Thus, Sir John Dalrymple, in passing on the news of the battle sadly commented that, 'I fear few will either get off or get quarter except some of the horse who ran first, and the foot officers ther servants ar all com away with ther horses.' Not surprisingly he added that; 'this makes a great consternation heir'. Family tradition certainly holds that Lieutenant Colonel John Fergusson of Craigdarroch, the second-in-command of Kenmure's Regiment, died at Killiecrankie precisely because his servant had indeed run off with his horse, while conversely Mackay's cavalry must have gotten away virtually unscathed for they were back in action within days, and in October it was noted that both of the troops were then only ten men below their authorised establishment of fifty.[10]

In the meantime, the General related in a little more detail that: 'Having passed through the croud of the attacking Highlanders, he turned about to see how matters stood, and found that all his left had given way, and got down the hill which was behind our line, ranged a little above the brow thereof, so that in the twinkling of an eye in a manner, our men, as well as the ennemy, were out of sight, being got doun pall mall to the river where our baggage stood.' Afterwards, being Hugh Mackay of Scourie, he piously reflected that, 'resolution and presence of mind in battle being certainly a singular mercy of God, he denyeth and giveth it when and to whom he will, for there are seasons and occasions, that the moft firm and stout-hearted do quake and shake for fear: As Solomon saith, "The wicked flee when none pursueth, but the righteous is bold as a Lyon."' Or, as Colonel August Kaust rather more pithily wrote of the American Civil War: 'In battle men are apt to lose their heads and do very absurd things.'

Nevertheless, although there is no doubting the horror of the initial onset, once the clansmen had routed his left wing, the lure of the 1,200-odd pack horses and their loads, still standing in the cornfield by what is now known as the Claverhouse Stone, proved an irresistible distraction from the slaughter.[11] Craigdarroch may have fallen, but Lord Kenmure himself escaped and only two other officers of his regiment, Captain James Donaldson and Lieutenant James Nisbet, are known to have become casualties – and what is more both were taken prisoner unhurt. Even the gunner, James Smith, despite 'many wounds in his head and body, survived to successfully petition the Privy Council for his back-pay!'[12]

As to the rest of Mackay's left wing; Brigadier Balfour lost his horse early on and was killed 'labouring with a few persons by him to get off, after his regiments had abandoned him'. Apparently, he died somewhere near Aldclune, where, according to legend, two highlanders got him up against a tree and then a third, traditionally identified as a minister of religion named Robert Stewart, came up and after he refused to surrender, killed him with a single blow.[13] Captain Thomas Erskine and Captain William Nanning of Balfour's Regiment also died trying to reach the river along with a Lieutenant Chambers, although Captain James Fergusson and Captain Bartholomew Balfour (Brigadier Balfour's son) were both captured. Ramsay's Regiment lost even more officers and men, with all four of its captains killed, namely; William Miln, John Gibson, William Douglas and John Clerk, while Captain-lieutenant Joost Van Beest was taken prisoner.[14] George Ramsay himself, however, somehow fought his way across the river, where he rallied the survivors and began wondering what had happened to his general.

Mackay, as it happens, was having an uncomfortably adventurous time, more appropriate to a dashing young subaltern than to a general officer of mature years:

> The General observing the horse come to a stand, and firing in confusion, and the foot beginning to fall away from him, thinking happily that the horse would be pricked to follow his example, and in all cases to disengage himself out of the croud of Highlanders which came doun just upon the place where he was calling to the officers of the horse to follow him, spurr'd his horse through the ennemy, (where no body nevertheless followed him, but one of his servants, whose horse was shot in passing,) where he judged, by the way they made for him, tho' alone, that if he had had but fiftie resolute horse, such as Colchester's, he had certainly, by all human appearance recovered all, notwithstanding the foot was just flying over all.

It was a truly extraordinary, perhaps unprecedented, and certainly a ridiculous situation. In the space of a few minutes, his army, had to all appearances not only fled, but had quite literally left him standing in the midst of the battlefield, surrounded but ignored by the enemy: 'At which sad spectacle,' he ruefully admitted, 'it may be easily judged how he was surprized, to see at first view himself alone upon the field, but looking further to the right he espyed a small heap of red coats.'

His left flank and part of his centre may have collapsed, but over on his right flank the fighting was still very far from over and the rebels had in fact suffered something of a disaster. Balhaldie tells us that during the period of waiting which preceded the battle, Dundee went along the line, and: 'Each Clan, whither small of great, had a regiment assigned them'. This, he says, was done at Locheil's suggestion, and claims that the Camerons were instructed to deal with Mackay's Regiment, clearly identified by what was claimed to be the Prince of Orange's standard.[15] However, if this was indeed the case, it meant that instead of going straight down the hill against Leven's Regiment, Locheil sent his men slantwise across their front. Pride may have played its part in choosing to tackle the opposing general's own regiment and there is no doubting Locheil was a proud man. He may also have been less than keen to co-operate with Glengarry after the Glen Urquhart business, but whatever the reasoning there is no doubting the consequences of his decision. Feeling the weight of his sixty-three years he himself was unable to keep pace with his men, but according to the ever loyal Balhaldie, 'leaving them to the protection of God, he satt down by the way, and deliberately pulling off his shoes that pinched him, had the agility to get up with them just as they drew their swords'.

This was probably just as well, for in anticipation of the attack, Mackay had earlier, 'commanded the officers, commanding battalions, to begin their firing at the distance of 100 paces by platoons, to discourage the approaching Highlanders meeting with continual fire.'

Platoon firing was a Dutch innovation intended to facilitate a steadier and more effective rate of fire. Ever since the invention of gunpowder troops armed with muskets had been trained to fire by one rank at a time, in the expectation that by the time that the last rank had fired the first one would have been able to reload in readiness to commence the sequence anew. There were a number of variants on this basic technique but the general adoption of the firelock or flintlock musket in the latter half of the seventeenth century speeded up the loading process, and so reduced the number of ranks needed for the firing cycle, which in turn meant more men were firing at a given time. Then the Dutch took it a stage further. As all three or four ranks could now fire simultaneously, the men in the firing line were told off into platoons, each thirty or forty strong, with the intention that instead of firing by ranks, all the men in each platoon would fire a volley one after the other in a ripple, or rather a series of ripples along the battle-line.

Although the technique itself was never quite so effective as its proponents then or afterwards claimed it to be, platooning was conceived as a method of conducting a sustained firefight against other regular soldiers, not a mob of fast moving Highland clansmen intent on performing a creditable impression of the wolf coming down on the fold. As General Mackay put it: 'the Highlanders are of such a quick motion, that if a battalion keep up his fire till they be near to make sure of them, they are upon it before our men can come to their second defence, which is the bayonet in the musle of the musket.' In brutally simple terms, the spluttering ripple of fire by platoons might indeed be 'continuall' but that did not guarantee that it would kill enough of the onrushing Highlanders quickly enough to stop them.

Yet Mackay's men, or at least those who stood their ground, may have come close to doing just that. Steep as the slope was, it was far from unbroken. The ledge up by Orchil and Lettoch where the clansmen deployed was not the only terrace on the hillside. There was another one just thirty metres ahead of Mackay's battle-line and the patterns of musket balls recovered during the 2002 excavations have revealed that the Highlanders' breasting of the terrace was the signal for a last devastating ripple of platoon fire, or more likely a massed volley, delivered at point-blank range by the redcoats, which quite literally mowed down those in the front rank, including all-too many of the leaders.

So many fell, that Mackay certainly had some justification for claiming afterwards that far from sweeping all before them: 'The enemy lost on the field six for our one, the fire to our right having been continued and brisk, whereby not only Dundee, with several gentlemen of quality of the countys of Angus and Perth, but also many of the best gentlemen among the Highlanders, particularly of the Macdonalds of the Isles and Glengarie were killed, coming down the hill upon Hastings, the General, and Levin's regiments, which made the best fire and all the execution; particularly the Generals battalion made great fire, being well exercised thereto by his brother.'

Like Locheil's people, both Sir Alexander Maclean's and MacDonald of Sleat's regiments initially directed their advance against Mackay's Regiment, but as they came running down the hill across his front, Hastings refused or swung back his left flank in order to shoot into them more effectively. As a result, although young Sleat himself came through unscathed, his military advisor and second in command, Sir George Barclay, was wounded and five of his 'near relations' were killed 'and a multitude of others whom it were tedious to recount.' Similarly,[16] in Sir Alexander Maclean's Regiment, young John MacDonald of Lairgie and his Tutor were killed, 'along with several gentlemen of the same family'. Another casualty was Charles Farquharson of Balmoral, who according to Deeside tradition, was crippled while serving under Inverey at Killiecrankie. So bad were the casualties, that Dundee's left wing was effectively stopped cold in its tracks. Some men may have succeeded in joining with Locheil's Camerons in breaking Mackay's Regiment but, for most, the enfilade fire from Hastings' was too 'hot' and for a time they were compelled to take cover amongst the walls and buildings at Orchilmore.

Further in towards the centre it was just as bad and Balhaldie admitted that, 'Locheil lost in this action one hundred and twenty of his men, which was just one half of his number, and was occasioned by a furious fire that he received in the flank from Leven's battalion.'[17] This was probably the highest proportionate loss out of any of the rebel units on the field and certainly one that would not be equalled, far less surpassed, until the bloody debacle at Culloden half a century later. Yet, notwithstanding their terrible losses, the Camerons still came tumbling down the brae. On level ground the sudden impact of so many simultaneous casualties ought to have halted them just as the regiments to their left were. Instead, not just raw courage but physical momentum and the sheer difficulty of actually stopping running down that steep slope, still carried them forward to pile into Mackay's Regiment.

Murderously effective though the platoon-firing might have been; there was general agreement that once the Highland charge actually impacted on the thin red line it was a very different matter and that, 'few or none of them [the clansmen] were killed after they drew their swords, and that the greatest part of them fell within a few paces of their enemy when they received the last fire, before they themselves discharged; after which, their loss was inconsiderable'.[18]

At this point, General Mackay famously asserted that his men were defeated by an unforeseen technical flaw in their weaponry. The musketeers at this time were equipped with dagger-like plug bayonets which were jammed directly into the muzzles of their pieces, effectively turning them into short pikes. Indeed, the weapon-handling drill for these hybrid weapons was directly adapted from that used by pikemen, and once the bayonets were fixed the musketeers were expected to level their weapons 'breast high', forming what was (hopefully) an impenetrable hedge of points. Unfortunately, of course, once the bayonet was stuffed into the muzzle, the musket could not be fired – and it probably took some effort to lever the bayonet out again afterwards. The conversion of the musket from a missile weapon to a bladed one therefore needed to be delayed until the last possible moment. Yet with no time to do so after delivering that final point-blank volley many of the Redcoats ran 'and the fire ceasing on both sides, nothing was heard for some few moments but the sullen and hollow clashes of broad-swords, with the dismall groans and crys of dyeing and wounded men'.

Naturally enough, Mackay's Regiment suffered badly as the clansmen took their revenge with little quarter being asked or given. The most prominent casualty was the General's brother, James Mackay, 'who, being his lieutenant colonel, commanded the battalion, and was killed on the spot with severals of the old souldiers pikemen, who stood by him after the shot had run away'. The 'several' others included Captain Alexander Lamy from Forfar and Captain Angus Mackay – both of whom according to the General were first shot down and then, having been abandoned by their men were 'dispatch'd with broadswords'. Two other captains were wounded. One was the General's nephew, Captain Robert Mackay, who collected no fewer than eight broadsword cuts before being fortunate enough to be hoisted on to the back of the Earl of Leven's horse. The other may have been George Connock who was serving with the regiment in 1688 but afterwards disappears from the rolls, but there is no direct evidence he was at Killiecrankie and it is more likely Mackay was referring to Captain-Lieutenant Mackenzie, who died during the retreat. In the end Mackay lamented that all the captains of his regiment were, 'either killed or do bear the marks of their good behaviour. Besides I lost six very good subalterns and brisk fellows'.[19]

It is unlikely that the doomed stand by Lieutenant Colonel Mackay and his pikemen lasted long before fugitives and pursuers alike rolled down the hill towards the baggage train and into the Pass beyond, once again leaving much of the battlefield proper strangely deserted apart from the dead, the wounded and stragglers from both sides. Yet, extraordinary as it seems, after that brief spasm of extreme violence, the battle was still not over after all. Hastings' Regiment had thus far escaped virtually unscathed and the remaining wing or battalion of Leven's was also still standing firm and serving as a rallying point for survivors from the other units.

It was at this juncture, when Mackay saw that 'small heap of red coats'; and 'whither galloping, he found it to be a part of the Earle of Levin's regiment, with himself, his Lieutenant Colonel, Major, and most of his officers upon their head, whom the General praised for their stedfastnes'. Leven's, and as soon became apparent, Hastings' Regiment as well, had for the moment weathered the worst of the storm and were being studiously ignored by their equally battered opponents. This was just as well, for Mackay quickly discovered that, although still holding their position, Leven's men were badly shaken and probably on the verge of dissolution: 'Seeing the men in confusion,' he continued:

> there being some few of other regiments got among them, [he] prayed the Earle with his officers to see to get them speedily in condition to receive the ennemy, whom he minutely expected, while he galloped further to a part of Hastings, which the Colonel was marching up to their first ground, which he affirmed to have lost in

pursuit of the ennemy, who, thinking to fall in his flank, he wheeled with his pikes to the right upon them, whereby they leaving him, repaired to the rest of their forces, which they saw among the baggage at the river-side, the plundering whereof gave time to many of our runnaways to get off, and having joined Hastings with the rest of Levins, he dispatched a nephew of his[20], captain of his regiment, seeing him on horseback, (tho he had eight wounds with broad swords upon his body) after his runnaways to exhort all officers, whom he could meet with, to keep up their men, and labour to bring them back to joyn him, in which case he assured them of advantage.'

Nevertheless, although there were evidently scattered parties of officers and men from the broken regiments still keeping together, he complained that it was difficult to get anyone to listen to him and take a grip of the situation, 'having in all about 400 men which wee could not possibly bring in any order, and receiving notice that none of the officers could persuade their men to stand, much less to return back'.[21] He did briefly consider barricading them all in Urrard House and its associated outbuildings and walls (quaintly referring to it as a garden), but 'presently changed his purpose, considering, if succour failed, as readily would fall out, there was no hope of escaping out of the ennemy's hands by defending an inclosure so far from new relief'.

Now was the time for the rebel officers to rally their own men and finish off the remaining redcoats while at least some light remained, but there was an appalling problem. Not only had far too many of the clan leaders, great and small, been killed or wounded by those last point-blank volleys of musketry, but Dundee himself was also down.

The timing and the circumstances of his fall and of his subsequent death were deliberately obscured by his own officers at the time, but can be satisfactorily reconstructed to a degree. Balhaldie has a plausible story that before the battle Dundee was urged by Locheil and the other chiefs to keep out of harm's way, but stoutly responded that it was necessary in this first battle to demonstrate to the clansmen 'that I can hazard my life in that service as freely as the meanest of them'. Accordingly, he took post in the centre of the battle-line with the intention of engaging Mackay's cavalry with his own. In the event of course, the Redcoats fled and so instead Dundee, together with the Earl of Dunfermline and about sixteen other companions, rode into the gun-line and set about the hapless artillerymen, while Colonel Wallace rather more sensibly swung most of the troop around and helped collapse the left of Leven's Regiment.[22]

Having captured, or at least ridden over the guns, Dundee also spotted that 'small heap of red coats' still standing firm further over to his left, and quite naturally decided to ride across and rally his own men against them. All of this took place in the space of just a few minutes and, ironically, it is possible that having both been momentarily deserted by their men, he and Mackay were only within a few metres of each other at the time. They certainly set off in the same direction, but for Dundee it was a fatal decision. Writing long years afterwards, Balhaldie felt compelled to deny what was then still a current story that Dundee was shot while vainly trying to get the two regiments on the left moving again, in order to deal with Leven's battalion. Instead he ingeniously claimed that it was an aide de camp who was sent, but, 'not having courage enough to pass through the interval betwixt them and Locheil's men, where the enemy's fire was very hot, he called out to such of them as were nearest, that the Generall wanted them, and they not understanding the orders, and their being entangled among dykes and houses, occasioned some confusion'.[23]

In point of fact, Dundee must indeed have being trying to reach the two regiments pinned down at Orchilmore, for he and his escort galloped towards them directly across the front of Leven's battalion. Unsurprisingly, they were saluted with a volley, and Balhaldie very circumstantially recorded that, 'The fatall shott, that occasioned his death, was about two hands-breadth within his armour, on the left side; from which the gentlemen concluded that he received it when he raised himself upon his stirrups, and streatched his body in order to hasten up his horse.'[24] If he was shot in the left side he must momentarily have turned to face back the way he had come, perhaps realising his danger, yet amidst the smoke and confusion his fall must at first have gone unnoticed, for his remaining troopers carried on going until they ran into Hastings' Regiment.

This came as another nasty surprise. Mackay recalled that at just this point, 'Hastings was marching up to their first ground, which he affirmed to have left in pursuit of the ennemy, who, thinking to fall in his flank, he wheeled with his pikes to the right upon them.'[25] In actual fact, Hastings refused his left and wheeled *backwards* on his right, and thereby swung his regiment round to face to his left. This, as we saw enabled him to shoot up Dundee's left and force it to take cover, but at the same time meant that he was not only disconnected from the rest of the battle-line, but he was further downhill and thus at first unseen by Dundee and the other rebel leaders riding across from the centre.

Halted by Hastings' men, Balhaldie next related that Dunfermline, 'proposed to gather together about fifty or sixty Highlanders, whom they observed straggling through the field of battle looking after their dead friends, and to attack them.' There was an embarrassing problem, however, in that none of the Lowland gentlemen concerned could speak Gaelic, but eventually with the help of Locheil's son-in-law, Alexander Drummond of Balhaldie,[26] they; 'made shift to get so many of them together, that they adventured to march against Hastings' half battalion. But that of Leven's, which stood att some distance, observing this motion, advanced to their assistance; and the Highlanders, whereof many were rather followers of the army rather than souldiers refuseing to engage, the gentlemen were obliged to retreat, and on their way discovered the body of their noble General, who was just breathing out his last.'

As there were 'some small remains of life' they naturally attempted to carry him off with the aid of a trooper named Johnston, but Leven's Regiment had, in the meantime, advanced close enough to deliver another withering volley into the cluster of officers, which shot Dunfermline's horse from under him and fatally wounded a prominent Angus laird named David Haliburton of Pitcurr. At that they all fell back in confusion, abandoning their badly wounded general for a second time. More reluctant stragglers were then rounded up for another attempt to recover him, perhaps about sixty men in all who were persuaded to march down in a body, but finding that the redcoats apparently standing firm, they quickly gave it up as a bad job. Whether Dundee himself, if he had not been shot down, might have done any better at wrapping up the battle than Dunfermline, Colonel Alexander Cannon and the other officers achieved, is an open question, but on balance it seems unlikely. It is possible that if he could have put himself at the head of his shaken left wing he might have essayed a renewed attack, but time and the gathering darkness would have been against him; the rebels were simply far too scattered, almost leaderless and all but overwhelmed by their own casualties.

Mackay, for his part, was oblivious to the rebels' unexpected plight, and had more than enough troubles of his own. As he had quickly realised there were a surprising number of his officers and men still standing on the battlefield, but bringing them under some kind of control proved unaccountably difficult as darkness fell:

> While he was in those irresolutions, in expectation of his nephews return, he brought at last news that all was gone clear away out of all reach, and that such as he had spoke to, noticed him not ; mean time he espyed numbers of men as it were forming themselves along the edge of the wood which was on Balfour's left, and where Lawder

had been posted with 200 men, and because he had not as yet been particularly informed of the behaviour of that wing, and it being already after sun-set, he was doubtful whether those men might not be some of his own men, who had retired to the wood upon the Highlanders descent ; so, exhorting the officers to labour to get their men in a condition to make at least one discharge if they were attacked, galloped up to the wood to view those men nearer, which having discovered to be ennemy's, he stepped back softly to his men, and bid them have special care to march off very softly, whereby happily the ennemy judging they were resolved to receive them briskly, would have respect; for them and let them retire quietly, the obscurity hindring them of a full view of our number, but that if they would offer to run, they should be sure to have the Highlanders among them; so, leading them softly down the hill he past the river, where he halted a little to get over all his men, and to observe whether the ennemy would approach the river after him. A little before his retreat the Lord Belhaven with the Earle of Annandales Lieutenant and Cornet[27] and some four or five horsemen came up to us, which served for scouts to discover during the retreat.

By this time the rebels were all too happy to let them go; marching steadily down the hill and over the battlefield, quietly picking their way through the dead and dying as they made their way in the dusk not down to the Pass but directly across the river.

Behind them, unknowingly, they left Colonel Lauder and his fusiliers still grimly holding out in the birch wood. Mackay's personal reconnaissance had been far too hasty and he had not approached them closely enough, (had they shot at him he would certainly have mentioned it to his advantage) and he far too readily decided that the men dimly seen in the trees were rebels. Afterwards he quite literally wrote off the hapless fusiliers by dismissively declaring that 'Lauder's detachment of 200 men, gave ground, or rather fled without any firing'. Yet this battalion, largely comprised of grenadiers and hardened by tough campaigning in the north, was by far the least likely of all Mackay's regiments to run away without fighting as he so ungenerously pretended. As to Lauder himself, running away would also have been very much out of character for that intrepid and resourceful officer, and in time Mackay acknowledged his error by recommending him for promotion.

Nevertheless, although closely questioned after his escape, Lauder does not, alas, appear to have made an official report or left any other written account of his experiences at Killiecrankie, but the truth, happily, is revealed by Balhaldie, who relates that the men brought off by Mackay were not the last formed body of troops to leave the battlefield. Instead, in his admittedly second-hand account, he quickly glosses over Mackay's successful retreat across the river by claiming that the general swiftly galloped away from the battlefield with only a handful of horsemen. However, he then goes on to tell an intriguing story of how, 'About the middle of the night, the [rebel] army returned from the pursute, but the enemy took the opportunity of retreating in the dark, and as they were marching through the Pass, the Atholl men … keeping still in a body, attacked them, killed some and made all the rest prisoners.'[28]

This last body of redcoats were evidently neither Mackay's nor Ramsay's men, since both parties had retreated directly across the river rather than attempt the Pass. Nor, once they had gone, were there any other substantial bodies of regular troops left standing on the open battlefield, which therefore means that the men described by Balhaldie marching down the Pass can only have been Lauder and his elite fusilier battalion, first by-passed in their wood when Sir John Maclean swept away Balfour's brigade; and then afterwards left well alone while the victorious clansmen got in amongst the unresisting temptations of the baggage train. There, forted up amidst the birch trees, they held out until darkness provided at least a chance of getting away down the Pass. It was perhaps inevitable, however, that it was Ballechin and his Athollmen who caught up with them in the end and forced most of the battalion to surrender, although Lauder himself got away – and indeed was the only senior officer to escape down the Pass. Having effectively abandoned them on the battlefield after mistaking them in the dark for the enemy, it is perhaps little wonder that Mackay should gloss over their fate afterwards.

At any rate, for his part, he was rather luckier and, having successfully broken contact with the rebels, he, 'met in the obscurity [darkness] about two miles off the field of battle with Colonel Ramsay, who had kept up the matter of 150 runnaways[29] altogether almost without arms, and knew not in the world how he would best get them off; whom the General having joyn'd into his party, continued his way up a little river, which fell into that which he had crossed before, till he came to some little houses where he saw light, and having got out the man of the house, enquired of him concerning the ground and the way to Strath Tay and the Laird of Weem's lands, who was our friend, his eldest son having been in the action with a company of 100 Highlanders, which he levied for their Majesties service.'[30]

Thus, supplied with directions, he set off once more for the eventual safety of Drummond Castle. Behind him he left a battlefield which with the coming of daylight horrified even his opponents:

> The enemy lay in heaps almost in the order they were posted; but so disfigured with wounds, and so hashed and mangled, that even the victors could not look upon the amazeing proofs of their own agility and strength without surprise and horror. Many had their heads divided into two halves by one blow; others had their sculls cut off above their earres by a back-strock like a night-cap. Their thick buffe-belts were not sufficient to defend their shoulders from such deep gashes as almost disclosed their entrails. Several picks, small swords, and the like, weapons, were cut quite through, and some that had scull-capes had them so beat into their brains that they died upon the spott.[31]

Lying amongst them all, they eventually found John Graham of Claverhouse, Viscount Dundee, stark and dead with a bullet 'betwixt his eyebrows', an unsettling discovery which compelled his surviving officers to compose a well-known, but entirely spurious, letter to King James, purportedly dictated from Blair Castle by a mortally wounded general, in order to cover up their own acute embarrassment at carelessly losing their general on the battlefield and leaving him alone to be murdered by his own stragglers.[32]

Beyond the numerous named officers and clan gentlemen, the other casualties are impossible to assess with any accuracy. Some 1,200 of Mackay's men were claimed by the rebels to have been killed, wounded and captured on the field. According to reports sent to Ireland some 800 of those were prisoners, of whom the rank and file were shortly afterwards released – largely because the rebels were incapable of feeding or accommodating them. Others escaped capture, including one fugitive who famously leaped over the river, but there may have been as many more of them knocked over the head as they scattered across the countryside. Against that, Balhaldie reckoned the rebels' own loss at about 700 and the spurious Dundee letter put the death toll even higher at 900, including far too many officers. In the end, Mackay's assertion that; 'The enemy lost on the field six for our one' might have been a touch exaggerated but was no mere braggadocio, for leaving the prisoners on one side, the rebels may have suffered twice as many killed and wounded as their opponents. Killiecrankie was undoubtedly a victory, but it was a too dearly bought one.

NOTES

1. Balhaldie, p.267.
2. See Stevenson and Caldwell, *Leather Guns and other Light Artillery in mid-17th Century Scotland*, Proceedings of the Society of Antiquaries of Scotland, Vol.108, pp.300-317. There were even some four-barrelled ones.
3. Mackay, *Urquhart and Glenmoriston*, p.202. See, however, the discussion of the fate of the Shewglie brothers in the previous chapter.
4. Balhaldie, p.266.
5. Tomasson & Buist *Battles of the '45* (Batsford, London, 1962), p.54. Oddly enough, this later incident once again involved a party of Camerons, and took place on the day before the battle of Prestonpans. Artillery fire compelled them to abandon a similar outpost in Tranent kirkyard and on that occasion Lord George Murray countered the reverse by immediately sending them forward again to occupy a different position, which was equally advanced but out of the line of General Cope's artillery.
6. A snaphans, snaphaunce was an early form of firelock which had been popular in Scotland and, although obsolete for military use, was still widely found on sporting guns such as those ornate brass stocked ones noted by Almerieclose.
7. 'A Short relation as far as I can remember, or what passed before, in and after the late defaite in Athole, of a parte of their Majesties forces under my command.' Strathbogie, 17 August 1689, in Mackay, *Memoirs of the War*, pp.264-5.
8. ibid.
9. Hopkins, p.154, quotes a Maclean bard as praising the bravery of Purcell's Irishmen, but comparing their charge to the stampede of a herd of cattle. As this exactly how a Highland charge is popularly imagined it is a little hard to understand what he meant. Possibly the Irish simply rushed straight down the hill without troubling to halt and deliver a volley of musketry before drawing any swords they may have possessed.
10. *Register of the Privy Council of Scotland* 1689, p.668. Mackay, *Memoirs of the War*, pp.250-251. Tradition also rather eccentrically holds that by way of divine punishment for failing to die in his master's stead, the colonel's servant and his descendants were cursed with poor eyesight. Be that as it may, the unfortunate colonel's saddle is still preserved at Craigdarroch.
11. According to tradition this ancient standing stone marked the spot where Dundee fell, but of course actually predates the battle by some 3-4,000 years. (A recent suggestion that he died sitting up against the stone is as ingenious as it is improbable.) As to the pack horses, it should be borne in mind that whilst the animals were valuable enough of themselves, and some of them were certainly carrying officers' effects, most of them were laden with oatmeal rather than the riches of the Indies.
12. *Register of the Privy Council of Scotland*, p.351.
13. Fergusson *Scots Brigade*, pp.483-4. Supposedly Balfour was offered quarter but his soldier-like refusal and robust language enraged the clergyman.
14. Fergusson *Scots Brigade*, p.484; *Register of the Privy Council of Scotland*, pp. 280, 379, 391 & 452. Other known casualties included Sergeant Andrew Murray, Sergeant George Lawson and Corporal Thomas Walker.
15. Balhaldie, p.266. The form of this standard is not revealed, although it is quite possible that it was the post-union royal standard, quartering the old lion rampant carried by Dundee's forces, with the English and French arms.
16. ibid, p.268.
17. ibid, p. 271.
18. ibid.
19. Mackay, pp.56-59 & 281-282. Fergusson *Scots Brigade*, pp.479 & 515. The alleged murders of

the wounded officers at Killiecrankie would be paralleled by the murder of Colonel Robert Monro at Falkirk in 1746; an act considered the more heinous because not only did the clansmen murder him in cold blood while he lay injured, but his brother Dr. Monro was also murdered while dressing his wounds. It is also worth noting that all three Dutch regiments appear to have had just four captains present, the others presumably being with their second battalions, left behind at Stirling.

[20] This was of course Captain Robert Mackay. According to the General this was his first time in action, but although he survived to later command the grenadier company and was a colonel of foot by 1694, his death two years later was attributed to ill-health resulting from his Killiecrankie wounds.

[21] 'A Short relation' etc. in Mackay, *Memoirs of the War*, pp. 265-6.

[22] Balhaldie, p.265. Wallace was later rather unfairly scapegoated and accused of cowardice by generations of historians for not following Dundee. Yet the general achieved nothing beyond cutting up a few gunners before recollecting that his job was to command the army, not a troop of horse. Wallace on the other hand was engaged in real work.

[23] ibid, pp.272-3. It is intriguing that Balhaldie refers to a gap between Locheil's and Maclean's regiments for that would obviously imply that the former had not yet charged down the hill. On balance, the course of the battle as reconstructed here seems likelier.

[24] ibid, p.269.

[25] Mackay, *Memoirs of the War*, p. 57.

[26] Therefore not by any means to be confused with the John Drummond of Balhaldie (probably a son) who penned the *Memoirs of Sir Ewen Cameron of Locheil* so frequently quoted here.

[27] As noted, Lockhart of Cleghorn actually commanded the troop at Killiecrankie. The cornet was John Johnstone of Westerhall, a "near relative" of Annandale. Dalton, C. *English Army Lists and Commission Registers*, Vol.3, pp.38-9.

[28] Balhaldie, p.270.

[29] In his August 1689 account Mackay put the number of men rallied by Ramsay at 200.

[30] Weem and his company do not appear to have been actively engaged and afterwards got away unscathed, either down the Pass or perhaps over it. They were, more or less, local men of course and the Athollmen, as neighbours, no doubt tacitly let them go without interference.

[31] Balhaldie, p.271. The reference to skull-caps is interesting. These were not issued to infantrymen in Scots or English regiments, but were normally worn by cavalrymen. In this case however they may have been worn by pikemen of the Dutch regiments.

[32] Hopkins, pp.176-7, cites Lieutenant Smith's letter confirming Balhaldie's account and describing another wound 'betwixt the eyebrows'. He also cites a letter from Dundee's brother asking Colonel Cannon to assist in the recovery of his personal effects from the Camerons, who were clearly suspected of being his killers.

Chapter 6

Holding the Line:
The Battle of Dunkeld

On 28 July, the Duke of Hamilton breathlessly advised Lord Melvill, King William's London-based Secretary of State for Scotland, that:

On Fryday last Major Generall Mackay marched from St. Johnston with about 4000 foot, 4 troops of horse and dragoons, and was at Dunkeld that night, where he received intelligence that Dundie was come to Blair in Atholl; he marched on Saturday towards him, and within two miles of Blaire about 5 at night they ingadged, and by feverall inferior officers and souldiers that is come here this evening, gives us the account, that after a sharp ingadgement Dundie being much stronger, the Major Generall was quite defeat, and I have yett heard of no officers of quality that is come of but Lieutenant Colonel Lauther, who my Lord Ruthven spoke with as he came from St. Johnston this day and gives the same account of there being wholy routed, but the confusion is such here that the particulars is hardly to be got. Wee have given orders at Council this afternoon to draw all the standing forces to Stirling, and has sent to the Weft countrey to raise all the fencable men, and Sir John Lanier has write to the English forces in Northumberland to march in here, and is goeing to Stirling to command, for Mackay is either killed or taken by all the account we have yett got, but you shall quickly have another flying packet or an express. I am sorry for these ill neues I send you to acquaint his Majestie with, and my humble opinion is, that his Majestie must first beat Dundie and secuir this kingdom or he attempt any other thing, and now Dundie will be master of all the other side of Forth where there are so great numbers of disaffected to join him, so the King must make hast to assist us to reduce him,

for I fear wee shall not be able to defend this side of Forth long, and
the King will know what new men is after a ruffle given.[1]

To all intents and purposes, General Mackay and all his army had
marched into the Pass of Killiecrankie and simply been swallowed up.
Of the 3,000-odd men who entered it, only a few scattered fugitives
emerged again to tell a dreadful tale of disaster. There could have been
as many as eighteen field officers with the army; majors, lieutenant
colonels and colonels. Only one had escaped. 'We doubt not', wrote Sir
William Lockhart, 'but the Major Generall, Ramsay and Ballfour, with
all the officers of ther regiments that wer ther, L. C. Lauder one
excepted, are cut off; it seems to be mostly chargable att my Lord
Murrays door, who not only refused to joyn McKay, but when his men
began to give ground fell on them. My Lord Kenmoor and Bellheaven
are certinly killed.' Similarly, Sir Patrick Hume of Polwarth agreed that,
'the falsehood of pretended friends led honest Mackay in the snare to
his ruine,' and Sir John Dalrymple was equally quick to assert that, 'ther
hath been treachery in the leading them to that place and the siege of
Blair, and my Lord Murrays raising his men hath all been concerted.'[2]
The Marquis of Athole, who had been trying so very hard to avoid any
kind of awkward entanglements, must have had a conniption fit and
was promptly arrested at Bath and afterwards imprisoned in London
for several months.

More happily, the early reports of Mackay's death were exaggerated
of course, and he was safely back at Stirling on Monday 29 July, dashing
any secret hopes Sir John Lanier might have entertained of being
appointed commander-in-chief Scotland and hero of the hour. What
was more, although there was no disguising the fact that he had been
heavily defeated, Mackay did not for a moment believe himself *beaten*.
His soldiers may have unaccountably run away from him but his self-
confidence was unshaken and he himself was still game. Like Queen
Victoria two centuries later, Mackay was 'not interested in the
possibilities of defeat'. Instead, he immediately set to organising a
counter-attack.

Three infantry regiments; The Earl of Mar's, Lord Bargany's and Lord
Blantyre's, were already at Stirling and, on receiving news of the
disaster, the Council summoned Argyle to return from the West
Highlands with three more, as well as calling out the West Country
fencibles[3]. Given a few days grace, Lanier could have pulled another
field army together to defend the capital, equal at least in numbers to
the one which had been lost, but General Mackay had very different
ideas. Moreover, whilst he was supposedly answerable to the Scots

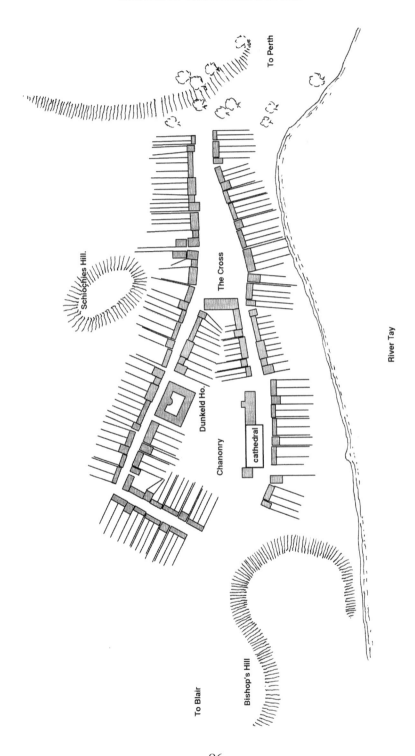

Government and addressed it with proper deference, his real master was Dutch William. He was acting in the King's name and with the King's authority which no-one was presently minded to challenge.

For a start, he lost no time in 'discharging … the west country men, whereof some thousands were gathering together upon the news of the defeat, the General not willing that those people, whose pretensions appeared already exorbitant enough, should have ground to think that the King could not without them maintain his government'.[4] When Sir William Lockhart loftily opined that, 'its pitie to give green men to good men, for ther running was the loss of all [at Killiecrankie]'[5], it is not difficult to guess where he had picked up that view, for it mirrored exactly Mackay's feelings about the April levies.

Instead, experience of campaigning in the north had convinced him that, no matter the cost in horseflesh, cavalry was the only effective answer to dealing with Highlanders, and from now on his infantry were to be relegated to a purely defensive role, providing garrisons for burghs and other key points. Accordingly, on 30 July, little more than forty-eight hours after the battle, he ordered; '8 troops of new levied horse, 4 of dragoons of the same sort, and the Lord Colchester's regiment of horse, to march to Stirling, Wednesday morning, not exceeding in all 500. Colchester's regiment being very weak, and the new troops not compleat.' As soon as they were assembled he going to head north again.

The rebel victory, meanwhile, stunning as it was, had inevitably left them with a number of problems in its wake, not least the rather obvious fact of their losing their charismatic leader. In the late evening of 27 July, while the battle of Killiecrankie was spluttering to an uncertain close, a certain Colonel Alexander Cannon unexpectedly found himself elevated to the command the rebel army. Surprisingly, almost nothing is known about him, other than the fact that he was a professional soldier from Galloway who had spent almost his entire career in the obscurity of the Dutch service as a colleague of Mackay. In 1685, however, while commanding one of William's English regiments during its brief sojourn in England at the tail end of the Monmouth rebellion, he was invited to transfer to King James' service, first as lieutenant colonel and then colonel of the newly formed Queen Consort's Regiment of Dragoons.[6] At the Revolution, colonel and regiment parted company, with the latter declaring for Dutch William and the colonel coming to Scotland via Ireland with the cadre for an

Opposite: The Battle of Dunkeld, 21 August 1689

intended regiment of dragoons. Unfortunately, both horses and men were promptly snaffled by a detachment of Argyle's Regiment, but nevertheless Cannon himself joined the rebel army along with Purcell's Regiment just two or three days before Killiecrankie, and there, on the battlefield, he succeeded Dundee simply by virtue of being the oldest or most senior officer on the spot. Alas, while he appears to have been a perfectly competent professional soldier, he was also completely unknown to his men, let alone to anyone else and was therefore quite incapable of providing the inspirational figurehead which the rising so badly needed.[7]

Aside from the appointment of a new general, there were a host of other practical problems facing the rebels, not least the post traumatic shock which Balhaldie describes setting in after daylight revealed the full horror of the battlefield. This lethargy, allied to the fighting only ending late at night and in darkness, meant that the entirety of the following day was spent in clearing the battlefield. The dead needed to be buried, albeit all too many were simply thrown into the river, but there were still the many wounded to be gathered in and somehow attended to, the prisoners needed to be dealt with and the battlefield itself scavenged for useable weapons and equipment, as well as the more obvious plunder of the baggage train. The companies and regiments, indeed the army as a whole, needed to be re-assembled from the drifting crowds and to a degree re-organised under new officers. Even without these mundane but necessary tasks, the victorious army could not simply pick up its feet and continue south at a few hours' notice, especially as the dash to Blair had seriously dislocated the rebel concentration and it was vitally necessary to let the tail catch up, if only to fill the terrible gaps in the rebel ranks.

Sensibly enough though, they did first shuffle forward as far as the burgh of Dunkeld, a short distance below the Pass, where they halted to sort themselves out and wait for those reinforcements to catch up. Several hundred more Camerons (no less than 500 of them according to Balhaldie) came in on Tuesday 30 July along with the Stewarts of Appin, the Glencoe MacDonalds, some 250 Macphersons and various other minor contingents, which more than replaced the casualties from Killiecrankie. All in all, by the time all the new men were added the rebel army mustered a reputed strength of some 5,000 men, and next day Colonel, now Major General, Cannon sent forward an advance guard comprising all his cavalry and some 300 Athollmen under Alexander Robertson of Strowan, in order to secure Perth.

At first, the rebel operation went smoothly enough. The government garrison, comprising Lord Bargany's Regiment under Lieutenant

Colonel Patrick Graham, had incontinently abandoned the burgh and fallen back on Stirling as soon as the Killiecrankie survivors came through.[8] The Fair City was therefore occupied without a fight. The magazines of oatmeal left there were also secured and, satisfied with a job well done, the Highlanders proceeded to get drunk, blissfully unaware that the government counter-attack was already underway and that General Mackay was closing in fast:

> On Wednesdays morning, having got his horse and dragoons to the park of Stirling, and passed them in review, and leaving order with a new battalion of foot to follow him, he marched out of Stirling about two in the afternoon, taking his way straight to Perth, from whence nevertheless he could not possibly get any news, all the country betwixt it and Stirling being in arms, and most part absent from their houses. He halted a part of that night for fear of ambushes in a village half way to Perth, and next morning at the break of day pursued his way toward the water of Earn, a little river three miles short of Perth, where four of his scouts, not above a musket shot before the party, according to their order, (lest they being surprised should discover our motion to the ennemy) met with two brisk horsemen of the ennemys party, who, attacking our men with a loud 'qui vive', made them fire upon the ennemy in a surprize, and happened to shoot the one dead, and the other so that tho he spake some words, he had no sense of what was enquired of him.
>
> This encounter made the General judge that happily the ennemys main body was not far off, wherefor he quitt the road and enlarged himself over a steep hill above which there was a great heath, where the Marquis of Montrose had obtained a notable victory over the Parliament's forces in the reign of King Charles the First, and having, about this place, got notice that some foot and horse of the ennemy were come to Perth, instead of moving straight toward the toun, he took his way to the left to fall in betwixt them, and the gross of their party camped at Dunkeld, 14 miles below the place where he had fought, and being advanced in sight of the toun of Perth, he discovered the matter of thirty horse of the ennemy already passed the river of Tay, and so out of reach ; but within one half mile without the said toun was a final party of foot about 300, who, upon the discovery of our party, came to ane halt as irresolute what to do.

Someone had warned them. Even as Mackay rode up, the rebels had already evacuated the place and were hastily falling back, but they had left it too late, as he continued;

The General, knowing the river to be low and fordable about that place, detached the four troops of dragoons to gallop all their best down to them to prevent their passage; at which motion the party of the ennemy returned toward the toun again, and the General, not knowing what number they might have in the village, where he had first discovered them, not having any sure intelligence where their main body lay to prevent their entry into the town, having no foot by him to force the entry upon them, he detached three troops of Colchester's horse at the gallop to fall in betwixt them and that retreat following close with the rest in good order ; after he had left detachments upon the heights, where they could discover to all hands from whence ane ennemy could approach. At the appearance of those detachments the ennemy threw themselves into the river, where the horse and dragoons mixed with them, and killed the matter of 120, and took 30 prisoners. They were all Athole-men, and were so opiniater or stupified that not one of them called for quarters. We lost but one man in the action, who followed indiscreetly 4 or 5 Highlanders a great way from his comrades.[9]

Rounding off the successful operation, two infantry regiments, the Earl of Mar's and Lord Bargany's, followed after the cavalry to form a new and stronger garrison for Perth under George Ramsay.[10] All in all, it was a brisk little victory, and all the more remarkable for its following just four days after the disaster on the other side of the Pass. What was more, while it hardly ranked as one of Scotland's greatest battles, it had far-reaching consequences, for it immediately stopped the rebel advance in its tracks and inspired the Government (at Mackay's suggestion) to offer a pardon and indemnity to all those Athollmen prepared to surrender their arms.

They were not quite ready for that yet, but any thought of advancing into the low country was abandoned and instead the rebels turned east and then north rather than threatening Stirling and Scotland below the Forth. The burgh of Dundee may at first have offered an alternative objective, but Berkeley's Dragoons were already marching south from Aberdeen and, with Mackay coming up fast behind, Cannon headed further north instead, aiming for a rendezvous with Farquharson of Inverey at Braemar. There, in the north-east, he hoped it might still be possible, with the Earl of Dunfermline's help, to raise the Aberdeenshire lairds and above all the cavalry he now so desperately needed, but Mackay was soon doggedly in pursuit.

Whereof the General being for certain advertised and apprehending for the northern counties, ordered Sir John Lanier, with the horse and dragoons which he expected out of England, to come with all diligence to Perth, (where the General left two battalions of foot,) where he was to post himself till further advertisement from him ; who, passing the River Tay, marched to Cowper, [Coupar Angus] ten miles from Perth, a little country town in Angus, not far from the foot of the hills, and there having spoke some of his men who escaped from the ennemy upon their march, was told that they continued their march further north, which obliged him to advance toward Forfar, within eight miles of Glenisla, where he understood the ennemy was camped; from whence Canon moved to Clova, much about the fame distance from the General's quarters, who, being but weak, and most part new levies, placed himself in the fields every night, and in the morning after he sent out some scouts, and placed his sentries upon the heights about his quarter, did let his men rest and refresh themselves.

After he had been two nights at Forfar, he got sure intelligence that Canon had passed a very high mountain, called Mount Capel, [Cairn o' Mounth] into Braemar, where the General had a garrison in the House of Abergeldie, from which place he might, with equal convenience and prospect of success, turn either toward Inverness or Aberdeen, where their party had many friends and well-wishers. Therefor, to hinder as much as possible the ennemy's progress till more forces could be had, he wrote orders to Sir John Lanier to come to Forfar, lest the ennemy, making a feint to draw him to the north, might suddenly return the fame way south, and into Angus again; and took his way straight to Aberdeen, where he arrived the second day to the great joy of the most part of the inhabitants, who otherwise expected the Highland army in their town that very night. [10 August]

There he was advertised by an express from the master of Forbes that Canon had taken a very strong post upon his father's ground, where he had the Highlands at his back, a wood to cover him, and free communication with his friends in the plain country of Aberdeen and Banff, which made the General judge, that the ennemy, knowing him to want foot, and his horse and dragoons but small in number, took that post of purpose to secure the junction of their friends in those countries, to make up a body of horse, with their foot, which at this time we judged odds of 4000 foot, with 150 horse, wherefore he presently dispatched an express to Sir Thomas Livingstone to leave the command of the forces in and about Inverness to Sir James Leslie, and to repair over Spey and toward Strathbogy, 24 miles benorth Aberdeen, with his regiment of dragoons, ordering him in case he found the ennemy to approach to that rout, to take his march more to the left over the plains, and to fend continual expresses to give account of his diligence, dispatching at the same time orders to Sir John Lanier to send Hayford's regiment of dragoons to Aberdeen, where he should find further directions; by the junction of which regiments he doubted not to overturn all the designs of the ennemy.[11]

Actually, he was doing pretty well already, for if he had not actually pitched into the rebels since the action at Perth, his constant attendance on their movements had not only frustrated any hopes of their regaining the initiative, but just as importantly his presence had warned off a number of lords and lairds, great and small, who might otherwise have joined with them – and most obviously, that included the Earl of Breadalbane, who was already distancing himself from any imputation of disloyalty. The feared general uprising had been frustrated after all.

As a result, once Sir Thomas Livingstone and his dragoons from Inverness rendezvoused with Mackay, the disgruntled clans all but gave up the ghost and insisted on holding a council of war at Auchindoun Castle. Once again, they proposed the futile campaign in Argyllshire and Kintyre which Dundee rejected in favour of marching to his fate at Killiecrankie. Locheil and his supporters justified the proposal by citing long outdated instructions from King James to facilitate the transfer of substantial bodies of troops from Ireland, and in an attempt to frustrate opposition to the motion (which was already rendered pointless by the lifting of the siege of Londonderry), Locheil also proposed that the 'Low-country officers, who acted as volunteers without any command,' should have no vote. He argued that 'it was unreasonable that simple Captains and subalterns, who brought no accessions of strength to the army but their own persons, should have equall powers with those that actually had regiments, or att least very considerable bodys of good men.'[12] Supposedly, most of the other chiefs loudly cheered him on, but at the end of the day Dunfermline succeed in rallying enough support to ensure that both this subterfuge and the chimeric expedition to Kintyre were blocked. Locheil thereupon returned home in a huff, leaving his son John, and his cousin John Cameron of Glendessary in charge of his clansmen. Afterwards, a period of some more or less futile dodging about the north-east followed, with other chiefs soon following Locheil's lead and, in the case of Keppoch at least, beginning to put out feelers about submission. Total disintegration of the rebel forces was looking increasingly like only a matter of time, but then suddenly

General Cannon broke contact and marched south again with a decision and energy totally at odds with his torpid reputation.

In the Lowlands, in the meantime, some strange things had been happening. From a military point of view Mackay's decision to follow and steadily wear down the rebel army was absolutely correct, but the political gentlemen in Edinburgh were decidedly nervous about his absence in the north and downright anxious at the prospect of the rebels coming out of the hills while he was gone. Sir John Lanier too was becoming increasingly keen to make a name for himself and some of the recent levies were also getting increasingly restive.

This was particularly true of the three regiments recalled from the West Highlands. Argyle, as it happens, was at odds with his lieutenant colonel, Sir Duncan Campbell of Auchinbreck, but that was in the nature of a family quarrel and had no significant overtones. The Earl of Angus' and the Earl of Glencairn's regiments on the other hand were a different matter. Like most of the new levies, both regiments were comprised of Westland Whigs and in the case of the latter a fair number of equally intractable 'Scotch-Irish' Ulster Protestant refugees. Both represented trouble. It was not merely a case of their being Presbyterian fanatics, but the fact that they drew little or no distinction between the exercise of religion and politics. Just as a kirk administered by the elders of local presbyteries was incompatible with a formal hierarchy of bishops, so that same democratic spirit sat ill with a military hierarchy requiring submission and obedience to the officers set over them. This destructive anarchy had been a major factor in the Covenanters' defeats at Rullion Green and Bothwell Brig, and now it was threatening to tear apart the present levy.[13]

Both regiments needed to be separated from each for the good of the service and, fortunately, a splendid opportunity arose to do so. Lanier and the Council were soon agreed between themselves on the necessity to mount an expedition to seize Blair Castle, (which was by then garrisoned by Purcell's Irish regiment), in order to bridle casual raiding out of Atholl and Balqhidder. First, however, there was the tedious necessity of sending north to obtain Mackay's authorisation as Commander-in-Chief. This consent was duly forthcoming, although he professed himself unconvinced as to the necessity for the operation, but naturally enough it all took time.

In anticipation, George Ramsay was informed by the Council on 5 August that he was to obey any orders given to him by Sir John Lanier, but it was not until a week later, on 12 August, that the Council was actually able to 'ordaine Livetennant Collonell Cleilland to march the Lord Angus regiement under his command from Downe and Dunblaine and wher they are now quartered to Dunkell, and upon ther aryvall at that place appoynts the said Livetennant Collonell to acquant Major Generall Lanier and the commanding officer of his Majesties forces at Pearth and to receive and prosecute such ordors and directiones as Major Generall McKay, the said Major Generall Lanier or the commanding officer of the forces at Pearth [Ramsay] shall give or send to him.'[14]

Afterwards, it was darkly insinuated that the Council intended they should play the part of Uriah the Hittite; that they were to be placed in the very forefront of the battle in order that the Highland clans might obligingly wipe out the lot.[15] In fact the posting was only intended to be a stepping stone in the Atholl expedition and once they had secured Dunkeld for him, Lanier was ordered on 19 August to concentrate his forces and march.[16]

Unfortunately, a bleak comedy of errors and miscommunication followed.

No sooner were the Cameronians settled in Dunkeld on the evening of Saturday 17 August, than their young commanding officer, Lieutenant Colonel William Cleland (who we last encountered fighting for the Covenant at Bothwell Bridge) decided, with some justification, that he was in an awful position and dangerously exposed. Next morning, however, he began digging in, and an immediate appeal to Ramsay at Perth brought two troops of horse (the Earl of Eglinton's and William Bennet of Grubbet's) and three of dragoons all under Lord Cardross. Like the Cameronians, most of the new arrivals were comprised of Westland Whigs, but Cardross appears to have had his cavalry properly in hand and was not best pleased to find that Cleland and his men had already alienated to locals by plundering and generally throwing their weight about. If they were not hostile before Cleland arrived they were certainly hostile now, so he commenced sweeping the surrounding hills with his dragoons, dispersing parties of 'insurgents' and capturing half-a-dozen prisoners. It only made matters worse, of course, and in response Stewart of Ballechin's brother, Alexander, sent round the fiery cross, and reputedly raised some 600 men overnight; not rebels intent on overthrowing the state, by any means, but simply acting as a neighbourhood watch to try and curb the Cameronians' depredations:

> Tuesday morning, many people appeared on the tops of the hills, and they were said to be in the woods and hills about Dunkeld, more than 1000 men. About eight of the clock, the horse, foot, and dragoons made ready to march out, but a detach'd party was sent

before of fourty fusiliers, and fifteen halbertiers, under command of Captain George Monro, and thirty horse with Sir James Agnew, and twenty dragoons with the Lord Cardross his own cornet; after them, followed ensign Lockhart, with thirty halbertiers. The halberts were excellent weapons against the Highlanders' swords and targets, in case they should rush upon the shot, with their accustomed fury. They marched also at a competent distance before the body. One hundred fusiliers were under the command of Captain John Campbel, and Captain Robert Hume, two brave young gentlemen; and upon the first fire with the enemy, Captain Borthwick and Captain Haries, with 200 musquetiers, and pikes, were likewise commanded to advance towards them; the Lieutenant-Collonel having proposed, by this method, to get advantage of the enemy in their way of loose and furious fighting. The body followed, having left only 150 foot within the dykes.[17]

The ensuing skirmishing was proclaimed as satisfactory; the sweep did not actually manage to properly engage with the insurgents, who obligingly gave way when pressed, but by way of demonstrating their determination the Cameronians admitted to having an officer and three men wounded (of whom one died) and claimed to have been told afterwards that the insurgents lost thirty! Meanwhile, unbeknown to them, Cannon was closing in fast with the real rebel army. Clashes between some of Cannon's cavalrymen and Lanier's patrols near Fettercairn, and a vicious little fight at Brechin, alerted Sir John to the fact he was in the uncovenanted presence of the main Jacobite field army. Any thought of going into Atholl was hurriedly abandoned and Ramsay was immediately instructed to pull back his cavalry to ensure the security of Perth. Therefore, when Cardross returned to Dunkeld on the evening of 20 August, he found orders waiting for him from Ramsay, ordering him to fall back. In fact, he 'received two peremptory orders for that effect. The second was sent to him, upon his answer to the first, by which answer, he told they were engaged with the enemy, and it was necessary he should stay.' Obediently, the cavalry marched that night, abandoning the infantry, who had received no such orders.

Afterwards everyone seemed inclined to blame George Ramsay for this dereliction. However, while Cleland was told that he was 'to receive and prosecute such ordors and directions' that might come from Mackay, Lanier or Ramsay, there is some doubt as to whether the latter considered Cleland to be under his command at all. Similarly, although Mackay claims that Lanier was aware Cleland was at Dunkeld, the orders sending the Cameronians there came direct from the Council and it is possible that he too may have been uncertain as to his own authority over them.

Mackay's very sensible remarks on the matter are worth repeating, as he was not directly involved and was therefore able to analyse the debacle with a degree of detachment:

> In this business the Council failed, by giving special order for the posting of forces, which they ought to have left to the judgment of officers. Ramsay failed (happily by too much respect for the Council's order, which he ought to have considered conditionally) first, by not stopping the regiment at Perth, giving the Council reason of his so doing, 2dly, that, upon the approach of the Highlanders, he did not either march with all the forces, which he had at Perth, to maintain the post if he judged it of consequence, or provided Cleland with orders, if he found not the place tenable against such numbers as he could expect against him, to make a timely retreat, giving at the same time advertisement to him that he might make a motion up the river to favour his retreat; for all officers, who are not tyed by express orders from their superiors in command, are answerable for the neglects of the service, as much as the chief commander, tho' he were present, when they by their rank fall to command in chief a body of the forces. Ramsay complained also, that Sir John Lanier delayed his resolution too long after he had given him account of the pressing danger of the post of Dunkeld. [18]

Colonel Cleland himself, however, was ultimately culpable. On 12 August, he had been directed by the Privy Council of Scotland to take his regiment up to Dunkeld and await further orders. Now, without such orders, from Ramsay or anyone else, he refused to abandon the place. While it might seem easy to dismiss him as a pompous fool, his stubborn pig-headedness reflected both his background and the present state of his regiment. Cleland was just twenty-seven or twenty-eight-years-old at the time and ten years earlier had fought in the debacles at Glasgow and Bothwell Bridge, where factional infighting and an endemic refusal to obey orders had doomed the Covenanters just as surely as the efforts of Claverhouse and the rest of regular army. That same chronic indiscipline was not only tearing his own regiment apart, but his withdrawing from Dunkeld without orders could give the government the excuse it needed to disband it.

He therefore decided to stay put, which inspired quite understandable consternation amongst his men, who might have been fanatics but had no pressing desire to add their names to the long roll of Presbyterian martyrs, and therefore all but mutinied:

> After the horse and dragoons were marched, some of the officers and souldiers of the Earl of Angus's Regiment, proposed that they might also march, seeing they were in an open useless place, ill provided of all things, and in the midst of enemies, growing still to greater numbers; the vanguard of Canon's army having appeared before they came off the field. The brave Lieutennant Colonel, and the rest of the gentlemen officers amongst them, used all arguments of honour to perswade them to keep their post; and for their encouragement, and to assure them they would never leave them, they ordered to draw out all their horses to be shot dead.

It is very doubtful that the argument was conducted quite so politely as this semi-official account blandly suggests, but although Cleland and his officers successfully faced down the dissidents, they still had a formidable task in front of them. Dunkeld lay entirely on the left or north bank of the River Tay, hemmed in by the surrounding hills. The street plan, paralleling the river from east to west, can be likened to a figure Y or rather something like a tennis racquet, with a single main street widening first into the market place and then splitting into two branches enclosing an inner core of buildings and yards including the semi-derelict cathedral and the four-square pile of Dunkeld House.[19] This inner core had once formed the chanonry or cathedral close, and as soon as the Cameronians arrived they camped within it and 'began some Retrenchments within the Marquess of Athol's yard-dykes, the old breaches whereof they made up with loose stones, and scaffolded the dykes about', albeit according to Mackay, they were 'in most places not above four feet high'. The chanonry was thus turned into an all-round defensive position, anchored on Dunkeld House itself, which provided an obvious strongpoint.

There is a fair degree of uncertainty, however, as to just how many men Cleland actually had on hand to man the perimeter and its outposts. An aggregate of the various detachments enumerated in the account of the previous day's sweep produces a total of 535 soldiers plus an unspecified number forming the 'main body'. Lieutenant John Blackadder claimed a round figure of 800 men in total and was at pains to explain that the regiment was thus 400 men short of its establishment, because they had been detached to serve in the West Highlands, although he neglected to admit there was also a quite frightening level of desertion.

With the decision made to stay, a tense night was spent under arms until at about 06.00 hours on the morning of 21 August, first light revealed the entire Highland army standing ranged around them in a suitably intimidating manner, while the rebel baggage train, carried on those 1,000-odd pack horses captured at Killiecrankie, passed by on its way to Blair. There is some uncertainty as to how strong the rebels really were with estimates ranging upwards from about 2,500 all the way up to 5,000 men or more, so Balhaldie's assertion that they were some 3,000 strong is probably as close to the truth as we are likely to get. All the Killiecrankie regiments were still with the army, with the exception of Purcell's Irishmen, sitting up at Blair, but others such as the Athollmen had since joined, of course. There were now four small troops of horse, and men had been found to man the guns taken from Mackay[20], but there were still no low-country foot and Sir Alexander Maclean's men were the only regulars. It is a measure of the rebel failure to broaden the revolt that the army was still to all intents and purposes a Highland army, and one which was badly suited to the operation about to commence.

It was not until at about 07.00 hours that various detachments were sent to attack, or at least push their way into the various entrances to the town. In anticipation, Cleland had established a ring of outposts forward of his main position in the chanonry, but all these were quickly beaten in, as the regimental account relates: 'A Lieutenant was posted at the east end of the town with men, who had three advanced sentinels, ordered, upon the rebels closs approach, to fire and retire, which accordingly they did; and the Lieutenant, after burning of some houses, brought in his party. Lieutenant [Henry] Stuart was plac'd in a baricado at the cross, with twenty men, who, seeing the other Lieutenant retire, brought his men from that ground, and was killed in the retreat, there being a multitude of the rebels upon them.' [21]

He had left it too late, for while he was covering the withdrawal of the unknown lieutenant at the east end, more highlanders came crashing into the town behind him and into the Scots Raw on his left.

The rebel dispositions are tolerably vague, but we do know that Cannon planned a general assault, covering all the entrances to the town. At the outset, the Appin Regiment and two troops of horse were sent around the back of the town to cut off any possible escape over a ford near the cathedral. There they found one of Cleland's outposts comprising twenty-four men under Lieutenant John Forrester and an Ensign Campbell, who, 'fired sharply upon the enemies horse, until great numbers of foot attack'd their dykes, and forc'd them to the church, where were two Lieutenents, and about 100 men.' That bastion at least was solid enough and it must have been some of the Appin men who then spread along the street to fall upon Lieutenant Stuart's detachment at the cross.

However, the main rebel attempt was directed towards Dunkeld House. Just forward of it was another outpost, under Captain William Hay and an Ensign Lockhart placed on Shiochie's Hill – an isolated mound overlooking the backs of the houses on the north side of the Scots Raw. The ground between the backs and the hill was a warren of dykes and yards and middens, so Ensign Lockhart was ordered forward with twenty-eight men to line a stone dyke at the foot of the hill. His tiny detachment was quite literally a forlorn hope. No sooner were they in place than a heavy assault column came rolling in from the north, comprising Sir Alexander Maclean's firelock-armed regulars, headed by a company of picked men, 'all armed with back, breast, and head piece' and armed with broadsword and targe – filling the place of grenadiers in a more conventional regiment.[22] The regiment was backed up by another battalion (probably Sir John Maclean's Regiment) and two troops of cavalry, and, as this formidable storming party roared in, all that Hay and Lockhart could do was pull their men back, fighting from dyke to dyke until they regained the dubious safety of the chanonry. It was a vicious encounter in which both Sir Alexander Maclean and Captain Hay each had his leg broken by a musket ball and Maclean's captain-lieutenant was shot dead.

Afterwards as Lieutenant Blackadder told his brother, 'the Highlanders came swarming in on all sides, and gave a desperate assault in four places all at once, first firing their guns, and then running in on us with sword and target. But it pleased God, that they were also bravely repulsed, our men still firing on them, where they came on thickest … In this hot service we continued above three hours.'

There is an impression given by many historians that the Highlanders came piling into the town, fired the 'traditional' single volley, drew their broadswords and then spent the next few hours impotently waving them at the barricades, before eventually giving up in disgust. Indeed, Mackay comments that 'the Highlanders are not of passive courage, so that when they meet with any thing to stop their first fury, and hinder their running upon their ennemys with sword in hand, they are foon rebated, and cannot stand before fire tho' never so irregular and small, whereof this is a great instance; for tho' they lost not twenty men in the attack, Canon could never bring them to it the second time.'[23]

No doubt broadswords were used by those who had them, when driving in the outposts, just as the Cameronians fought back with pikes and halberds, but after Killiecrankie the Highlanders were as well provided with military firelocks and matchlocks as their opponents, and the wit to use them. Cleland went down early on, struck by 'two shots at once, one through the head, and another through the liver', which sufficed to kill him before he could reach the shelter of Dunkeld House. Immediately afterwards Major James Henderson also fell with several wounds, which first disabled him and eventually killed him four days later. Three other captains were wounded, one fatally, at about the same time; 'Captain Caldwal was shot in the breast, and is not like to recover. Captain Borthwick was shot through the arm, going with succours to the church; and Captain Steil got a wound in the shoulder, which he caused pance [treat] and returned again to his post.'

Within an hour of the battle beginning, the Cameronians had all been forced back into the chanonry, and their defences were quite literally starting to crumble, as the clansmen tore at the loose rubble walls and flimsy barricades. In desperation, the Cameronians' senior surviving officer, Captain George Monro, initiated a counter-attack of sorts by sending out 'small parties of pikemen, with burning faggots upon the points of their pikes, who fired the houses.'[24] It is unlikely that many were trapped in the burning houses, since back doors are generally as common as front ones, but the fires which soon spread throughout the town, and together with the thick smoke which choked the streets, proved an effective barrier. Only the width of the Scots Raw and what is now Cathedral Street separated the two forces, but to attack, the rebels needed to assemble a storming party in the backs and then debouch through houses and vennels. This was difficult enough in itself and all but impossible once the houses were ablaze. Only at the cross was there space for an assault, and no matter that the Jacobite cavalry in the market place tried to force the Highlanders forward, the attacks became increasingly futile.

Instead, both sides blazed away at each other, but amidst the swirling smoke and an understandable reluctance to take careful aim, it was, as Balhaldie said, like thunder; noisy but ineffective. Remarkably both sides not only optimistically claimed to have slain 300 of their opponents, but only admitted to only losing eighteen or nineteen of their own officers and men killed. Mackay afterwards confirmed this by stating in his memoires that 'they lost not twenty men in the attack' although in reality, rebel casualties may have been higher, for in addition to Sir Alexander Maclean's wounding, and the death of his captain-lieutenant, there were two of Sir John Maclean's captains killed and 'some other officers of note[25].

At all events, the losses were not as crippling as at Killiecrankie, but, as the hours wore on, everyone was soon running short of ammunition and in the Cameronians' case they were dependent on 'the diligence of a good number of men who were imployed, all the time of the action, in cutting lead off the house, and melting the same in little furrows in the ground, and cutting the pieces into sluggs to serve for bullets'.[26]

No such resource was available to the Highlanders, and at about noon that same shortage of ammunition compelled them to withdraw. Good leadership could have seen them resuppied, re-organised and led in again, but Sir Alexander Maclean, who might have done it, was down and General Cannon was incapable of rousing them for that one last effort. Instead the Highland army more or less spontaneously withdrew, while their equally exhausted opponents threw their bonnets in the air, flourished their colours, beat their drums and jeered. At Blair, six days later, the clans elected to disperse and return home, ostensibly to gather the harvest, but although they signed a bond agreeing to rendezvous again in September, few can have believed they would come out again before winter.

NOTES

[1] Mackay, *Memoirs of the War*, pp.248-9. In terms of the shock caused, the Killiecrankie disaster might easily bear comparison with the destruction of the East India Company's Army in the Khyber Pass 150 years later.

[2] ibid, p.250.

[3] Argyle's, Glencairn's and Angus' regiments.

[4] Mackay, *Memoirs of the War*, p.62. The newly raised dragoons belonged to Lord Cardross's Regiment, while the eight troops of horse included Eglinton's, Grubett's, Belhaven's and probably Annandale's as well. Afterwards, Belhaven himself was given the honour of carrying Mackay's report of the victory to Edinburgh, by way of demonstrating that the General's confidence in him was undiminished after Killiecrankie.

[5] Lockhart to Melville, 29 July 1689, in Mackay, ibid, p.253.

[6] Later the 3rd (King's Own) Dragoons.

[7] His surname itself is obscure, being largely confined to Galloway and in any case according to Dalton, (*English Army Lists and Commission Registers*, Vol 2, p.11) should more properly be rendered as *Canan* or *Cannan*. Needless to say, he had no Gaelic and no understanding of Highlanders.

[8] Cardross to Melville, 30 July 1689, in Mackay, *Memoirs of the War*, p.258.

[9] Mackay, ibid, pp.63-4. The 'great heath, where the Marquis of Montrose had obtained a notable victory over the Parliament's forces in the reign of King Charles the First', was Tibbermore, the scene of Montrose's first battle in 1644.

[10] Mackay to Hamilton, 2 August 1689, in Mackay, ibid, p.259. Rather confusingly Mackay refers to Bargany's Regiment as 'Balbeignies'.

[11] Mackay, ibid, pp.65-6.

[12] Balhaldie, pp. 284-5; Hopkins, Paul, *Glencoe and the End of the Highland War* (John Donald, Edinburgh, 1986), p.182.

[13] Privy Council to Argyle 6 August 1689: instructions regarding trouble in the regiments of

Glencairn and Angus. *Register of the Privy Council of Scotland*, Vol. 14 (1689-1689), p.20.

[14] ibid, p.34.

[15] ibid, pp.12 and 35.

[16] ibid, p.83.

[17] Crichton, Andrew *The Life and Diary of Lieut. Col. J. Blackader: Of the Cameronian Regiment* (H.S. Baynes, Edinburgh, 1828), pp. 42-46. The use of armoured halberdiers to try and deal with Highlanders was not new. In 1647, the establishment of each Scots infantry regiment was ordered to include seventy-two men carrying halberds and wearing body armour and helmets. There is no reference to this in the surviving documentation for the 1689 levies but Cleland was clearly following this earlier practice rather than consulting his own fertile genius. *Acts of the Parliament of Scotland* 6, Pt.1, pp.708-9.

[18] Mackay, *Memoirs of the War*, p.71.

[19] With the exception of the ruined cathedral and some buildings still fronting on to the Cross, nearly all of the area defended by the Cameronians has been cleared and now forms a well-tended public park!

[20] The artillery saw no real use during the battle and it was claimed afterwards the rebels had no cannonballs – which would be consistent with their being leather guns only intended to fire case-shot.

[21] Crichton, pp.42-46. The account is entitled '*The Exact Narrative of the Conflict at Dunkeld, betwixt the Earl of Angus' Regiment, and the Rebels, collected from several Officers of that Regiment, who were Actors in, or Eye-witnesses to, all that's here narrated in reference to these Actions.*' It constitutes a remarkable if not unique account of a seventeenth century action at a regimental level. A full transcript is provided in Appendix 3.

[22] Crichton, p.93. The use of armour by Highland troops appears unprecedented. It was presumably scavenged from Killiecrankie, perhaps from the pikemen of the Scots Brigade, or from any detachments of halberdiers belonging to Leven's and Kenmure's regiments – see note 17 above.

[23] Mackay, *Memoirs of the War*, p.70.

[24] While not specifically alluded to, it would be strange if the Cameronians' pikes had not been shortened in anticipation of fighting in such a confined space.

[25] Balhaldie, p.287; Crichton, p.99; Mackay, *Memoirs of the War*, p.70; Hopkins, p.189.

[26] Crichton, p.99.

Chapter 7

The End of an Old Song:
Cromdale and After

Drifting homeward by way of Loch Rannoch and seemingly stealing everything that was moveable along the way, the Highland Clans soon dispersed and something of a winter of discontent ensured.

Mackay, for his part, was determined to ensure that they did not break loose again and once more assembled a large force at Perth, from whence he marched north again on 26 August with seven infantry regiments, four regiments of horse and dragoons and three troops of militia horse. Two days later he again negotiated the Pass of Killiecrankie and this time arrived safely at Blair, which had been abandoned by the rebels after he threatened 'to leave not a standing house in Athole, and to burn and destroy all their corn if the House of Blair, where he designed a garrison, should be burned by the ennemy'. Afterwards he sourly grumbled, it was only heavy rain which prevented the rebels from burning it, but be that as it may, he duly installed his garrison, mainly drawn from Mar's Regiment and surrounded it with a ditch or covered way and palisade. His entry into the Highlands was at last secure. The Athollmen, despite Ballechin's efforts, hastily surrendered their arms in expectation of the indemnity promised at the beginning of August – and then found themselves plundered unmercifully by Argyle and his regiment, in grim revenge for the ravaging of Argyllshire in1685.

Another month of this kind of pressure confirmed that there was to be no general rendezvous after the harvest, and on 11 October, Mackay reported that his forces were dispersed in their winter quarters:

> Stirling: two battalions of his own regiment (rebuilt with new recruits and returned prisoners), with Blantyre's Regiment and

Eglinton's and Ross's troops of horse.

Perth: Balfour's two battalions and Argyle's Regiment at Perth with Grubbet's and Newbattle's troops.

Dundee: Ramsays two battalions with Annandale and Belhavens troops.

Montrose, Arbroath, Brechin and Forfar: Angus' Regiment [two battalions but very badly depleted] and Cardross's Dragoons.

In the North East, Livingstone's Dragoons and six other troops of horse were scattered across Aberdeenshire, Banff and Moray, with Leslie's, Grant's and Strathnaver's regiments quartered in Inverness, Forres and Elgin, 'to be drawn together upon advertisment of the commanding officer in those quarters.'

In the Edinburgh area Leven's Regiment with six companies of 'Beuuridge'(Kenmure's ?) were quartered immediately outside the capitol in in Leith and the Canongate, and as to the rest, five companies apiece of Mar's, Glencairn's and Bargany's regiments were in the garrisons of Blair, Finlarig and Weem, and the remaining companies of each, which were 'scandalously waik' were lodged in Coupar, Inverkeithing and Dunfermline where they could hopefully be brought up to strength.[1]

To a degree Mackay now began to find himself a victim of his own success. He was only too aware that the rebel threat had only been contained, but it had not yet been destroyed and, surprisingly enough, there was still the potential for a more general uprising in favour of King James. The revolution in March and April which saw him deposed was something in the nature of a coup and as the months went by James's supporters started entering into conspiracies, both amongst themselves and with disappointed protagonists of the original coup, who were becoming increasingly dissatisfied with William's lack of interest in Scotland, its problems – and their advice. The intricacies of the various plots need not trouble us here, but the government was inevitably weakened by the shifting loyalties and increasing factionalism. Money for the army was in short supply and that was particularly unfortunate because if he was to give the rebellion its quietus Mackay still needed a substantial army to undertake his pet project of marching into the heart of Lochaber and planting a garrison at Inverlochy to overawe the clans once and for all. The money, or at least the bulk of it, would have to come from England and the problem was to justify such an apparent diversion of funds and other resources at a time when the situation in Ireland was deteriorating badly. There,

Londonderry was eventually relieved on 28 July, the day after the battle of Killiecrankie was fought, but although William's commander, the Duke of Schomberg, had then proceeded to clear King James' forces out of Ulster, he had been stopped by Tyrconnell at Dundalk. Since then his army had effectively fallen apart in its squalid winter quarters, losing as many as 6,000 men to disease and neglect. Mackay had already parted with Lanier's Horse, Heyford's Dragoons and Hastings' Foot, urgently needed to reinforce Schomberg, while Colchester's Horse and Berkeley's Dragoons were returned to England in order to be recruited back up to a respectable strength before following them. Livingstone's Dragoons and Leslie's Foot seemingly only remained part of the Scots army because of the practical difficulty of recalling them from Inverness. Yet, notwithstanding these substantial reductions, Mackay was still under pressure to make economies and so he set out his own appreciation of the situation and his recommendations in a lengthy letter to Lord Melville the next day:

> I received your Lordships of the 5th from Newmarket, insinuating his Majesties order to have from me the true state of the forces on foot in this countrey, with what regiments and troops are fittest to be kept up, since ther is no money to pay the whole; 'tis not possible for mee at present to answer to the former, because the nature of the countrey and the service doth require their sepperation at no lesse distance than betuixt Glascow and Indernesse in a half circle, bordering the Highlands, in all which bounds I must take my measures so that where the Rebells (whose strength when together is all in one body,) doe turn head or move, I may have presently together wherewithall to make head to them, so that the regiments which lye be north Spey, I have not seen since the midle of July last, after the Highlanders had separate and I had formed a deseyn to goe to Lochaber, though I confess too late for any preparations I could get to effectuat it, but in generall I may say, that though many of the regiments are little worth, yet the disbanding of them might be of evell consequence till things be further advanced in Ireland, and my raison is, first, that the name of them doth keep the countrey in som aw, at least the low countrey, of which benorth Tay wee are not very sure except som feu familys; nixt the great distance of countrey to garde over all, at least 200 miles, and the manifold garifons to mantaine requires many men, besyds that wee must have hors and foot over all to forme a body where those High landers appeare and fall down, so that wee must make account to be oblidged to keep at least triple the number that they can be able to put together to withstand their attempts over all; the Highlands

lying in a masse contiguous together, and surrounded with the low countrey, so that making a feinte-to draw our forces north or south, they may (cutting short through the hills,) surprise other parts before the fame body could be bak again to oppose them; this is the true notion of this sort of war, and the situation of the kingdom will let your Lordship or any other see it in the map, so that my opinion is clearly that none of the hors or dragouns be disbanded this winter, if his Majestie resolve not to send others in their place, and that 6 battaillons of the new levied foot or at least five be keept on foot, for our regements and the Earle of Levens ought to be keept disingadged from garifons to forme one body or more (according to the nature of the ennemys interpryses) when occafion might require; for if a competent number of forces in the kingdom be wanting, ther shall appeare more ennemys then doth appeare as yet; the only aprehension of the forces and Duke Schombergs passage to Ireland being that which discouradged them, so that my opinion is, that his Majestie ought rather to be at som expences to keep a formidable body on foot for this winter, then to hazard a longer continuation of the troubles of this kingdom, which is not yet so very setled as could be wished, though forces being layd as I have and fhall further appoint them; I am persuaded the ennemy for this yeare cannot doe much harme; if his Majestie resolve to break som of the foot, his favour ought to regulat it, for ther is litle difference, only that I beleeve the regements of Mar, Glenkarne and Blantire to be of the worst sort, also a battaillon of Angus might be brock; but one good might be made of it if ther were a man of service put vpon the head of it, for the men are good, and ther may be for that number of good officers of som service, and not of their wilde principles got among them, I beleeve that Strathnaver and Grant have as good men as any of the rest; I had no tyme all this yeare to look after the modelling of them, being continually ingadged against the Rebells since I came to Scotland except a feu weeks the beginning, and though my indeavours had not all the succes which humanly one might propose to himself in my chief ingadgement with them, neverthelesse the Kings affaires hath suffer'd nothing by it through Gods blessing vpon my present diligence to hinder the ennemy from the advantage which he proposed to himself thereby, and which certainly he had obtained if he had not met with present opposition, though my number was but very small, not exceeding 450 hors and dragouns most new and ill armed men...

But to return to the consideration of the forces, I pray your Lordship whatever the King resolve as to the foot, let not the hors and dragouns be reduced to a smaller number for a while yet, till things be better fixed in Ireland, and if his Majestie break more than 4 battaillons, they might be confider'd thus; of Angus one battaillon, Glenkarns regiment, Mars regement, Blantires and Kenmores, for certainly they are the worst, and Angus though the men be good it can make but one battaillon at present ; if the hors be keept ther is a necessity to regement them, for they shall not otherwyse be capable of serving so well nor be so well cared for.[2]

By and large Mackay's suggestions were taken on board. On 18 December King William went ahead with the remodelling of his Scottish forces. Six of the regiments; the Earl of Angus', Earl of Argyle's, Glencairn's, Kenmure's, Strathnaver's and the Laird of Grant's were ordered to be re-organised to comprise thirteen companies apiece (including a grenadier company) while an entirely new regiment was to be formed under Colonel Richard Cunningham. The necessary personnel for this reorganisation were to be found by disbanding three other regiments; Mar's, Blantyre's and Bargany's, and reducing the Earl of Angus' Cameronians from two battalions down to one battalion.[3] The exercise was not entirely successful in that although Cunningham's Regiment was duly formed, there were insufficient men to provide most of the additional companies required for the other regiments. The King was unimpressed and muttered darkly about 'false musters', but it scuppered his original intention of taking four of the regiments to Ireland.

By the time Mackay wrote to Hamilton and Melville, it was clear that despite the promises that had been made at Blair, the Clans were not prepared to rise again until the spring. There was some raiding, almost as a matter of course, often sanctioned by written orders to emphasise that those involved were legitimate combatants and not mere banditti who might be hanged out of hand by the civil authorities. For the same reason, the raiding was as far as possible aimed at government supporters, such as Lord Cardross, but all too often the real aim was to secure food. The Highland economy was heavily dependent on the exchange of cattle for oats – a trade totally wrecked by the war. Except in localised areas there might not yet be actual starvation, but it was all but impossible to assemble supplies for large bodies of men and for military operations. Thus the 3,000 rebels who fought at Dunkeld were overnight reduced to just two small regiments; Purcell's Irishmen and what was left of Sir Alexander Maclean's regulars, both of whom were quartered on Mull and soon virtually starving.

The Clans were not yet ready to surrender but all that sustained them were illusory promises of reinforcements, money and supplies from

Ireland. Unfortunately, whilst Schomberg's offensive there had completely stalled, the loss of the Ulster Coast and the Government's hold on Kintyre rendered any large-scale reinforcements impractical. On the contrary, Tyrconnell now argued, with some justice, that far from the Irish army sustaining the Scots, a substantial success in Scotland was needed to relieve the pressure on Ireland.

In response, as Mackay had predicted, the rebels did indeed 'interprise' in the north of Scotland, but it was a half-hearted and indeed wholly impractical affair which sought to call the clans together in winter for an offensive against Inverness. The original grandiose intention was to march down both sides of the loch, and eventually join with the Mackenzies and other northern clans. The Earl of Seaforth was in Ireland, where he was appointed James' secretary of state in succession of Melfort, but as Christmas approached his uncle Coll Mackenzie was said to be calling out his people and it was reported in Inverness that Glengarry was arrived in Glen Urquhart with 500 men, with whom he laid siege to Urquhart Castle on 3 December 1689.

Despite its dramatic location on the shores of Loch Ness, and its imposing fortifications, the castle had an unfortunate knack throughout its history of being captured by every army and every marauding band of MacDonalds that happened by. This time was different. It soon transpired Glengarry could only call upon 120 men, with the rest simply marauding up and down the glen in search of food and shelter, so that a detachment of the Laird of Grant's Regiment under the command of Captain James Grant, (with the aid of late reinforcement twelve men and a sergeant of Leslie's Regiment arriving in a leaky boat), successfully bid him defiance for nearly two weeks, until the rebels retired in disgust.[4] That in turn scuppered plans for the rendezvous further north, where Coll Mackenzie was forced to disband his nephew's people with little or no prospect of getting them out again.

But then came Major General Thomas Buchan, a professional soldier from Aberdeenshire and sometime commanding officer of the Scots Fusiliers, who had served King James as brigadier of the Scots infantry ordered south in 1688.[5] When the army fell apart outside London he opted to remain loyal to James and early in the following year was earmarked to take a brigade of Irish troops to Scotland. Between one thing and another, however, it was not until 24 January 1690, that he sailed from Dublin in the *Janet* (formerly of the Scots navy) with some professional officers, a quantity of ammunition and £900 in hard cash.

Working hard, by April of 1690, he had assembled token contingents of around 100 men sent in from various clans and after a menacing lunge towards Inverness, seemingly in search of food, he began

Above left: General Hugh Mackay of Scourie and (right) John Graham of Claverhouse, Viscount Dundee

Below left: This Victorian imagining of Dundee leading a cavalry charge at Killiecrankie is reasonably accurate but errs in depicting him wearing a broad-brimmed hat instead of a fur-trimmed helmet.

Below right: The fall of Dundee as depicted by Stanley Berkeley highlights a minor mystery in that the general was reported to have been shot through the left side, under his armour while galloping from west to east across the battlefield. This means he must either have reversed his course, perhaps to urge on laggard followers, or was actually passing in the *rear* of Leven's Regiment at the time.

Above left: A collection of ironmongery said to have belonged to Dundee: the breastplate may be authentic, but the bullet holes were apparently added by an estate carpenter at Blair Castle. The helmet is rather too old while the pistols are highland ones with belt-hooks rather than the horse-pistols which a cavalry officer would have carried. Above right: A romantic depiction of Dundee being carried from the field by his sorrowing followers; in fact, it was not until broad daylight that his murdered corpse was discovered, and the flag which covers him appears to be the English royal standard rather the Scottish one!

Above: Contemporary view of Dunkeld from the by John Slezar. The cathedral is clearly seen while the now vanished Dunkeld House is the square building slightly to the left of centre. Left: Dunkeld market place; the buildings facing, or their predecessors were held by the Cameronians, while those on the left were occupied by the rebels and latterly. The cramped nature of the "battlefield" is readily apparent by the width of Cathedral Street separating the two.

Above left: Dunkeld Cathedral; one of the two strongpoints still held by the Cameronians at the end of the battle. The photograph is taken from within the Chanonry area held by the Cameronians. Above right: Cavalry and Infantry; typical of the Killing Time rather than Killiecrankie. Note the musketeer's collar of bandoliers; according to Sir James Turner this was worn under the loose overcoat on the march in order to keep the powder dry.

Right: Collar of bandoliers; ordinarily each container or flask held a single charge of powder, while the musket balls were carried separately in the pouch seen in the centre. The slightly larger flask under the pouch could hold finer powder which was dribbled into the flash pan as a priming charge. The drawbacks of loosely suspending individual flasks by cords can easily be appreciated,

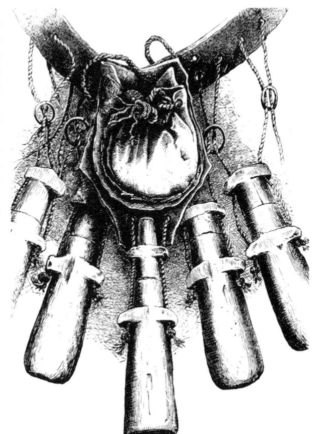

Left: Grenadiers were the elite troops of their day, equipped with modern firelocks or fusils, bayonets and hatchets, and distinguished by their caps and other embellishments.

Centre left: Grenadier of the Scots Brigade from a contemporary water colour. His red coat lacks the lace loops sported by most British grenadiers, but he is distinguished by a fur trimmed cap. All three figures wear red coats with red cuffs and are not individually identified but this one has a different style of pocket flap and a fur cap – a suitable distinction perhaps for Mackay's Regiment as the senior unit in the brigade. Centre middle: Another Grenadier of the Scots Brigade from the same series, this time wearing a low-fronted cap more typical of the Dutch Army. Note that although his ammunition is carried in a patronash or cartridge box on his right hip, he still has a small powder flask suspended from his belt for fine grained priming powder. Centre right: The third Scots Brigade figure appears to have the same style of pocket flap as the preceding one but wears a broad-brimmed hat. While the Gerpines camp list of 1691 cites blue linings for Mackay's Regiment and white for Ramsay's, these sketches suggest that all three regiments in the brigade had red coats with red cuffs.

Bottom left: Although based on a much later sketch dating from 1745 this figure gives a pretty good idea of the appearance of the Cameronians who defended Dunkeld, wearing traditional Scots blue bonnets rather than soldiers' hats. Bottom right: Another regiment wearing bonnets rather than hats was the Laird of Grant's. Raised and stationed in the north of Scotland it took some time to get the regiment properly clothed and equipped and in the meantime Mackay recommended that it be armed with Highland weapons such as this Lochaber axe.

Left: The style wheellock carbine and pistols place him at an earlier period but this this trooper is still typical of the cavalry of the Killing Times, armed with sword, carbine and pistols and wearing a buff coat and helmet, the latter being of the style worn by Dundee with the addition of a fur turban. [INSET] Almerieclose referred to Dundee wearing a fur-covered helmet, presumably like this one worn by a German cavalryman, sporting a fur band or turban which will have helped to distinguish him in battle.

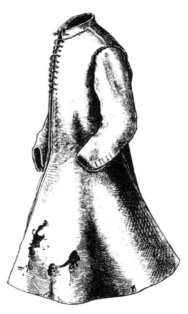

Right: Cavalryman's buff leather coat of the style seen in the preceding illustration and still worn to an extent during the Highland War, chiefly by officers.

Below left: Surviving double-barrelled leather gun, usefully illustrating its construction with a metal core bound with rope and covered by a leather skin. Below centre: The core of a leather gun; a sheet iron barrel with iron rings shrunk on to prevent the welded tube bursting apart. Below right: A gunner with a round flask for fine-grained priming powder and a linstock with slow-match to touch off the priming. This individual is a blue coated Dutchman but Scots gunners will have differed only in having red coats and grenadier style furred caps.

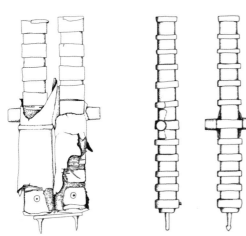

Right: Highland Gentleman in trews by McIan. Trews or tartan trousers were widely worn and especially by the better off.

Below right: Another Highlander in trews, this time with his plaid tightly bundled up for action rather than draped elegantly over his shoulders. Below centre: A romantic and far from realistic view of combat between a tartan clad Highlander and a red-coated Presbyterian, but nevertheless an evocative one. Below right:: The less than romantic reality presented by a ragged rebel soldier with a Lochaber axe.

Right: Far from wielding basket-hilted broadswords, most ordinary clansmen according to Almerieclose appear to have been armed with Lochaber axes and pikes or half-pikes. Far right: In describing the muster at Dalmucomir also refers to Glendessary's ruddy banner. This in fact survives at Achnacarry; a red banner with a green panel in the middle bearing the Cameron arms, but bearing Glendessary's arm and sword crest rather than Locheil's bunch of arrows. Locheil would appear to have had an undifferenced banner with four red and three yellow bars.

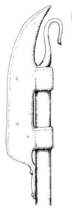

Above right: No clan regiment was of course complete without its pipers such as this one [a McCrimmon of course] depicted by McIan. Above left: This view of Edunburgh Castle from the Lawnmarket amply emphasises the degree to which the Castle dominated the capital, much to the embarrassment of the Scots government.

Below: The Covenanters' victory at Drumclog 1679

Above: William and Mary

Right: Argyle; although this playing card supposedly depicts the Marquess' grandfather, it actually provides an excellent illustration of Lowland Scottish dress of the Killiecrankie period, with plaids draped for effect

Queen Mary. WV King William.

Argyle a muckle Scotch Knaue in gude faith Sir.

marching eastwards into the high country of Upper Strathspey, eventually hoping to reach his native north-east, where he was assured that preparations were underway for a general rising. His force was pitifully small and initially by his own estimate amounted to no more than 8-900 men, including his own regiment, which must itself have been formed by combining the tattered remnants of the two regular units; Sir Alexander Maclean's Regiment and James Purcell's Irishmen.[6] The majority of his men were of course Highlanders and included parties of MacDonalds, MacLeans, Camerons, Grants of Glenmoriston (and perhaps Glen Urquhart as well), some MacNachtans and ultimately some MacPhersons, which may eventually have pushed Buchan's numbers up to something like 14-1500 men, although Keppoch was the only chief to come out in person. Afterwards Buchan complained that they were 'the very worst men amongst the Clanns, the Chiefes never venturing their best but where they goe themselves'.[7] That particular judgement may sound unfair, but most of Buchan's little army was effectively a collection of inadequately officered detachments rather than proper regiments. Like all such ad hoc forces, whether regular or irregular, his band was inevitably ill-discipled, well-nigh uncontrollable and ultimately extremely brittle.

His opponent, Sir Thomas Livingstone, was no great military genius, but he knew his duty and marched from Inverness on 27 April with a rather more homogenous force comprising 'a detachment of four hundred men of Sir James Leslie's, six companies of Grants, the Highland company of Captain Mackay, three troops of my dragoons, and my Lord Yester's troop of horse, and camped that night near Brodie, where I was forced to stay two days, for my baggage horses coming in very slow from the country, as likewise for the three other troops of dragoons from Elgin, and Captain Burnet's of horse.'[8]

Buchan quickly had word of their coming and indeed may even have deliberately enticed them out of Inverness, in the mistaken belief that he could raise the country against them in the name of King James. Equally fatally, for some reason, Buchan had also gained the notion that with the Laird of Grant absent in Edinburgh, even the Grants would rally to King James' banner. At any rate, in a council of war held at Culnakyle on 29 April, he insisted on marching his little army down to encamp on the open ground at Cromdale, in full view of Ballachastell (Castle Grant), despite its being held held by a company of foot under Captain John Grant of Easter Elchies. However, whether Buchan was deliberately inviting a confrontation or merely raising King James' standard at a prominent rallying place, he was making a fatal error in both his expectations and his dispositions.

The Haughs of Cromdale 1 May 1690

Buchan's position was an outwardly strong one, with most of his army encamped on rising ground by Lethendy Castle, situated about a mile back from the right or east bank of the swift flowing river Spey and separated from it by a broad and fairly boggy area of flat haughland, or alluvial plain. The impression given is that the camp was pretty loosely spread about. Keppoch and his people certainly insisted on camping further to the north around the nearby village of Dalchapple and as a result they were to play no real part in the battle. Between the main camp and Ballachastell was a known ford over the Spey hard by Cromdale kirk, and Buchan's officers discovered two other usable crossing points a short distance above and below the main one. All three were picketed with detachments of forty-five men apiece under two officers named Brodie and Grant, whose names suggest they were local men and therefore acquainted with the area. The picquets in turn were supported by a main guard of 240 men under an un-named lieutenant colonel which was posted by a watermill on the Cromdale Burn, at what is now the village of Cromdale about halfway between the river and the main camp. Outwardly, it was all done very much by the book. If the pickets were attacked they were to give warning, and then would fall back on the main guard which would in turn resist long enough to allow the army to be roused and formed into a battle-line. Unfortunately, and possibly because Buchan was an infantryman, he failed to take account of the likelihood that Livingstone might drive in the outposts with his cavalry so quickly as to frustrate any delaying action.

So indeed, it turned out. Livingstone was determined not to let the rebels escape. He and has men had been operating in the area for nearly a year by then, and with the aid of some local guides from Grant's Regiment he was confident enough to march them directly across the hills under cover of darkness. At about 02.00 hours on the morning of 1 May he arrived on the hill above Ballachastell. There half an hour's rest was allowed to his men while Captain Grant explained the layout of the rebel camp by reference to the campfires clearly visible below them, and then, as he proudly related, he 'called the officers together, and told them my resolution, so that they might examine the soldiers, if they were able to do it, who unanimously told me they would stand by me to the last man, and desired me earnestly to go on.'[9] They might be tired after the long approach march over rough country and in the dark, but they sensed that victory was finally at hand.

With Grant and his company leading the way, the dragoons, then descended the valley of 'Auchinarrow', or Allt an Fhithich to the ford by Cromdale kirk. The outpost there was duly tripped and local tradition says the bells in the kirk were rung to warn the rebels. Much good it did them. Livingstone relates that; 'we passed the river by three o'clock in the morning at one foord where there was a church; the enemy keeped a strong guard, where I sent some foot (presumably the Grants as they were the only regular foot present) and a few dragoons to fire upon them and amuse them, and in the mean time passed the river at another foord below it; two Troops of Dragoons, and Captain Mackay's Highland Company was already passed before the Enemy perceived us, and then we see them run in Parties up and down, not knowing which way to turn themselves, being surprized.'[10]

The rebel main guard fell back on the watermill, on the site of the present village, and gamely held out there for a time, but as for the rest, according to Shaw, they made no attempt to stand, for the remainder of Livingstone's Dragoons came up with them; 'before they could all get into their clothes, who fled precipitately about a half mile, many of them quite naked; at the foot of the hill of Cromdale, they eventually faced about and made a faint defence, but were soon routed; and had not the hill been so steep that the horse could not pursue, few would have escaped.'[11] Livingstone himself reported that once all his cavalry were over the Spey; 'I commanded all the Horse and Dragoons to joyn, and pursued them, which affrighted them, so that they took themselves to the Hills, and at the foot of Crombdel we overtook them, attacked them, killing betwixt three and four hundred upon the place, and took about 100 Prisoners, the greater part of them Officers, the rest got off by a Mist, that came just at that time upon the top of the Hill, so that we could scarcely see one another, otherwayes the Slaughter would have been greater.'[12]

At that point, Livingstone sensibly decided to quit while he was ahead and fell back on the rebel camp, where amongst a considerable amount of other booty he found the rebels' royal standard (presumably the same lion rampant carried at Killiecrankie), Cannon's and Dunfermline's highly incriminating correspondence and a gratifyingly large quantity of oatmeal and claret. The latter was promptly drunk by the victors, who also mounted green leaves in their hats, to celebrate both their victory and May Day and, in this happy mood, Livingstone accepted the surrender of Buchan's regulars in the mill and at Lethendry Castle. The party in the castle under Captain James Buchan[13], the general's nephew, at first made a show of resistance, but Sir Thomas soon settled the business by calling for grenades and very loudly discussing the proprieties of shooting prisoners taken after they had refused quarter, whereupon Captain Buchan took the hint and very sensibly surrendered without making any further difficulty.[14]

Shaw summed it all up by declaring that: 'There were above 100 killed and about 60 were made prisoners, who were found in the Castle of Lethindie and the mill. It deserves to be remarked that Colonel MacDonald of Keppach, who was ever keen for plunder, but never once fought for his King, would not encamp with the other rebels, but with his men quartered in Garvlin, half a mile distant, and thereby escaped without loss. Such of the rebels as climbed up the hill could not be pursued. But a party of Camerons and MacLeans, who next day crossed the river, were pursued, and on the Muir of Granish near Aviemore some were killed, and the rest taking shelter in Craigelachie, and Keppach, who, with their banditti, attempted to reduce the Castle of Lochinelan in Rothiemurchus, were by that laird and his tenants beat off with loss.'

It was a sorry end to Buchan's offensive and afterwards Livingstone sat down and penned a justifiably cocky despatch announcing to General Mackay and to the world in general that; 'Buchan got off without hat, coat, or sword, and was seen that day, and in that posture, in Glenlivet, very much fatigued … Cannon got away in his night-gown … We have taken all their baggage and ammunition, and the soldiers have got considerable plunder, as I thought they carried about with them. Their king and queen's standard, where they cited the country people to repair to, are taken: there are said to be some people of note that are killed, but of this I can give you no certain account, being that when we came to visit them, they were all naked.'

As to his own casualties, he reported he had none killed and just 'three or four wounded, but not dangerously either, and about a dozen of horses, but many horses disabled'. By way of a postscript he explained his lack of any pursuit not on that sudden mist (or the claret) but the fact that a heavy rain had set in and that, 'The weather is so horrible that I fear I shall be obliged to give it over.' That, in itself, was sufficient to destroy the scattered remnants of the rebel army without any further intervention by him. The fugitives had fled in their shirts (if they were lucky), not only abandoning their weapons, but their plaids and other outdoor clothing and, with no protection against the horrible weather, the demoralised rabble drifted homewards and afterwards showed no inclination whatever to come out again.

Nevertheless, although the rebels had been decisively defeated the rebellion was not yet over. On 20 May the Earl of Seaforth turned up aboard the ubiquitous *Janet*. He had succeeded Melfort as King James' secretary of state and now armed with a major general's commission, a company of Irish grenadiers to act as his bodyguard, and the customary supply of officers, oatmeal and ammunition, he was expected to raise the north. Instead, he promptly returned home to Kintail and displayed a decided reluctance to move far from his fireside.

Fort William

This was probably just as well because General Mackay was still intent on carrying out his old plan of marching into Lochaber and planting that garrison at Inverlochy. As a first step, Captain Edward Pottinger RN[15], with a detachment of troops under Major John Fergusson,[16] was set to cruising the Western Isles, showing the flag, mounting punitive expeditions and generally disrupting traffic and discouraging the Hebridean clans from engaging in exciting adventures on the mainland. By June, Mackay was at last ready. Three battalions were left to cover Edinburgh and the ever-nervous government. Glencairn's Regiment was assigned to garrison Perth and the still shattered remains of Kenmure's Regiment left to look after Stirling[17]. With the remainder; comprising all six battalions of the Scots Brigade, Argyle's Regiment and four troops of horse, he set off on 21 June. A feint was made by a detachment in the direction of Atholl, but rather than attempt to bludgeon his way straight through the Highlands, this time Mackay swung the long way around by way of Strathardle, Braemar, Strathdon and Strathavan, picking up at least a part of Lord Angus' Regiment in the by-going, and making a rendezvous with Livingstone at Culnakyle in upper Strathspey. Livingstone brought his own dragoons, together with the Laird of Grant's and Lord Strathnaver's regiments, two Highland independent companies under Menzies of Weem and Ross of Balnagowan, and an additional 300 of Lord Reay's people. After a brief conference, it was decided to leave Strathnaver's Regiment and the Reays to look after Inverness, and two troops of horse (Bennet of Grubbet's and Yester's?) to remain at Elgin, while with the rest of the army, Mackay at last turned south for Lochaber.

Avoiding the passes, and the clansmen who might otherwise have tried to oppose him, he followed Livingstone's example and came directly over the hills and into Inverlochy by way of Glen Spean, untroubled except by the odd sniper. Commencing on 5 July, he and his men then built what became Fort William in just 11 days! It was by all accounts a pretty sorry, jerry-built affair, down by the water, consisting of little more than a wooden palisade erected on the crumbling foundations of the long-abandoned Cromwellian fort. Some guns were landed from Pottinger's ships in case the French might one day come sailing up the loch, but otherwise it was an awful place. Badly sited, it was overlooked by high ground, it was damp but at the same time lacked a proper water supply, the ramparts were horribly unstable and there were only tents to accommodate the garrison. This comprised nine companies of the Laird of Grant's Regiment, four each of Angus' and Argyle's regiments, and the two Highland independent companies. Having figuratively dusted his hands, Mackay marched out again two days later with the rest of the army (including Livingstone's Dragoons) and by 27 July was safely back in Perth.

While he was unmolested on his expedition, and rather to the astonishment of all concerned, the sickly and soon mutinous garrison of the Fort was afterwards left well alone by the local clans, Buchan and Cannon proceeded to do exactly what the Government had always feared they would do. In Mackay's absence, Buchan rode east with just seventy cavalrymen, hoping to raise his native north-east for King James, while Cannon headed south into Balqhidder, threatening Stirling and beyond. Both threats quickly ended in fiasco. Buchan was checked by the Master of Forbes, while further south the beleaguered Government once again turned to its first and most dangerous resort; the Covenanters of the south-west. As always, they eagerly responded to the call to turn out the fencibles with what was, in effect, another insurrection. Just as in the previous year, as many as an alleged 14,000 volunteers quickly flocked to their old banners. Most of them were of course unarmed or at best provided with the usual bucolic assortment of more or less lethal farm implements and old muskets, but the Government, fearing them almost as much as the rebels, insisted on most of them being sent home, retaining just 4,500 of the better armed ones to hold Glasgow, Falkirk and Stirling until Mackay returned.

However, once he had been re-joined by Cannon, Tom Buchan tried again. This time, from Glenlivet he passed into Upper Deeside where he was joined by the Black Colonel with about 600 Highlanders, and, leaving 160 of them to blockade the garrison in Abergeldie, they marched across to Kildrummy in Strathdon. Forbes' original four troops of horse and dragoons had, in the meantime, had been reinforced by four troops of Cardross's Dragoons under Lieutenant Colonel Robert Jackson, but Buchan succeeded in magnifying the appearance of his forces, by ranging his infantry over a large extent of ground, and interspersing his baggage horses among them. This subterfuge convinced Forbes and Jackson that they were heavily outnumbered and, after a hasty council of war, they hurriedly fell back on Aberdeen in something of a panic. The burgh had no defences of its own other than a half-demolished Cromwellian fort overlooking the harbour, but the militia were called out, the streets barricaded and some cannon mounted, while they anxiously awaited the arrival of Colonel Richard Cunningham. He was supposedly marching north with three and a half battalions of infantry and some cavalry, but halted at Montrose to wait for Livingstone's Dragoons, only for Sir Thomas to fall gravely ill with dysentery. Unwilling to push forward alone, Cunningham then stayed where he was, until General Mackay himself caught up with a battalion each of Ramsay's and Lauder's regiments.[18]

Fortunately, Buchan and Cannon had, in the meantime, come no closer than Inverurie, ten miles north-west of Aberdeen and, rather than get embroiled in a fight for the burgh which was liable to be costly in both military and political terms, they essayed to push south into the Mearns and even rather hopefully summoned the great coastal fortress of Dunnottar Castle. Thus far, their Highlanders had been astonishingly well-behaved, taking only horses and provisions rather than indiscriminately plundering, in a futile hearts and minds operation. There was, outwardly at least, a great deal of sympathy for the rebels, but ironically enough many of their putative supporters declined to come out because none of the western clans had come east, and without that necessary show of force they were unwilling to expose themselves. On the contrary, Tom Buchan's younger brother John, was back in Aberdeen as lieutenant colonel of Cunningham's Regiment and making the most of his local contacts to actively dissuade the waverers to accept the new regime and refrain from doing anything foolish.

By 17 August, Mackay had advanced the length of Brechin and at that point Buchan, finding none of the local support he had counted on, decided that the game was up and fell back into the hills once again. Pausing briefly at Aberdeen to pick up some supplies, Mackay then turned west, going into the hills by way of Deeside to relieve his lonely little garrison in Abergeldie Castle. In a last futile stand, the Black Colonel tried to stop him on 21 August 1690 in a notorious defile known as the Pass of Ballater, only to be peremptorily brushed aside, as:

> ...the Major General sent a detached party of two troops of Sir Thomas Levingston's Regiment of Dragoons, under the command of Major Aeneas Mackay, to attacque that party that had posted themselves at the pass, whilst another detachment should attacque the Rebels that lay before the Castle. The Rebels made what defence they could on both sides; but our men behaved themselves so courageously & successfully, that they soon took the pass, & forced the rest to fly, having killed about 100 of them on the place, & taken most of the chief Officers prisoners; amongst whom was the young

Laird of Innerey, his father having fallen, & being left for dead on the place, who they say, after three or four hours stay amongst the dead bodies, & whilst our men were in pursuit of the Rebels, made a shift to get up & make his escape, leaving his head-piece, target, blunderbuss, & other arms behind him. Some of the officers that were in this engagement say that we have not lost one man in all this action. This happened on Thursday, the 21st instant, about two o'clock in the afternoon.[19]

It was an inconsiderable affair, but it was also, as it happens, the last pitched battle in the Scottish campaign, for the rebellion was dying on its feet, and in Ireland King James had been decisively defeated at the battle of the Boyne on 12 July.

Closely followed by Mackay, Tom Buchan doubled back towards Inverness, hoping to rendezvous with Seaforth and, even now at this late stage, take the Highland capital, which had been denuded of most of its garrison. Unfortunately, by now Seaforth was thoroughly convinced of the hopelessness of the position and having briefly raised his people, disbanded them again and surrendered to Mackay at Strathpeffer on 3 September. For their part Buchan and Cannon retreated up Loch Ness, but the bright, youthful enthusiasm of Dalmucomir had died in the bloody slaughterhouse of Killiecrankie and 'Lochaberians' flatly refused to come out again. In a last effort Buchan moved into Menteith with all his cavalry but just 100 foot. The Government called his bluff and mustered enough men under Lord Drumlanrig to face him off, and Buchan once again retreated on 12 September, dismissing the last of his foot and breaking his horse into small parties. There were some despairing attempts to establish small garrisons in remote castles which might perhaps hold out over the winter, but all were quickly mopped up long before the first snows.

It took another year of plotting and intrigue, while the Highland chiefs, who had indeed been bridled by Fort William, breathed defiance while simultaneously sitting quietly in the hills. The surrender of Limerick on 3 October ended the Irish war but to all intents and purposes the Highland war was already long over, and the chiefs tentatively began to formally submit and swear loyalty to King William. James, for his part, delayed giving his consent to do so for as long as possible, and the last surrenders therefore took some time. A last campaign was in contemplation but, in the end, it took the squalid massacre in Glencoe on 13 February 1692 to bring in the last holdouts, such as Glengarry, and see Buchan and Cannon granted passes to go abroad into exile.

Then, in a remarkable postscript to the story of Killiecrankie, Locheil's second son, Donald Cameron, obtained a lieutenant's commission in Mackay's Regiment on 1 August that year.[20] Sadly, it was only a truce, and war would return again to Lochaber.

NOTES

1   Mackay to Hamilton 11 October 1689. Mackay H. *Memoirs of the War*, pp.283-4.

2   Mackay to Melville 12 October 1689, ibid, pp. 284-7.

3   King William to Earl of Leven, Hugh Mackay and Sir George Monro 18 December 1689, ibiid, pp. 308-310.

4   Leslie to Melville 6 December 1689. Mackay, ibid, pp.299-300; Mackay, W. *Urquhart and Glenmoriston* (Inverness, 1914), pp.206-211.

5   Thomas Buchan was one of three brothers from Aberdeenshire. The first, James, succeeded their father (who died young) as laird of Auchmacoy in 1661, Thomas, the second son, served in the Scots army until the revolution and thereafter remained loyal to King James. The third brother John, served in the Dutch army, and has already been encountered in this narrative first as commander of the fusilier battalion and latterly as lieutenant colonel of Mackay's Regiment in succession to James Mackay, slain at Killiecrankie.

6   Purcell himself decided that he had enough and sailed back to Ireland on the *Janet.*

7   Hopkins, Paul, *Glencoe and the End of the Highland War* (John Donald, Edinburgh, 1986), p.214.

8   Livingstone, Thomas, *A true and real account of the defeat of General Buchan and Brigadeer Cannon, their High-land Army, at the Battel of Crombdell upon the 1st of May; 1690. In a Letter from Sir Thomas Livingstone to General Mackay* (Edinburgh, 1690). Lord Yester's troop was one of those commissioned on 18 April 1689 and ordered to be raised in Haddington and Berwick. The dragoons from Elgin will presumably have been the other half of his own regiment, while 'Burnet's' may have been William Bennet of Grubett's troop of horse, although Mackay recorded them quartered at Perth in October. Surprisingly, Sir George Gordon of Edinglassie's troop does not appear to have been present.

9   Livingstone, ibid; Shaw, Lachlan, *History of the Province of Moray* (New Edition Thomas D. Morrison, Glasgow, 1882), Vol.3, pp.129-30. The manuscript of Shaw's history was actually written at some time before his death in 1777. He was a meticulous historian with a good knowledge of the local topography and traditions. Although a secondary source he has every appearance of being a reliable one.

10   Livingstone, op. cit. The actual disposition of Livingstone's forces is not entirely clear. Although he refers to two troops of dragoons crossing by the lower ford, it is possible that they were in fact Yester's and Grubett's troops and that he kept all six troops of his regiment together. Similarly, although there is no doubt that some highlanders were mounted behind the cavalry it is uncertain as to who they were and when they were mounted. On balance, the scenario outlined here is most likely and that it was Captain Mackay's company which was mounted in order to provide some firepower for the diversionary attack over the lower ford. There is no suggestion, incidentally, that the upper ford was attacked at all.

11   Lachlan, Vol.3, pp.129-30.

12   Livingstone, op. cit.

13   He was the second son of James Buchan of Auchmacoy, the eldest of the three brothers discussed in note 5; At the revolution, he was Captain-lieutenant of Thomas Buchan's Regiment (Scots Fusiliers) and followed his uncle to Ireland. Family tradition accords him

the Jacobite rank of major but that may relate to later service in the French army. Dalton, Charles *English Army Lists and Commission Registers*, Vol.2, pp.218-219.

[14] Where the grenades came from might at first sight seem puzzling since Leslie's Regiment and its grenadier company had been left far behind and did not actually fight in the battle. However, Livingstone's Dragoons, being equipped as mounted infantry, still included a grenadier troop at least as late as 1705 and it was they who no doubt furnished the grenades and very ostentatiously lit and tossed them.

[15] Mackay, *Memoirs of the War*, pp.322-324.

[16] Taken prisoner at Killiecrankie as a captain of Balfour's Regiment but since exchanged and promoted. Curiously enough his grandson, Captain John Fergusson RN, would attract a fearsome reputation while similarly employed in the Hebrides in1746.

[17] Kenmure's regiment never recovered from Killiecrankie and in October was still so shattered and unfit for service that Mackay did not bother to include it in his list of quarters, unless its name was as mangled as its condition to be recorded as 'Beuuridge's'.

[18] *Highland Papers Vol IV* (Scottish History Society 3rd Series, Edinburgh 1934), pp.108-110; Hopkins, pp.241-243.

[19] *Highland Papers Vol IV*, p.112. An unlikely local tradition claims that Inverey escaped by riding his horse up the near vertical side of the pass.

[20] Fergusson, J. *The Scots Brigade in Holland* (1899), Vol.1, p.571. This is his earliest recorded commission in the regiment – he was a captain a year later – and there is no evidence to support the popular legend that he was already with the regiment at Killiecrankie and exchanged pointed remarks with Mackay about his father's people standing on the hillside above.

Appendix I

The Scots Army of 1689

An entirely new Scots Army had to be created in 1689. Aside from various ad hoc militias the first regiment to be raised was the Earl of Leven's, required to blockade Edinburgh castle, but on 22 April a further eight infantry regiments were authorised by the Council:

> The estates of the kingdom of Scotland, considering that viscount of Kenmure has made an offer to levy a regiment of 600 foot to be commanded by him as colonel, and to be employed in the service of his majesty William, by the grace of God, king of Great Britain, France and Ireland, and the estates reposing special trust and confidence in the fidelity, courage and good conduct of the said viscount of Kenmure, have therefore nominated, constituted and appointed and, by this commission, do nominate, constitute and appoint the said viscount of Kenmure to be colonel of a regiment of foot appointed by the act of the said estates of the date of this commission to be levied by him, as said is, consisting of ten companies and sixty men in each company, with full power to the said viscount of Kenmure to nominate the lieutenant colonel and major of the said regiment, and the captains and inferior officers of the several companies, and to grant commissions accordingly and to command and exercise the said regiment, both officers and soldiers, carefully and diligently and to keep them in good order and discipline, and to do and act all things competent and incumbent for any colonel of foot to do and perform, requiring and commanding hereby all officers and soldiers of the said regiment to give due obedience to the said viscount of Kenmure as their colonel and to their respective commanding officers...[1]

After the initial surge of enthusiasm, it proved difficult to maintain this establishment and on 18 December 1689. King William ordered a remodelling of his Scottish forces. Six of the regiments; the Earl of Angus', Earl of Argyle's, Glencairn's, Kenmure's, Strathnaver's and the Laird of Grant's were to be re-organised to comprise thirteen companies apiece (including a grenadier company), each consisting of 3 officers, 2 sejeants, 3 corporals, 2 drummers and 57 soldiers, while a new regiment was to be formed under Colonel Richard Cunningham. The necessary personnel for this reorganisation were found by disbanding three other regiments and reducing the Earl of Angus' Cameronians from two battalions down to one battalion.[2] Otherwise both Leven's and Angus' regiments were considered to be untouchable after their fights at Killiecrankie and Dunkeld respectively and both of them survived the next round of cuts on 13 November 1690, when Glencairn's, Grant's and Kenmure's regiments (and an Independent Company commanded by Robert Menzies of Weem) were amalgamated to form a new regiment commanded by Colonel John Hill, which was to form the garrison of Fort William.

The schedule set out covers all infantry regiments serving in Scotland in 1689 and 1690. Naturally enough the greater number were Scots units, but three Dutch and two English regiments are also included.

SCOTTISH INFANTRY REGIMENTS

Lord Angus' Regiment

James Douglas, Earl of Angus, was commissioned by the Estates on 19 April 1689, and his regiment was raised in Ayrshire, Dumfries and Galloway, largely from amongst those militant Presbyterians calling themselves Cameronians. Most regiments authorised in April had an establishment of 600 men, but in this case, there was sufficient enthusiasm for two battalions to be raised.

The regiment was completed by 12 May and duly mustered into the service by Major Nicol Buntine, Muster Master General, at Douglas in Ayrshire on 14 May 1689. It was then assigned to service in Argyllshire before finding itself defending Dunkeld against the whole Highland army on 21 August 1689. However, from the very beginning, religious fanaticism manifested itself in an anarchic approach to disciple which in turn led to chronic desertion, and at the beginning of October 1689, Mackay reported that the regiment, 'is not above 600 men at present; with all I am certainly informed that the said Earles own companie was never in being: in my opinion it were best to reduce them to ten companies, for which ther might be found good officers and men of som service in the regiment, and who are not of the wilde principles; but if it be continued a regement, ther ought presently be sent a good Lieutenant Colonel, a man of service.'[3] His recommendation was partially accepted with a reduction in size to one battalion of thirteen companies as part of the general consolidation ordered on 18 December 1689. The companies to be disbanded were chosen by lot and their personnel drafted into the remaining ones. Once the campaign was over, the regiment went to Flanders where it was briefly taken into Dutch pay, but survived to become part of the British Army.

It is not entirely clear whether the required 1,200 coats were provided before the regiment marched up to Dunkeld, but a complaint made in August 1689 that shoes had been provided when the regiment was raised but that stockings and hats had not, would imply that they had been. Coats at this period were red with white facings rather than the yellow adopted by this regiment later. The statement that hats were not initially supplied is confirmed by Blackadder's account of Dunkeld in which he refers to the soldiers throwing their caps (blue bonnets) in the air when the Highlanders retreated.

On 4 July 1689, just as the regiment was about to march north, an order was given for it to be provided with the equipment then deficient, viz; 400 obsolete bandoliers, 400 swords and belts, 800 bayonets and 100 tents. Whether it actually received any or all of these items is not stated, but it had earlier received 400 pikes, 500 firelocks and 40 sergeants' halberds out of the magazine at Stirling. Equipment issued to the grenadier company in 1691 included grenadier caps and cap badges, which shows they were wearing fur caps with metal grenade badges rather than the embroidered cloth caps favoured by English units.[4]

No particular description survives of the regiment's colours at this period, but all Scots infantry regiments appear to have carried the traditional white cross of St. Andrew on a blue field.

Officers[5]

Colonel	James Douglas, Earl of Angus*
Lieutenant Colonel	William Cleland (killed at Dunkeld)
Major	James Henderson (killed at Dunkeld)
Captain	Daniel Ker of Kersland
	George Monro*
	John (Roy) Campbell of Moy
	William Hay
	John (Dhu) Campbell, younger of Moy
	William Borthwick of Johnstonburn (grenadier company)
	Gavin Cochrane of Craigmuir*
	John Haldane
	William Herries
	James Lindsay
	Ninian Steele
	James Gilchrist*
	John Mathieson*
	John Caldwell (died of wounds at Dunkeld)
	John Stephenson*
	William Grieve*

*Company disbanded December 1689.
Cleland was replaced as lieutenant colonel by Captain John Fullartoun of the Earl of Leven's Regiment, while Captain Daniel Ker (who had not been at Dunkeld) succeeded Henderson as major.

Earl of Argyle's Regiment
Archibald Campbell, Earl and later 1st Duke of Argyle, was commissioned on 19 April 1689 and his regiment was chiefly recruited from amongst the Highlanders he had earlier brought to Edinburgh. A cadre was also drawn from Lord Bargany's Regiment to provide NCOs who could discipline it, probably as a result of a cryptic comment by

Mackay that, 'Argil's Regiment needs mending, which he has promised to doe.'[6] Subsequently, the grenadier company was also formed of drafts taken from other Lowland Scots units. Initially it served in the West Highlands. Only the grenadiers, commanded by Captain Thomas Drummond, and Captain Robert Campbell of Glenlyon's company, were involved in the infamous massacre of Glencoe in 1692. Afterwards the regiment went to Flanders and was eventually disbanded in 1698 after the Treaty of Ryswijk ended King William's War.

Other than the wearing of blue bonnets, with an embroidered boar's head and coronet badge, (and fur caps for the grenadiers) the clothing was entirely conventional. Unusually the red coats had yellow rather than the customary white facings, and these were set off (initially at least) by yellow stockings. The colour of their waistcoats is uncertain. It should be noted that while they were made of plaiding the term denoted woollen cloth woven to half the width of broadcloth, not tartan. While the possibility cannot be ruled out that tartan material was used, the waistcoats were most likely red.[7]

A colour taken at Dixemunde in 1692, which can be attributed to the regiment by a process of elimination, was the usual blue sheet with a white saltire overall, distinguished by a large golden thistle in each quartering.

On 20 May 1689, 200 firelocks were ordered for the regiment and patronashes (cartridge boxes) were to be made in Glasgow according to a pattern supplied by Lieutenant Colonel Sir Duncan Campbell of Auchinbreck. As he had previously served with the Scots Brigade the pattern was probably a Dutch one. Otherwise information on its early equipment is lacking, although it is likely that all of the rank and file were armed with muskets without any admixture of pikes.

Officers[8]

Colonel	Archibald Campbell, Earl of Argyle
Lieutenant Colonel	Sir Duncan Campbell of Auchinbreck
Major	Robert Duncanson
Captain	Archibald MacAuley of Ardincaple
	James Campbell, younger of Ardkinglas
	Archibald Lamont of Lamont[9]
	Archibald Campbell of Torrie
	Archibald Campbell of Barbreck
	Hector Bannatyne, younger of Kames
	Robert Campbell of Glenlyon
	Thomas Drummond grenadier company
	John Campbell of Airds
	James Ure of Shirgarton[10]

Lord Bargany's Regiment

Lord Bargany was commissioned to raise his regiment on 19 April 1689. Some were presumably raised in his native Ayrshire, although afterwards Mackay started that, 'Barganys is composed of good men, but most of them Scots Irish, who came over last somer'.[11] A substantial detachment of 200 men was sent on the expedition to Kintyre in May 1689, under Captain Young, but the remainder of the regiment served in the Stirling area and afterwards formed part of the garrison of Perth. It was reduced into Colonel Richard Cunningham's Regiment on 18 December 1689.

No details survive as to the regiment's clothing, but Bargany afterwards complained he had not been reimbursed for the costs of it. As to equipment: on 25 April 1689, 'The estates of this kingdom ordain the keepers of the public arms at Ayr to deliver to lord Bargany, or his order, 200 muskets with bandoliers and match conforming and 160 picks, upon his receipt, for the use of the regiment to be levied by the said lord for the service of the public.' However, muskets must have been in short supply for between 25 April and 6 May 1689, 360 pikes were issued but only 280 (matchlock) muskets and 340 collars of bandoliers.[12] On 21 May Lieutenant Colonel Patrick Grahame was authorised to draw 200 bayonets and '200 patronashes for musquets for the use of the detachment under the command of Captain Young in Kintyre.'[13]

Officers[14]

Colonel	John Hamilton, Lord Bargany
Lieutenant Colonel	Patrick Grahame
Major	William(?) Hamilton
Captain	William Thompson
	William Hamilton

Lord Blantyre's Regiment

Another south-west regiment; Lord Blantyre was commissioned to raise his regiment on 19 April 1689 and, like his colleague Lord Bargany, seemingly recruited it in part from amongst Protestant refugees from Ulster. A detachment under Captain Young went to Kintyre in May 1689. The regiment was then in camp at Stirling when Mackay marched north to Killiecrankie but otherwise saw no real service and was ordered reduced into Colonel Richard Cunningham's Regiment on 18 December 1689.

No details are available as to the uniform worn by the regiment, but the officers declared in a petition to the Privy Council in 1690 that they had raised and clothed their several companies at their own expense.

In July 1689, Blantyre had himself petitioned the Privy Council, declaring that he had, according to his commission, levied 480 musketeers and 150 pikemen and requested that the government supply them with swords and bayonets. In response, however, only 200 bayonets were ordered![15]

Officers[16]

Colonel	Alexander Stewart, Lord Blantyre
Lieutenant Colonel	William Baillie, Lord Forrester
Major	William Buchannan
Captain	Durhame
	Charles Swinton of Mersington
	James Sleigh
	William Rowan
	Alexander Hume
	Alexander(?) Young[17]
	William Baillie of Hardingtoun
	Alexander Dunbar

Colonel Richard Cunningham's Regiment

When Bargany's, Blantyre's and Mar's regiments were reduced in December 1689 the remaining personnel were consolidated into an entirely new regiment to be commanded by the then Captain Richard Cunningham of Lauder's Regiment, of the Scots Brigade. His lieutenant colonel (and successor in December 1690) was another Dutch officer, Major John Buchan of Mackay's. The regiment, thirteen companies strong was originally intended to go to Ireland, but the threat posed by Buchan's campaign in the north-east saw it detained for service in Scotland; first in garrison at Aberdeen and afterwards at Braemar, before eventually going to Flanders in 1693 and being disbanded after the Peace of Ryswijk in 1697.

Officers[18]

Those officers listed below were newly commissioned into the regiment in December 1689 and apparently do not include officers with existing commissions transferring across with other personnel from the disbanded regiments. For example, Captain William Baillie killed in 1695 while commanding the grenadier company was most probably the same officer earlier serving in Lord Blantyre's Regiment.

Colonel	Richard Cunningham
Lieutenant Colonel	John Buchan

Major	Stewart[19]
Captain	James Orrock
	John Montgomery
	Archibald Dunbar

Earl of Glencairn's Regiment

The Earl of Glencairn was commissioned to raise his regiment in the south-west on 19 April 1689, but like Bargany's and Blantyre's regiments was said to be substantially comprised of 'Scotch-Irish' refugees from Ulster.[20] No doubt to their dismay they were sent with Argyle's Regiment to the West Highlands, but as a consequence survived the original round of cuts until 1691 when it was ordered to be reduced into Colonel John Hill's Regiment.

An order dated 29 April 1689 directed forty muskets and twenty pikes to be issued to Captain William Blair's company.

Officers[21]

Colonel	John Cunningham, Earl of Glencairn
Lieutenant Colonel	John Houston of that Ilk
Major	Archibald Burnett of Carlops
Captain	Robert Dickson
	William Blair
	John Mackay
	Sir Alexander Livingston
	Nicol Buntein of Ardoch
	Gavin Hamilton
	James Hamilton

Laird of Grant's Regiment

Ludovick Grant of Grant, otherwise known as the Laird of Grant, was another commissioned to raise his regiment on 19 April 1689. Recruited in the Inverness area, Mackay declared in October that, 'I doe judge that my Lord Strathnavers and the Laird of Grant's regiments are the best and completest.'[22] Nevertheless in 1691, it was reduced into Colonel John Hill's new regiment, probably for no better reason than at the time all but one company was already serving on the garrison of Fort William.

While quickly recruited, it evidently took some time to get Grant's Regiment properly clothed and equipped. Mackay recalled that while he was in the north in May of 1689; 'He ordered also the Lord Strathnaver and the Laird of Grant to levy their regiments, for which they had taken commissions, with all speed, and to arm so many of them as they could, with such arms as usually Highlanders make use of, most of them being of that sort of people.' Nevertheless, as late as early December, Sir James Leslie wrote that: 'Lord Strathnaver's regiment and Colonell Grant's haue no cloathes as yet, and ar very ill arm'd, … they are very good bodyes of men, but haue neither swords nor bagganetts.' Leslie did, however to on to say that, 'I have given an order for Colonell Grant to take out his armes and cloathes out of the ship above eight days agoe, soe hope, by this time, they will have got them, and then they will be in a better condition to doe service then they are att present.'[23] The clothing was seemingly furnished by several Edinburgh merchants. Coats were probably the usual red ones with white linings and as no reference is made to hats the men most likely wore blue bonnets.

Unusually, and probably because he was so remote from the magazines in Stirling and Edinburgh, Grant was authorised to purchase the necessary arms for his regiment without waiting for the government to supply them: 'The meeting of the estates (25 April 1689) having considered an offer made by laird of Grant to import 600 stand of arms for the public service, providing the price thereof be repaid to him, they give warrant to the laird of Grant to buy and import 600 stand of arms for the public service, and declare that the price thereof shall be repaid to him by the public with their conveniency, he making the arms forthcoming', and in December he duly requested payment of his outstanding accounts, declaring that he had purchased 600 bayonets, patronashes and belts made by a beltmaker named Robert Handasyde, and also 500 firelocks.[24]

Officers[25]

Colonel	Ludovick Grant of Grant
Lieutenant Colonel	Patrick Grant
Major	Hugh Mackay
Captain	Alexander Grant[26]
	John Grant[27]
	John Forbes
	Laird of Burgiss
	George Gordon
	Robert Grant of Dunleugus
	Robert Ross

Colonel John Hill's Regiment
Hill was an Englishman who had served in the original Cromwellian garrison of Inverlochy in the 1650s, building up what was regarded as a useful rapport with local chieftains such as Locheil. On the strength of

that, he was appointed governor of Fort William and made colonel of a regiment of foot to serve as its garrison. Pragmatically this regiment was formed on 13 November 1690 by consolidating the understrength regiments and detachments already holding the Fort; Grant's, Glencairn's and Kenmure's, together with Menzies of Weem's Independent Company. Its official establishment was twelve companies, each comprising three officers, 2 serjeants, 3 corporals, 1 drummer and 77 soldiers, plus a grenadier company with 3 officers, 3 serjeants, 3 corporals, 2 drummers and 77 grenadiers.

As to clothing and equipment, 1,000 'piecoats' and a like number of pairs of stockings and shoes were ordered for the regiment in anticipation, and on 20 October, 1,000 firelocks.[28]

Officers[29]

Colonel	John Hill	
Lieutenant Colonel	James Hamilton	(ex-Glencairn's)
Major	John Forbes	(ex-Grant's)
Captain	Robert Hunter	
	Alexander Anderson (grenadier company)	
	James Cunningham	
	Anthony Wilkie	
	Neil McNeil	
	Lord Kilmaurs	(ex-Glencairn's)
	James Menzies of Weem	

Independent Companies of Foot

A number of Independent Companies were raised during the campaign, usually for local defence purposes, and sometimes best described as irregulars. Those listed below appear to have been the only ones carried on the regular establishment: [30]

The Duke of Hamilton to be Captain and Commander of the Company in the Castle of Arran, consisting of 40 men, with power to appoint subordinate officers. Dated Edinburgh 22 April 1689.

Earl Marischal to be Captain of a Company of 60 men to garrison Dunottar Castle, with power to appoint subordinate officers. Dated Edinburgh 22 April 1689

David, Earl of Leven (Constable and Governor of Edinburgh Castle), to be Captain of a Company of Foot in garrison in Edinburgh Castle. Dated Hampton Court 4 July, 1689.

John Erskine to be Captain of a Company of Foot in Stirling Castle. Dated Hampton Court 26 July 1689.

Robert Menzies, Yr., of Weem, to be Captain of the Independent New Company in Scotland. Dated Hampton Court 22 August 1689.[31]

Lord Neil Campbell[32] to be Governor of Dumbarton Castle and Captain of the Company in garrison there. Dated Hampton Court 15 October1689.

William Erskine to be Lieutenant Governor of Blackness Castle and Lieutenant in the Company of Souldiers in garrison there. Dated Holland House 19 November 1689.

Viscount Kenmure's Regiment

Kenmure was commissioned to raise his regiment on 19 April 1689, and did so partly in his native Kirkcudbright-shire and elsewhere in the south-west and partly from amongst Protestant refugees from Ulster. Its most notable service, under Kenmure himself, was at Killiecrankie, where it was effectively destroyed, although the remains survived until November 1690, when it was ordered reduced into Colonel John Hill's Regiment.

There are no details available as to the regiment's clothing, but presumably they had red coats at Killiecrankie. There is, however some correspondence as to equipment, with 450 bayonets being required, indicating the usual ration of three musketeers to one pikeman. Patronashes were ordered for the corporals but the ordinary musketeers had to make do with obsolete collars of bandoliers. The regiment obviously had a mixture of firelocks and matchlocks, for in September 1689, when he was trying to rebuild the regiment after Killiecrankie, Kenmure petitioned the Privy Council to let him have 'what snapwarks [firelocks] muskets, bandoleers they wanted', together with pikes and bayonets. In response, he was ordered to be supplied with 200 muskets and 100 pikes.[33]

Officers[34]

Colonel	Alexander Gordon, Viscount Kenmure
Lieutenant Colonel	John Fergusson of Craigdarroch (killed at Killiecrankie)
Major	Alexander Gordon
Captain	James Donaldson (prisoner at Killiecrankie)[35]

James Gordon, younger of Craichlair
Alexander Gordon
John McCulloch of Ardwall[36]
Patrick Dunbar
Thomas Kennedy
William Gordon

Earl of Leven's Regiment

Enlisted by the Earl of Leven on 19 March 1689 from amongst the Westland Whigs and Cameronians then thronging Edinburgh. According to *The London Gazette* the regiment was fully recruited to a strength of 780 men within two hours and put to the task of blockading Edinburgh Castle. Although initially intended as a temporary formation, it was taken into the line in April and given a cadre of professional officers and soldiers. A detachment found itself reinforcing the garrison of Inverness, but most of the regiment fought well at Killiecrankie.

Linen, stockings and lining material was provided on 19 April, and there is an oblique reference in June to suits of clothes being provided by the New Mills Cloth Manufactory. We also have Mackay's testimony the regiment was certainly in red coats at Killiecrankie. There are no contemporary references to facings but most Scots units had plain white ones at the period so this seems more likely than the yellow facings worn by the 1740s. A white colour was certainly taken from the regiment by the French in the 1690s, bearing a representation of Edinburgh Castle in the centre, with the city's motto NISI DOMINUS FRUSTRA, but this probably dates from after Killiecrankie when the regiment was adopted by the city.[37]

Officers[38]

Colonel	David Melvill, Earl of Leven
Lieutenant Colonel	William Arnot[39]
Major	Robert Bruce
Captain	Archibald Paton
	Sir Robert Hamilton of Silverton, Lanark[40]
	Henry Verrier
	William Hill
	James Denholme
	John Fullartoun[41]
	James Bruce
	James Lundie

Charles Erskine
John Moncrief

Earl of Mar's Regiment[42]

Charles Erskine, Earl of Mar, who had once raised and commanded the Scots Fusiliers, was commissioned to raise a new regiment on 19 April 1689, largely to demonstrate his loyalty to the new regime, but he was already terminally ill and most of the work fell to his lieutenant colonel, David Erskine of Dun. Unlike most of the others, it was recruited not in the south-west, put partly in Aberdeenshire, where he had considerable estates, down the east coast and in the Stirling area. At least part of the regiment helped defend Dundee against the rebel raid in May, losing some of its drums and baggage. By October, the five strongest companies were in garrison at Blair Castle while the rest were at Coupar in Fife. Eventually, still designated as Mar's Regiment, it was reduced into Cunningham's Regiment that December.

No real detail is available as to its uniforms although Erskine of Dun stated that contracts for clothing had been placed with William Blackwood and Thomas Cussine of Aberdeen and that most of it was issued in August.[43] While the usual red coats lined with white were probably worn, it is worth noting that the earlier regiment raised by Mar, which eventually became the Royal Scots Fusiliers, had red facings rather than white.

Officers[44]

Colonel	Charles Erskine, Earl of Mar (d. natural causes 22 May 1689)
Lieutenant Colonel	Sir David Erskine of Dun
Major	Robert Forbes of Brux
Captain	Sir Thomas Nicholson of Tillicoultry
	John Nicholson
	George Preston
	David Bruce
	Alexander Hunter
	Hugh Kennedy
	John MacKenzie

Lord Strathaver's Regiment[45]

Commissioned on 19 April 1689, and largely raised in the far north, although at least two companies were recruited in Fife by Lieutenant Colonel Robert Lumsden. Mackay declared in October that, 'I doe judge that my Lord Strathnavers and the Laird of Grant's regiments are the best and completest.'[46] Based in Inverness throughout its existence until folded into Hill's Regiment in November 1690.

Little information is available as to clothing and equipment although 300 firelocks were ordered to be delivered to Lieutenant Colonel Lumsden on 15 May 1689, in place of matchlocks. According to Sir James Leslie in December 1689, 'Lord Strathnaver's regiment and Colonell Grant's haue no cloathes as yet, and ar very ill arm'd, … they are very good bodyes of men, but haue neither swords nor bagganetts.'[47]

Officers[48]

Colonel	John Gordon, Lord Strathnaver
Lieutenant Colonel	Robert Lumsden of Innergellie
Major	George Wishart
Captain	Sleigh[49]
	Salkeld
	Robert Monro of Foulis
	Adam Gordon of Dalfelly
	John Gordon of Embo
	George Gordon
	John Monro of Clynes

The Scots Brigade

The Scots Brigade which had been in the service of Holland since 1572, comprised three regiments by 1688; commanded by Hugh Mackay, Bartholomew Balfour and George Ramsay respectively. When they sailed from Holland each regiment comprised ten companies of fifty men but on being taken on the English establishment and therefore paid for by the English Treasury the opportunity was taken to increase their strength to 1,200 men in two battalions. Conversely, at just the same time this radical expansion was underway, some officers, NCOs and men were transferred away as cadres to stiffen and help train the new regiments.[50] This proved over-ambitious and initially Mackay only took one battalion from each regiment to Killiecrankie, albeit then dividing them in turn into two little battalions apiece for tactical purposes. Afterwards, however, there are references to both battalions of each regiment serving together later in the campaign. Nevertheless, by 1691, when they went to Flanders, the regiments were consolidated once again into a single battalion apiece, albeit now with thirteen companies rather than the original ten.[51] Upon the Scots Brigade's return to the Dutch service following the Peace of Rijswijk in 1697 the three additional companies were disbanded and they reverted once again to ten companies.

All three regiment wore red coats, clearly shown in a contemporary set of four sketches by an unknown artist. They principally differed from Scottish ones in being *pijj* or frock coats with a distinct waist, and the cuffs rolled well back to expose the facing-coloured waistcoat sleeves. Most wore broad-brimmed black hats trimmed with white, but grenadiers had brown fur caps with a red 'bag'.

The oldest known set of colours belonging to the Scots Brigade, as laid up in St. Giles' Cathedral in Edinburgh, take the form of a plain union flag distinguished only by a crowned thistle proper and below it a royal blue ribbon bearing the old Scots' motto NEMO ME IMPUNE LACESSIT. This corresponds very closely in style to an otherwise unidentified colour taken by the French at Le Quesnoy in 1712, which was a plain white saltire on blue, with a gold thistle and crown in the centre and a red ribbon over bearing the same motto. Those carried at Killiecrankie were presumably very similar but may not yet have featured a crown above the thistle.

Major General Hugh Mackay's Regiment

This was the senior regiment of the brigade, also known as the 'old regiment' since it could trace a continuous existence back to 1574 and by way of distinction the officers were said to wear orange sashes rather than red, as the other regiments did.

According to *An exact List of the Royal Confederate Army in Flanders, commanded by the King of Great Britain ... as it was drawn up at Gerpines Camp, July 27, 1691* Mackay's Regiment then had red coats lined blue. Waistcoats and breeches in the Dutch service were normally of the facing colour.

Officers 1689[52]

Colonel	Hugh Mackay of Scourie
Lieutenant Colonel	James Mackay(killed at Killiecrankie)
Major	John Buchan[53]
Captain	Walter MacDonald Bowie
	George Connock (killed at Killiecrankie?)
	Peter Watkins
	Charles Graham
	Everard (Edward) Halket
	Alexander Lamy (killed at Killiecrankie)
	John Mudie
	Robert Mackay (wounded at Killiecrankie)
	Angus Mackay (killed at Killiecrankie)
	William Sharp

Colonel Bartholomew Balfour's Regiment

Following Balfour's death at Killiecrankie, the regiment was taken over by his lieutenant colonel, George Lauder. It was not present in the Gerpines camp in 1691, but is presumably the Scots regiment with red coats lined red, with red waistcoat and breeches depicted in two of the sketches referred to above.

Officers 1689[54]

Colonel	Bartholomew Balfour
Lieutenant Colonel	George Lauder[55]
Major	Patrick Balfour[56]
Captain	James Fergusson[57] (prisoner at Killiecrankie)
	Walter Murray
	Thomas Erskine (killed at Killiecrankie)
	Alexander Livingston
	William Nanning (killed at Killiecrankie)
	Bartholomew Balfour (prisoner at Killiecrankie)
	Alexander Gordon[58]
	Richard Cunningham

Colonel George Ramsay's Regiment

This was Wauchope's Regiment until he defected to King James' service a few months before the revolution. The list of officers below is particularly incomplete and uncertain, as first a re-shuffle was necessary to replace those officers who left with Wauchope, and then a significant number of the remainder transferred to other regiments or raised units of their own. According to *An exact List of the Royal Confederate Army in Flanders, commanded by the King of Great Britain ... as it was drawn up at Gerpines Camp, July 27, 1691*, Ramsay's Regiment had red coats lined white.

Officers 1689[59]

Colonel	George Ramsay
Lieutenant Colonel	William Miln[60]
Major	William Murray[61]
Captain	John Clerk (killed at Killiecrankie?)[62]
	Walter Corbet
	William Douglas (killed at Killiecrankie?)
	George Hamilton
	John Gibson
	John Somerville

Scottish Cavalry Units

The cavalry engaged in the Highland War fell into two categories; the more prestigious were those designated as Horse, while Dragoons on the other hand were regarded as mounted infantry and equipped accordingly, even to the extent of fielding a grenadier troop. A broadsword and at least one pistol was carried in addition to full infantry equipment of musket and bayonet. Their horses were cheaper, smaller and sturdier than the large heavy animals favoured by the Horse and ironically proved to be far better for Scottish conditions – a point tacitly acknowledged when the independent troops of militia horse were eventually amalgamated to form two regiments of Dragoons. Both had an establishment of six troops, each comprising 3 officers, two sergeants, 2 corporals, 2 drummers and 50 dragoons. A peculiarity of cavalry units at this time was that although the six troops were each allocated to the colonel, lieutenant colonel and four captains, the major had no troop of his own.

Lord Cardross's Dragoons

Confusingly, although the regiment was authorised on 23 April 1689, the original officers' commissions were backdated to 19 April.[63] Like most of the infantry regiments it was largely raised in the south-west and its Cameronian sympathies were widely suspected to be the reason for the regiment being disbanded at the end of 1690 – ostensibly to make way for an entirely new regiment commanded by Colonel John Cunningham. Much of its service was in the Stirling area, watching the Braes of Balquhidder but it was ingloriously involved in the Dunkeld business and in the following year went north under Lieutenant Colonel Robert Jackson.

No information appears to be available as to clothing, but they presumably had red coats and probably white linings. A standard or guidon survives, swallow-tailed as was customary for dragoons, made of red silk with a gold fringe, bearing Cardross's embroidered crest; a hand holding a sword implanted wolf's head proper, all set on a coronet with a scroll over bearing the motto FORTITVDINE. By way of distinguishing it as a Scottish unit there was also a small blue canton displaying a crowned thistle.

Equipment included firelock muskets, swords ad bayonets, and patronashes or cartridge boxes for their ammunition, musket belts and buckets

Officers 1689[64]

| Colonel | Henry Erskine, Lord Cardross |
| Lieutenant Colonel | John Erskine[65] |

Major	John Guthrie
Captain	Sir Alexander Home of Kerse
	John Home of Ninewells
	Walter Lockhart of Kirktoun
	James Muir

Militia Horse

Ten Independent troops of horse were ordered to be levied on 22 April 1689:

> The estates of this kingdom, considering that by their act of the eighteenth instant they have ordained the number of 500 horsemen, or thereby, to be levied and raised out of the shires of this kingdom, according to the proportions therein expressed, and it being necessary that these horsemen be modelled in troops and officers nominated to command them, therefore the estates do ordain that there shall be ten troops of these horsemen, each troop consisting of fifty, to be commanded as follows:

Alex Montgomerie, Earl of Eglinton:	Ayr and Renfrew
Wm Johnstone, Earl of Annandale:	Dumfries, Wigton and Kirkcudbright
John Hay, Lord Yester:	Haddington (East Lothian) and Berwickshire
William Kerr, Lord Newbattle	Roxburgh and Selkirk
William Ross, Lord Ross:	Peebles, Linlithgow and Midlothian
John Hamilton, Lord Belhaven:	Lanark[66]
Andrew, Lord Rollo:	Forfar, Kincardine and Aberdeenshire[67]
William Blair of Blair:[68]	Perthshire
Sir William Hope:[69]	Fife and Kinross
William, Master of Forbes:	Banff and the Earl of Erroll's part of Aberdeenshire

On the following day an additional troop, this time of volunteer horse, was authorised to be raised by William Bennett, younger of Grubbet.

By the end of the year, however, General Mackay was recommending that the various troops should be regimented. To his disappointment, this took some time and it was not until early in 1691 that a substantial re-organisation of the cavalry took place. In late 1690, Lord Cardross's Dragoons were disbanded and in their place the various independent troops were re-organised into two regiments of Dragoons under Colonel Richard Cunningham and Lord Newbattle respectively. The latter were disbanded in 1697, but Cunningham's Regiment served until 1714, when it was reduced to a cadre before being revived during the Jacobite Rising of 1715 and becoming the 7th Dragoons.

A contract survives relating to the making of coats for two of the troops raised in 1689: 'the said George Home having mad bargone with the Earl of Annandale and Lord Ross for ther troopes viz:- ther coats lined with Aberdaines fingarrins dyed ride with eight dizen (96) of buttons for threty five shillings and mad coat.'[70] Although the body colour of the coat is not mentioned it too was presumably red and it is likely that the other troops wore the same to distinguish them (socially) from the infantry, who had white linings. This particular contract was drawn up on 22 June 1689, which suggests that Annandale's troop may not have been uniformed at Killiecrankie.

Royal Regiment of Scots Dragoons
Together with the Lifeguard troop this was the only regiment of the old Scots Army to serve in Scotland during the war, where its service was almost entirely in the north. At first its loyalties were dubious, but a purge of disaffected officers proved effective and it served well against the clans, most notably at Cromdale and the relief of Abergeldie.

Its uniform since 1685 was red coats lined with blue, and as cavalry they would have had blue breeches and waistcoats to match. Headgear is slightly uncertain. Some certainly appear to have had furred caps, with the usual red bag, but these may have been confined to the grenadier troop with ordinary troopers wearing hats.

There is no evidence as to their riding grey horses at this time, with the earliest reference dating from 1693, and a good theory has been advanced that they may have taken over the grey horses from the Dutch *Garde te Paard* when that regiment returned to Holland.

Officers[71] 1689

Colonel	Sir Thomas Livingstone
Lieutenant Colonel	William Livingston of Kilsyth[72]
Major	William Douglas[73]
Captain	John Strachan
	John Livingston[74]
	James Murray[75]
	William Creighton[76]

Officers 1689 (post conspiracy)

Colonel	Sir Thomas Livingstone
Lieutenant Colonel	William Douglas
Major	Aeneas Mackay[77]

Captain	John Strachan
	Henry Balfour[78]
	John Hay
	Sir William Douglas of Cavers

Artillery

The Scots artillery comprised a single company, of just twelve Gunners and Under-Gunners, commanded in 1688 by Captain John Slezar or Slessor. At the revolution, he was initially uncertain as to his loyalties and according to Mackay, 'absolutely denied to serve his Majestie' (King William). However, his successor, Captain James Smith, was badly wounded at Killiecrankie and so Slezar was reinstated (over Mackay's objections) as, 'Captain of the Artillery Company in Scotland and Surveyor of the Magazines', on 11 January 1690.[79]

In 1683 the Gunners had suits of fine scarlet cloth, lined with serge and decorated with long silk loops, silver buttons, buff belts with silver buckles, furred caps laced with gold galloon – metallic braid – and scarlet stockings. On ceremonial occasions at least, they were to carry halberds.

The Under Gunners were to wear suits, 'so laced' but their buckles were steel and they carried grenade bags and patronashes with the King's cypher.[80] As they also had bayonets they were presumably armed with firelocks.

ENGLISH INFANTRY

Colonel Ferdinando Hastings' Regiment

The only English unit to fight at Killiecrankie, Hastings's Regiment, was raised in Buckinghamshire in 1685 by the Earl of Huntingdon. At the revolution, it was in garrison at Plymouth where Huntingdon and a number of other officers were arrested and dismissed. One of two regiments brought north of the border by Sir John Lanier, it served with Mackay in the north, leaving a detachment at Inverness before serving creditably at Killiecrankie and afterwards going to Ireland. It eventually became the 13th Foot (Somerset Light Infantry).

At a muster on Houndslow Heath on 30 June 1686, it was noted to be dressed in red coats turned up with yellow, yellow breeches and grey stockings. Buttons were pewter and so their hats were presumable edged with white tape.[81]

The regiment's colours were yellow; the colonel's a plain sheet while the others bore a red cross overall edged in white.

Officers 1689[82]

Colonel	Ferdinando Hastings
Lieutenant Colonel	Robert Ingram
Major	John Tidcombe
Captain	Christopher, Viscount Hatton (grenadier company)
	Charles Hatton
	Sir John Jacob
	Charnock Heron
	Henry Waldron
	Michael Duncan

Sir James Leslie's Regiment

Raised in 1685 by Sir William Clifton, this was another regiment which lost a number of its officers at the revolution. The then colonel, Sackville Tufton, was replaced in December 1688 by Sir James Leslie, a Scot then serving as lieutenant colonel of the Queen Dowager's Regiment of Foot. Crossing the border with Sir John Lanier (less three companies left to hold Berwick upon Tweed), it served as part of the garrison of Inverness and was present at Cromdale in 1690. Eventually it became the 15th Foot. The regiment was not present at Houndslow Heath but a 1687 deserter description cites a red coat, lined red, white stockings and a grenadier cap edged with white with the King's cypher. Officers coats were still scarlet lined scarlet in 1690, although yellow facings were adopted at a later date. Despite the red facings, Clifton's colours in 1685 were a deep bluish green in the same style as Hastings but distinguished by various heraldic devices peculiar to Clifton. These had presumably gone by 1689.[83]

Officers 1689[84]

Colonel	Sir James Leslie
Lieutenant Colonel	Rupert Billingsley
Major	Charles Tankred
Captain	William Stow[85]
	William Barnes
	John Fowkes
	Phillips
	William Dobbins[86]
	William Hussey[87]
	Roger Kirkby
	Robert Leslie (grenadier company)
	Henry Paget

English Cavalry

Hon. John Berkeley's Dragoons
Formed in 1685 from a number of independent troops and designated Princess Anne of Denmark's Regiment. Came north with Lanier and were originally based in Angus, but then went north with Mackay on his initial expedition to Inverness, before returning to the east coast.
By the eighteenth century the regiment had green facings but whether this was so in 1689 is uncertain. In 1687 all Dragoons were required to be armed with, 'snaphaunce musquets strapt with bright barrels three feet eight inches long with buckets, cartouche boxes, bayonets, granade pouches and hammer hatchets.'[88]

Officers 1689 [89]

Lieutenant Colonel	Francis Hawley
Major	Hugh Windham
Captain	Henry Smith
	Giles Spicer
	Edmund Mortimer[90]

Lord Colchester's Horse
Originally raised by the Earl of Plymouth in 1685, the regiment was taken over by Colchester at the revolution and came north with Mackay early in 1689, only to be marched into the ground in short order. Notwithstanding the general's confidence in the regiment as soldiers, its large horses quickly broke down in Scottish conditions.

Eventually ranked as the 3rd Dragoon Guards the regiment was noted in 1686 to be wearing red coats lined with green. As Horse, they were equipped with broadswords, a pair of pistols and a carbine – the latter at this time were long barrelled weapons distinguished from muskets only by a smaller calibre and (latterly) no provision for fitting a bayonet. In theory, the troopers could wear body armour, but it is unlikely that they burdened their horses with the weight of it in Scotland.

Officers 1689[91]

Lieut. Col.	John Staples
Captain	Thomas Windsor
	Sir William Clerke
	William Wentworth
	Matthew Ducy Morton (major 31 May 1690)

Colonel Anthony Heyford's Dragoons

This was actually the 1st or Royal Regiment of Dragoons, raised in 1683 and ordered north after Killiecrankie.

At the Putney Heath review in 1684 they were noted to be coated and cloaked in red, faced with blue, with red saddle housings embroidered with blue and yellow.

Sir John Lanier's Horse

Raised by Sir John in 1685, and eventually ranked as the 1st Dragoon Guards, they were recorded in 1686 as wearing red coats lined yellow, otherwise as for Colchester's. The regiment saw no action in Scotland and soon departed for Ireland.

NOTES

[1] *Convention Parliamentary Register* 22 April 1689.

[2] King William to Earl of Leven, Hugh Mackay and Sir George Monro, 18 December 1689, in Mackay, *Memoirs of the War*, pp.308-10.

[3] Mackay to Hamilton 11 October 1689, in Mackay, ibid, pp.283-4.

[4] *Register of the Privy Council of Scotland* (1689), pp. 439 & 487; Acts of the Parliament of Scotland IX, pp.55-56; Lawson, C.C.P. *History of the Uniforms of the British Army* (Kaye Ward, London, 1969), Vol.1, p.65. A list of the regiments in camp at Gerpines in Flanders confirms that the regiment had white facings at this time.

[5] Dalton, Charles, *English Army Lists and Commission Registers*, Vol.3, pp.87-88.

[6] Mackay to Melvill, 22 October 1689, in Mackay, ibid, p.290.

[7] Prebble, John *Glencoe* (Secker & Warburg, London, 1966), pp.178-9.

[8] Dalton, Vol.3, p.89.

[9] Uncertain. According to Hopkins (151-2) he was nominated to a commission but declined it.

[10] Not listed in Dalton, possibly substitute for Lamont.

[11] Mackay to Melvill, 22 October 1689, in Mackay, ibid, p.290.

[12] *Register of the Privy Council of Scotland* (1689), p.55.

[13] *Convention Parliamentary Register* 21 May 1689. The Captain Young referred to actually belonged to Lord Blantyre's Regiment.

[14] Dalton, Vol.3, p.90.

[15] *Register of the Privy Council of Scotland* (1689), p.488.

[16] Dalton, Vol.3, p.91.

[17] There is some uncertainty as to this officer's identity. Dalton identifies him as the Alexander Young who later became lieutenant colonel of Lord Strathnaver's Regiment, but according to Hopkins his first name was *William*.

[18] Dalton, Vol.3, p.97.

[19] Possibly the Major Samuel Stewart serving as lieutenant to the Earl of Eglinton's Troop of Horse in April 1689.

[20] Mackay, ibid, p.293.

[21] Dalton, Vol.3, p.93.

[22] Mackay to Melvill, 22 October 1689, in Mackay, ibid, p.290.

[23] Sir James Leslie to Lord Melvill, Inverness 6 December 1689, in Mackay, pp.300-301.

[24] *Register of the Privy Council of Scotland* (1689), pp.228, 543-544. Interestingly, some of those firelocks survive in the Seafield Collection at Fort George. Most of the equipment forming the collection dates from the raising of the Strathspey Fencibles in the 1790s, but it also includes a small number of firelocks with the characteristic flare to the muzzle designed to accommodate a plug bayonet.

[25] Dalton, Vol.3, p.92.

[26] Unidentified, although Dalton insists he was not Alexander Grant, younger of Grant. Soon he left the regiment and was replaced by the Captain James Grant, who defended Urquhart Castle.

[27] Second son of Robert Grant of Elchies; fought at Cromdale.

[28] *Register of the Privy Council of Scotland* (1690), pp.493, 523, 565, 575. The term 'piecoats' was a corruption of the Dutch *pijjcoat*, which survives in English as pea-jacket. In this particular case, it appears to have been applied to what are now termed frock-coats, with a properly defined waist, rather than the older style of coat which hung down straight from the shoulders.

[29] Dalton, Vol.3, p.277.

[30] ibid, p.98.

[31] Menzies had commanded an Independent Company at Killiecrankie. This may indeed be a new one, or more likely this marks the point at which it was taken on to the regular establishment.

[32] Second son of Earl of Argyle.

[33] *Register of the Privy Council of Scotland* (1689), pp. 542-3.

[34] Dalton, Vol.3, p.94.

[35] Appendix to *Acts of Parliament of Scotland* IX, p.56.

[36] The lieutenant of his company, John Nisbet, was taken prisoner at Killiecrankie, ibid.

[37] *Register of the Privy Council of Scotland* (1689), p. 438; *Minute Book of the Managers of the New Mills Cloth Manufactory* (Scottish History Society, Edinburgh, 1903), pp.234, 209 & 211; Lawson, Vol.1, p.144.

[38] Dalton, Vo.3, pp.85-6.

[39] Not identified, but a *Lieutenant* William Arnot of Balfour's Regiment in the Scots Brigade was recommended for a captaincy after Killiecrankie. He was probably a relative, but the possibility cannot be ruled out that Lieutenant Arnot volunteered to 'discipline' Leven's recruits, Mackay, p.272.

[40] Previously in Dutch service with seniority as captain from September 1688.

[41] Lieutenant Colonel of the Cameronians in succession to William Cleland, killed at Dunkeld.

[42] Not to be confused with his earlier regiment raised in 1678 which eventually became the Royal Scots Fusiliers.

[43] *Register of the Privy Council of Scotland* (1689), p.156.

[44] Dalton, p.95.

[45] Not to be confused with his later regiment raised for service in Flanders in 1693, which remained in existence until 1717, and a subsequent one raised in 1702 and disbanded in 1713.

[46] Mackay to Melvill, 22 October 1689, Mackay, p.290.

[47] Sir James Leslie to Lord Melville, Inverness 6 December 1689, in Mackay, p.300.

[48] Dalton, p.96.

[49] Possibly the same James Sleigh listed under Lord Blantyre.

[50] Amongst the casualties in Leven's Regiment were two hautbois (oboeists) named Francis Hopteir and Lachland Ross. As their widows afterwards petitioned the Privy Council for

passage back to Holland, both men must have originally been serving with the Scots Brigade. *Register of the Privy Council of Scotland* (1689), pp.317, 351 & 421.

[51] Fergusson, J. *The Scots Brigade in Holland* (1899), Vol.1, pp.516-518. Fergusson mistakenly dates the change to the thirteen-company establishment to their arrival in Great Britain, but Mackay's narrative is unambiguous as to the two-battalion organisation being employed throughout the Scottish campaign.

[42] Fergusson, J. *The Scots Brigade in Holland* (1899), Vol.1, pp.511& 516; Dalton, Vol.2, pp.232-233.

[53] Not at Killiecrankie, presumably commanded second battalion at Stirling.

[54] Fergusson, pp.516-517; Dalton, pp.234-235.

[55] Lieutenant Colonel in succession to Sir Thomas Livingstone and colonel in succession to Balfour after Killiecrankie. He himself commanded Fusilier battalion there.

[56] Fergusson, Vol.1, p.517 – no evidence he was at Killiecrankie; presumably commanding second battalion at Stirling.

[57] Probably commanded regiment at Killiecrankie. Major in succession to Patrick Balfour afterwards, and lieutenant colonel (and later colonel) of the Cameronians 1692.

[58] Probably commanded grenadier company as he was appointed Governor of Abergeldie Castle with a company from the Fusilier Battalion serving as its garrison.

[59] Fergusson, pp.517-518; Dalton, p.236. Reconstructing the list of Ramsay's officers is extremely difficult due first to the number of officers who left with Wauchope to enter King James' service and also those who took up commissions in the new Scots Army; most notably Lord Cardross who gained a regiment of dragoons and Campbell of Auchinbrec who became lieutenant colonel of Argyle's.

[60] Fergusson, J. *The Scots Brigade in Holland* (1899) 1:517. Dalton appears to err in saying that he left the regiment in 1688.

[61] Uncertain given the upheavals but he served in Scotland and was appointed lieutenant colonel of the regiment at Namur in 1695. Another possibility is George Hamilton, who was confused in the original commission register with Gavin Hamilton of Balfour's Regiment, but later became a colonel of foot in the Dutch service.

[62] Both Clerk and Douglas appear on the April embarkation list but are not mentioned again afterwards.

[63] The estates of this kingdom, taking to their consideration the danger of the public peace and how necessary it is for security thereof that a competent force and number of horse, foot and dragoons should be levied and provided according to the exigence of the present juncture, together with an offer made to them by Henry, lord Cardross that the said noble lord should levy and cause be levied, for the service of the estates, a regiment of dragoons consisting of six troops with fifty dragoons in each troop, and furnish the said dragoons with horses and other necessaries suitable to the said service, providing the said dragoons should be furnished by the estates upon the public charge with dragoon arms only, and that the said Henry, lord Cardross should be allowed and empowered by the estates to name the whole officers to be employed in the command of the said regiment, and each particular troop of the same, excepting the colonel, the said noble lord being most willing that the person who shall command the same as colonel should be named and authorised for that effect by his majesty after his acceptation of the crown of this realm, as he in his wisdom shall think fit; therefore the estates have accepted of the said offer made to them in the terms foresaid and do approve of the said noble lord his good and faithful intentions in the public service and do, by this commission, authorise his grace, duke of Hamilton, their president, to subscribe particular commissions to such persons as the said Henry, lord Cardross shall name to be employed in the respective commands of the said regiment, excepting always in manner above-excepted, and for the encouragement of both officers and soldiers who

shall serve in the said regiment the estates declare that each troop of the said regiment, after the same is mustered and found to consist of fifty dragoons complete, shall be entered and received into the public pay conforming to the present establishment of this kingdom, and that for both officers and soldiers of each one of the said troops so mustered and completed, it being nevertheless the meaning of the estates that the colonel, lieutenant colonel and major of the said regiment shall not have the pay of colonel, lieutenant colonel and major until the completing and mustering of the whole regiment, both officers and soldiers, of the division and numbers above-expressed, without prejudice to them of their pay as captains of their respective troops after the completing and mustering of each troop in manner above-mentioned. And in regard the said offer was made to the estates upon 19 April instant, therefore they declare that the commissions granted, by virtue of this present act, shall be understood to be of the same dates with the other commissions granted since the said day.

[64] Dalton, Charles *English Army Lists and Commission Registers* 3: 36-37

[65] Replaced in June 1689 by William Milne, who was in turn replaced by Robert Jackson in August.

[66] "with thirteen out of the shires of Stirling and Clackmannan"

[67] More exactly, only the Earl Marischal's part of Aberdeenshire, comprising the burgh of New Aberdeen (but not Old Aberdeen) and the eastern and north-eastern parts of the shire.

[68] As related in the text, Blair was captured at Perth in the earliest days of the rising and eventually died in captivity. Subsequently his troop was given to Sir George Gordon of Edinglassie on 11 December 1689. Mackay to Melvill, 31 October 1689, Mackay H *Memoirs of the War carried on in Scotland and Ireland 1689-1691* (1833): 293.

[69] Originally assigned to Sir Charles Halket, but taken up by Sir William Hope of Kirkliston on 25 April 1689.

[70] *Minute Book of the Managers of the New Mills Cloth Manufactory* (Scottish History Society, Edinburgh 1903) :211. "Fingarrins" was a fine-grained woollen cloth.

[71] Dalton, Charles *English Army Lists and Commission Registers* 2: 213-4; 3: 30

[72] Headed the conspiracy in 1689 to defect to the rebels. Arrested and deprived of his commission but no further action taken. Succeeded his brother as Lord Kilsyth in 1706 and commanded a Jacobite troop of horse at Sheriffmuir in 1715.

[73] Did not have a troop of his own

[74] Arrested and deprived of his commission 1689

[75] Arrested and deprived of his commission 1689

[76] Arrested and deprived of his commission 1689

[77] Nephew of the general. Originally he served in the Scots Brigade but in early 1688 transferred to King James' service under Colonel Wauchope. This appears to have been a clandestine operation and as soon as the revolution was accomplished he once more entered William's service and was conveniently at hand when it was necessary to stiffen Livingstone's Regiment with a reliable cadre.

[78] Formerly of Balfour's Regiment of the Scots Brigade

[79] Dalton, C. *The Scots Army 1661-1688* (William Brown, Edinburgh, 1909): 166. Mackay to Melvill, 10 September 1689, IN Mackay H *Memoirs of the War carried on in Scotland and Ireland 1689-1691* (1833): 278. Mackay was keen to promote a Lieutenant Forbes, who had served very satisfactorily at the siege of Edinburgh, but Slezar obviously had friends.

[80] In King James' day that was a simple JR. Afterwards the cypher was MR for Mary Rex. Although William insisted on being King, and continued to reign alone after Mary's death, legally he was only her consort.

[81] Dalton, Charles *English Army Lists and Commission Registers* 2: 90

[82] Dalton, Charles *English Army Lists and Commission Registers* 2: 143; 3:142. As with the Scots Brigade this listing is tentative and since the last complete list dates from November 1687,

prior to the purging of the regiment at the revolution. As a detachment of the regiment had been left at Inverness, Hastings' himself is the only officer who can be identified with any confidence as serving at Killiecrankie.

[83] Cited in Lawson, C.C.P *History of the Uniforms of the British Army* (Peter Davis, London 1940) 1:78, 137

[84] Dalton, Charles *English Army Lists and Commission Registers* 2: 145; 3: 144. Once again this listing is somewhat tentative.

[85] Left regiment 1 November 1689

[86] Major 4 December 1690

[87] Replaced by John Price 1 March 1690

[88] Directions for musters 21 February 1687, quoted in Walton, Clifford; *History of the British Standing Army 1660-1700* (Harrison and Sons, London 1894): 799

[89] *An abstract of the muster of Lord Berkeley's Regt. Of Dragoons taken in Scotland by order of Major-General Mackay the 26 Sept. 1689* (Dalton, Charles *English Army Lists and Commission Registers* 3: 33)

[90] Killed Captain Smith in a duel at Louvain in 1692.

[91] *An abstract of the muster of Lord Colchester's Regiment of Horse taken in Scotland by order of Major-General Mackay the 26 Sept. 1689* (Dalton, Charles *English Army Lists and Commission Registers* 3: 22)

Appendix II

The Highland Clans with Sword in Hand

In the popular imagination, the Highland army is still largely pictured as a mass of fearless warrior clansmen, armed to the teeth with broadsword and targe, or the like, roaring down upon their foes in an avalanche of steel, to deal death and destruction upon their hapless foes. However, as the narrative has demonstrated, the truth behind this myth is at once rather more complex and far more interesting.

On the whole, the Highland army performed poorly. This might appear an odd and even perverse assertion in the light of its dramatic victory at Killiecrankie. There is certainly no doubting the fact of the victory, or the near total destruction of General Mackay's army, but a victory which cost the victor something in the region of 700 and perhaps as many as 900 dead out of no more than 2,500 men, was not one to celebrate. At a regimental level, Balhaldie asserted that, 'Locheil lost in this action one hundred and twenty of his men, which was just one half of his number.'[1] It is possible, and arguably likely, that in both cases the quoted losses encompassed both killed and wounded rather than the dead alone but, whatever the truth, it was a profoundly shocking experience which the Highlanders had no wish whatsoever to repeat.

Yet hurling themselves straight at the enemy was less a matter of choice than sheer necessity, for most clansmen were simply too ill-equipped to engage in more conventional tactics. This is all too apparent from the Atholl wapinschaw (literally weapon-showing) returns of half a century earlier, transcribed in full below.[2] There will, inevitably, be some changes in detail during the intervening period but whether that affected the overall picture is doubtful. We may be reasonably sure, that the numerous bows and sheaves of arrows listed in 1638 had disappeared by 1689[3], but on the other hand, given that those men

156

carrying bows were evidently farm servants and other comparatively humble men, it would be unwise to assume that a comparable number of them had obtained firearms instead.

Similarly, the fact that 448 men carry swords (or 451 if three two-handed swords are included) out of a total of 523 might be taken as confirmation of the popular picture of the Highland clans advancing sword in hand. Unfortunately, it is sadly contradicted by the fact that only 125 of those swordsmen had the essential accompaniment of a targe, which leads inexorably to the conclusion that the overwhelming majority of 'swords' were in fact Highland dirks, or sgians. Indeed, there is a very relevant comparison both in the Irish clansmen of a century before, who were mostly armed with skeans or long knives. To all intents and purposes, far from being as heavily armed as a battleship, or at least a pirate, most clansmen were effectively unarmed, and unless they could be equipped with muskets sent from Ireland or scavenged from the field of Killiecrankie they needed to be armed with the spears or rather pikes which featured so prominently at Dalmucomir.

The roll of the heretours of the Landis within the Parochin of Strowane, and of the number of thair men within the samen, and what vapins and armour they have.

1638

In the first place the *Laird of Strowane*, and tuttour of *Strowane*, Thair men of the lands within the parachin of Strowane ar in number....................fyftene
quhairof thair is ten that hes gunes, bowis, sheavis, swirdis and tairges, and the remanent five men hes bot swirdis.[4]

Neill Stewart of Grenycht, his men if his landis within the said parochin of Strowane ar in number....................thrie
quhairof ane hes ane gun, ane bow, ane shaif, ane swird and targe, and the uther tua hes bowis, shaiffis and swirdis.

Chairlis Robertsone of Achleikis, his men of his haill landis that he hes within the said parochin ar in number....................tuelf
theiroff thrie that hes gunes, bowis, sheaves, swirdis and tairges, and uther aucht that hes bowis, sheavis and swirdis, and ane that hes bot one suird.

The Laird of Faskeillie, his men of his landis within the said parochin of Strowane by his feuris Kylbrour ar....................sex
quhairof thair is tua that hes gunes, bowis, sheavis, swirdis and tairgis, and uther tua of thame hes bow, sheavis and swirdis, and the remanent tua hes swirdis.

157

Duncane Robertsone of Kindrocht, and his men ar......................thrie
and has ilk ane of thame ane gun, ane bow, ane sheaf, ane swird and tairge

Donald McInas VcPaull of Petildonycht, and hes men ar also
......................thrie
and hes ilk of thame ane sword, ane tairge, ane bow, ane shaiff

Paull Robertsone, portioner of Pettagowne, and hes men ar
......................thrie
himself hes ane gune, ane bow, ane shaiff, ane swird and tairge, and hes
tua men hes bowis, sheaves and swirds.

Alexr Robertsone of Calbrour, and hes men ar......................thrie
himself hes ane gun, ane bow, ane sheaf, swird and tairge, and his tua
men hes bot suirdis.

Patrick Robertsone of Blairfettie, and hes men ar in number
......................sex
quhairof four hes gunes, bows, sheavis, swirdis and tairges and the
remanant tua hes bowis, shaves and swirdis.

Alex. Stewart of Vraardbeg, his men of his landis within the said parochin
ar in number ....sex
quhairof ane hes ane gun, ane bow, shaiff, ane swird and tairge, and uther
tua hes bowis, sheaffis, and swirdis, and uther thrie hes but swirdis.

Neill Stewart of Urardmoir, hes men, viz: hes sones within the said
parochin, ar......................tua
quha hes gunes , bowis, sheavis, swirdis and tairges

John Stewart of Eister Innervak, he and hes men of the lands he hes within
the said parochin ar in number......................vij
quhairof thrie hes gunes, swirdis and tairges, and tua hes bowis, sheaffis
of arrowis and swirdis, and the remanant tua hes but swordis.

Alexander Robertsone of Lude, his landis of Clunemoir and Clunebeg
lyand within the said parochin of Strowane ar of men......................xij
quhairof tua hes swordis and tairgis, ane uther hes ane bow and sheaf
and swird, and uther sex bot swirds onlie, and the remanent thrie hes
nathing of vapins. There is of thame auld men.

The roll of the heretours of the landis within the Parochins of Lude and

Kilmawenog, and of the number of thair men within the samen, and quhat armour and wapins they have.

The Earll of Atholl, his men of his landis within the parochins Of Lude and Kilmawenog (by his feuers and Achgowall) ar in number ....ten
quhairof thrie of thame his snap vark gunes[5] and swirdis and tairges, and uther tua of thame hes bowis and sheavis of arrowis, and swirdis, and the remanent five hes bot onlie swirdis.

Alex[r] Robertsone of Lude, and his men of his landis within the saidis parochins of Lude and Kilmawenog ar in number .... fourtie sex quhairof his awin vapins and his household mane is tua gunes, tua tairges and tua suirdis, and uther tua of his men hes gunes, swirdis and tairges, and thrie hes bowis, sheaves of arrowis and swirdis, and the remanent thair is xxxj that bes bot swirdis, and uther viij of thame ar auld and hes na vapins.

Donald Robertsone of Kincraigie, his men and himself ar in number ....allevin
his vapins is ane swird, ane tairge, ane gun, and his men hes bot swirdis onlie, tua of them are auld

Jhone Stewart, minour, vodset haver of Achnagoull, his men ar Raknyt bot to....................tua
vquha hes tua bowis, tua swirdis, and sheaves of arrowis

Angus McIntoshe of Tereny, he and hes men ar in number ....thrie
his awin vapins is ane swird, ane tairge, and his tua men hes ilk ane ane swird and tairge.

The roll of the heretours of the landis within the Parochin of Mulling, and of the number of thair men within the samen, and quhat armour and wapins they have.

William Fergussone of Bellezoucone, himself and the men of his landis within the said parochin of Mulling ar in number....................iiij
his awin vapins is ane swird and tairge, four gunes, tua pistols, ane bow and sheaffis of arrowis, with ane habershoone, and ane of his men hes ane gun, ane swird, ane tairge, and the uther tua hes bot swirds.

Thomas Butter of Callemulling, himself and his men of Callemulling and

Delchoisney and Delnavard ar in numer ....ffour
quhairoff himself hes of vapins tua snap vark gunes, ane pistol, ane
bow, ane sheaf of arrowis, ane swird, ane poll aix, and hes men hes bot
swirdis onlie.

Jhone Conesone, vodset haver of half Ardgie (and David Ratray of
Tullochcuren the uther half) is of men.....................thrie
The said Jhone Conesone hes of vapins ane snap vark gun, thrie swirds,
ane bow, ane sheaf, ane poll aix, ane tairge, and the remanent tua men
hes bot swirdis onlie.

The said *David Ratray, Jhone Murray of Belnabrooch* and *David Murray his
brother*, thair men of the landis of Ediradour that they and thair tenentis
possess ar amongis thame.....................sevene
quhairof the said David Murray hes ane snap vark gun, ane swird, ane
tairge, and ane uther of the saidis men hes ane gun with ane swird and
tairge, and uther tua hes bowis, sheavis, and swirds, and the remanent
thrie hes bot swirdis.

Captain Peter Rollok, possessor of Pettarok, himself and his men theiroff ar
in number.....................thrie
The said Captane himself hes tua snap wark gunes, ane swird, ane jak,
ane habershone, ane poll aix, and the remanent tua hes bowis, sheaffis
and swirdis.

Robert Moncrieff, portioner of Kinhaird, himself and hes men of his haill
landis within the parochin of Mulling ar.....................nyne
The said Robert himself hes ane snap vark gun, ane bow, ane sheaf, and
swird, ane tairge, ane poll aix, and thrie with bowis, sheavis and
swirdis, and the remanent five hes bot swirdis onlie.

Thomas Butter, portioner of Kinhaird, his men and himself of his landis ar
bot.....................tua
his awin vapins is ane bow, ane sheaf, ane swird, ane tairge, and ane poll
aix, and his man ane bow, ane sheaf and ane swird.

The said *Thomas Butter* betuix him and *Johne Robertsone of
Croftmichie*.....................ane man with vapins.

Johne Butter of Myln and Myl landis of Petlochrie, himself and hes men
ar.....................thrie
his awin vapins is ane snap vark gun, ane swird, ane tairge, ane

habershone, and ane of hes men hes ane bow, ane sheaff and ane swird, and the uther hes bot ane swird.

Johne Robertsone of Lattoch, younger, himself and the men of Lattoch ar.....................thrie
the said Johne hes of vapins ane gun, ane swird, ane tairge, ane bow, ane shaiff, poll aix and head piece, and ane of hes men hes ane bow, ane sheaf, ane swird, and the third hes bot ane swird.

Duncane Robertsone of Ballegullane, he and hes men tharof are of number.....................thrie
and hes himself of vapines ane gun, ane bow, ane shaif, ane pistel, swird, tairge, and poll aix, and his tua men bes bot swirdis onlie.

Donald Robertsone of Belnacraig, he and his men theirof ar ....thrie
and he hes ane gun, ane swird, ane tairge, and ane of his said men hes ane gun, ane swird, ane tairge, and the third hes bot ane swird.

Johne Fergussone of Drumchorie, and his men ar also.....................thrie
himself hes of vapines ane gun, ane swird, ane tairge, with ane habershone and ane headpiece, and his tua men hes bot swirdis onlie.

Fargus Fergussone of Balledmond, himself and hes men of Balledmond and Petfourie ar in number.....................sex
and he hes of vapines ane gun, and swird, ane tairge, with tua tua handit swirds, and ane habershoone, and ane of his said men hes ane gun, and bow, ane sheaf, ane swird and ane tairge, and the remanent four hes bot ilk ane of thame ane swird.

Johne Stewart of Bonskeid, and Donald Stewart in Strathgarie,Wodset haveris and possessors of the saids lands of Strathgarie, the said Donald Stewart himself and the men of the saidis landis of Strathgarie (by the said Johne Stewart) aucht to be in number.....................fyve
the said Donald hes of vapines ane bow, ane shaiff, with ane swird and ane tairge, and ane uther of the said men hes bot ane swird, and the remanent thrie ar.....................[unarmed?]

Alex^r Stewart of Vrquhilbeg, himself and his men of his lands within the said parchin of Mulling ar in number.........................sex
himself hes ane gun, ane tairge, and swird, and the remanent fyve men hes bot onlie swirdis.

Robert Stewart of Urquhillmoir, himself and his men of his haill landis within the parochin of Mulling ar in number.....................twentie
quha hes of wapins, himself thrie gunes, ane swird, ane tairge ane head piece, and four of hes men hes gunes, bowis, sheavis, swirds and tairges, and threttene of the rest has bot swirds, and the uther tua nothing bot depaupent.

The Laird of Faskillie, his men of his landis within the Parochin of Mulling ar in number.....................nyne
quhairof tua hes bowis, sheaffis, and swirdis, and ane uther hes ane gun, ane swird and tairge, and the remanent sex hes bot swirdis onlie.

Donald Stewart for Cammoch, quhilk is for it.....................ane man
and hes of vapines ane swird, ane tairge, ane gun.

James Stewart of Vestir Cluney, for himself and ane uther is ....tua men
himself hes of vapines ane gun, ane swird, ane tairge, with ane bow, ane sheaf, and his man ane bow, ane sheaf, ane swird.

Donald Robertsone of Killechawie, for Drumchaber.....................ane man
with ane bow, ane shaiff

Jhone Stewart of Belnakeillie, and Jhone Stewart, younger, his son, haldis the saidis landis of Belnakeillie of the Abacie of Dunfermling recusantis quha hes of men, rakinnyng the said Jhone Stewart younger ane, because his father is auld.....................fyftene
The said Jhone Stewart, younger, hes of vapines tua gunes, ane pistol, ane bow, ane sheaf, ane swird, ane tairge, and poll aix, and tua of hes men hes gunes, swirdis and tairges, and uther tua swidis and tairges, and the remanent ten men hes bot onlie swirdis.

Androw Small, fiare of Dernean, and his men of Dernean ar all in number.....................sex
himself hes ane gun, ane swird, ane tairge, ane bow, ane shaif, and ane of hes men ane swird, ane tairge, and the remanent four men hes bot swirdis onlie.

Jhone Robertsone of Eister Straloch, his men of his landis within the said parochin of Mulling ar in number.....................auchtene
quhairof thair is fyve that hes gunes, bowis, sheaffis, swirdis and tairges, and uther thrie that hes bowis, sheavis, and swirdis, and the remanent ten hes bot swirdis onlie.

Leonard Robertsone, fiare of Wester Straloch, himself and his father's men
of the saidis landis ar in number.....................fyftene
The said Leonard hes of vapins ane gun, ane bow, sheaf, ane swird, ane
tairge, and tua of hes said men hes gunes bowis, schaiffis, swirdis and
tairges, and ane hes ane bow ane shaiff, ane swird, and nyne hes bot
swirds onlie, and uther tua is depaupent.

Alex^r McCoull of Eistir Kindroigney, and his men ar....................thrie
and hes himself of vapins ane gun, ane bow, sheaiff, ane swird and ane
tairge, and ilk ane of his tua men hes swirdis and tairges.

*The roll of the heretours of the lands of the Parochin of Logyreit, and of the number
of thair men within the samen, and quhat vapins and armour they have.*

In the first place Jhone Stewart of Killechassie, himself and his men ar in
number.....................tuelff
and hes of armour and vapins for himself and tua of the said men, that
ar within his hous, tua gunes with snap warkis, ane swird, ane tairge,
ane poll aix, ane pistolat, and thrie of his men hes ilk ane of thame ane
bow, ane shaiff of arrowis and ane swird. Ane uther hes ane gun with
ane snap wark, ane swird, aine tairge, and ane uther hes ane swird, ane
haberschun, ane steil bonet, and the remanent four hes ilk ane bot an
swird onlie.

The Laird of Weyme, his landis within the said parochin of Logyreit hes
of men therein.....................allevin
quhairof ane of thame hes tua swirdis, tua tairges, tua bowis with tua
shaiffis of arrowis, tua snap wark gunes, ane head piece & pleat sleeves,
and uther tua has ilk ane ane snap vark gun, and ane swird, and thrie
hes swirdis and tairges, and the remanent fyve of hes bot swirdis onlie.

The Erll of Atholl, his men of his landis within the said parochin of
Logyreit (by his feuaris) ar of number.....................thrie scoir [60]
quhairof seven of thame hes ilk ane ane snap vark gun, ane swird, ane
tairge, and sum pistols, and uther nyne hes bowis, sheaffis of arrowis,
and swirdis, and thrie hes swirdis and tairges, and the remanent fourtie
ane men hes bot ilk ane ane swird.

The Laird of Ballaquhane, his men of his landis within the said parochin
of Logyreit ar.....................auchtene
quhairof thair is ten that hes bowis, schaiffis of arrowis, and swirdis,
ane uther hes ane snap vark gun, ane swird, ane tairge, and ane bow,

ane schaiff, and tua with swirdis and tairges, and the remanent fyve hes bot swirdis onlie.

Jhone Stewart of Eister Clochfoldie, he and hes men ar....................sex quha hes for himself ane snap vark gun, tua swirdis, ane tairge, ane bow, ane sheaf of arrowis, ane pistol, ane habershun, ane head piece, and ane of his men hes ane bow, ane shaeff of arrowis, and uther thrie with swirdis onlie, and the sext hes nathing.

Jhone Stewart of Fandynet, he and his men ar....................aucht and his awin vapines ar tua snap vark gunes, tua swirdis, tua tairges, ane bow, ane shaiff, ane pistol, ane haberschune, and ane of his men hes ane bow, ane scheaff, and uther thrie hes bot swirdis, and the remanent thrie hes na vapines.

Jhone Cairdney, fiare of Petcastill, himself and his men ar ....aucht his awin vapines is ane snap vark gun, ane swird, ane tairge, and tua of his men hes gunes and swirdis and tairges, and the remanent thrie hes bot swordis onlie.

James Stewart of Fancastill, his men of his landis within the parochin of Logyreit ar....................aucht
quhairoff   [blank]

Henrie Reid of Petnacrie, himself and his men ar....................sex quhairof tua of them will have tua hagbuitis, uther tua of them will have tua bowis and tua scheavis of arrowis, and the third tua men will have tua swirds and tua tairges with ane habersone and ane head piece.

Adam Reid of Eister Tyre, himself and his men of his landis within the said parochin of Logyreit westir Dercullycht and all ar ....ten
quhairof   [blank]

Donald Robertsone of Killiechangie, himself and his men within the said parochin of Logyreit ar....................fyve
quhairof himself hes of vappins ane gun, ane swird, ane bow, ane sheaf of arrowis, ane tairge, with ane steil bonet, and tua of his men hes swirds, and uther tua hes n vapins.

Robert Fergussone of Westir Dunfallandie, himself and his men ar ....sex
his awin vapines and armour ar tua snap vark gunes, thrie swirds, ane

tairge, ane halberd aix, tua habershunes, and tua head pieces, ane of his men hes ane bow, ane sheaf, ane swird and tairge, and uther thrie of thame hes bot onlie swirdis, and the remanent na vapins.

The said *Robert Fergussone* and *Thomas Butter* of Callemulling hes in feu betuix thame equallie the landis of *Eister Dunfallandie* quhairin thair is of men.....................thrie
quhairof there is tua that hes ilk ane ane bow, ane shaif of arrowis, ane swird, ane tairge, and the uther bot ane swird onlie.

Archibald Campbell of Lagvinshak, his men of his landis within the said parochin of Logyreit, called Fundnabis ar.....................aucht
quhairof thair is tua that hes bowis, arrowis, swirdis, and ane uther ane bow with arrowis, and four of thame that hes swirdis, and the uther of the said aucht has na vapins.

Jhone Robertsone of Bellintume, hes men of the saidis landis and of the *west end of the Hauch of Dulshiane,* by himself, ar.....................four
quhairof ane hes ane bow, ane shaif of arrowis, and ane swird, and the remanent thrie bot swirdis onlie.

Patrick Fergussone, portioner of Dulshiane, beand ane auld man, his eldest lawfull son *Donald Fergussone,* answerable for his said Father. The said Donald, and his Fathers men of Dulshiane ar.....................fyve
The said Donald his vapines are ane bow, ane shaiff of arrowis, ane snap vark gun, with ane swird, and the uther four bot swirdis onlie.

William Fergussone of Bellezucone, his men of his landis within the parochin of Logyreit, by himself ar.....................thrie
his awin vapins ar givin up in the roll of the parochin of Mulling, and his thrie menis vapins heir ar ane with ane swird, and ane tairge, and the uther tua hes bot swirdis.

Jhone Robertsone, of Lattoch, and *Alex^r Camrone, feuris of Donevird,* extending of men to ....thrie
quhairof the said Alex^r Camrone his vapines ar ane bow, ane shaiff of arrowis, ane swird, ane tairge, and ane uther hes ane bow, ane shaiff of arrowis, and the third ane swird.

Alex^r McLauren, in Belnagaird, portioner of Dulshiane, his men of the saidis landis ar.....................thrie
hes bot swirdis only.

Adame Fergussone of Bellechandowy, and his men thairof, ar bot all …………………thrie
quhairof the said Adame hes of vapines ane tua handit swird, ane halberd aix, and his tua men hes bot swirdis.

Jhone Robertsone of Tenandrie, himself and his men of his landis that he hes in feu within the parochin of Logyreit ar …………………nyne
His awin vapines ar   [blank]

The Laird of Strowen, and tuttour thairof, his men of his Lands within the said parochin of Logyreit ar…………………thrie
Quha hes of vapins, bowis, sheavis, and swirdis.

Duncane Campbell, fiare of Lagvinshak, his men of his lands within the parochin of Logyreit, viz., *Drumquhene and Drumchastill*, ar in number …………………threttene
quhairof   [blank]

Parish	No. of Men	Guns	Hagbutts	Pistols	Bows and Sheaves	Pole-axes	Halbert-Axes	Two-Handed Swords	Swords	Targes	Head Pieces	Steel Bonnets	Plate Sleeves	Habergon	Jack
Struan	81	31			52				76	36					
Lude &c.	72	8			7				65	11					
Moulin	155	46		5	43	8		2	148	43	3			5	1
Logierait	215	25	2	6	47	1	2	1	159	35	5	2	1	6	
Total	523	110	2	11	149	9	2	3	448	125	8	2	1	11	1

NOTES
[1] Balhaldie, p.271.
[2] Atholl, John, Duke of *Chronicles of the Atholl and Tullibardine Families* (Edinburgh, 1908), Vol.1, Appendices x-xx.

³ Of the clans mustered at Dalmucomir, only the Macleods of Raasay were described as carrying bows but, as they do not actually appear to have been present, this reference must be considered doubtful to say the least. *The Graemid*, p.147.

⁴ Whilst it would be tedious to translate the whole document, rendering this initial entry from Scots into modern English will perhaps be helpful:

In the first place the *Laird of Strowane*, and tuttour of *Strowane*, Thair men of the lands within the parachin of Strowane ar in number .... fyftene quhairof thair is ten that hes gunes, bowis, sheavis, swirdis and tairges, and the remanent five men hes bot swirdis.

In the first place the Laird of Strowan and Tutor of Strowan Their men of the lands within the parish of Strowan are in number   15
Whereof there are 10 that have guns, bows, sheaves [or arrows], Swords and targes, and the remaining five have only swords.

In this case Robertson of Strowan's own men were well armed, but more typical was one of his neighbours:

Chairlis Robertsone of Achleikis, his men of his haill landis that he hes within the said parochin ar in number.............................tuelf
theiroff thrie that hes gunes, bowis, sheaves, swirdis and tairges, and uther aucht that hes bowis, sheavis and swirdis, and ane that hes bot one suird.

Of his 12 men only three had guns, bows, swords and targes, another eight had bows and swords and the last had only a sword, or more accurately in 1689 three of their sons and grandsons had the full fig of musket, broadsword and targe, while the rest ran only to dirks and perhaps a couple more muskets.

⁵ This is the first specific reference to a snap-work or flintlock, indicating the majority of muskets listed were matchlocks in 1638, but it is likely that fifty years later snap-works predominated.

Appendix III

General Mackay's Account of Killiecrankie

The following is from H. Mackay's *Memoirs of the War carried on in Scotland and Ireland 1689-169.* Other than replacing the archaic letter form f with the more modern s for the sake of clarity, both the original spelling and orthography have been left unchanged. Sadly, whatever his military talents, it will be apparent that Mackay was no great hand at writing, with a prose style that was frequently turgid, repetitive and sometimes downright unreadable, but yet withal, an absolutely indispensable source:

> The first day he set forward from St. Johnston [Perth][1] he lodged over against Dunkeld, where by 12 of the clock at night he received a letter from the Lord Murray[2] signifying Dundee's entry into Athole, and his own retreat from the castle of Blair, (which till then he made the fashion to keep blockt) and his passing a strait and difficult pass two miles below the said house, leaving it betwixt him and the ennemy, the farther side whereof he affirmed to have left guarded, for our free passage to Blair where he supposed Dundee to be already; altho Lieutenant-Colonel Lawder[3], whom the General commanded presently upon Murray's advertisement for the better securing of the pass, denied to have met with any of his men there. Next morning by the break of day the General marched, having dispatched orders to Perth to haste up the other six troops and come to the entry of the pass, which was eleven miles from his former nights camp, about 10 of the clock, where he let his men rest two hours to take some refreshment; having at his coming to a halt commanded 200 men more, under the Earle of Leven's Lieutenant Colonel[4] to fortify Lawder, with order to send back what

168

advertisement they could have of the ennemy, before he would engage himself in the pass, which was two miles long. The General had spoke with the Lord Murray a little below the pass; who being enquired how many men he had with him, answered that most of them were gone to the hills to put their cattle out of the way, so that he had at present but two or three hundred of them by him, which seemed reasonable as well as customary to that sort of people, when any forces, whether friends or ennemy pass through their country; which made the General not so apt to judge ill of Murray as others did. However it might be, he apprehended not the ennemy, though he should have met them much stronger than himself. Therefor after he had got a return from Lawder, that the pass was clear, he marched in the following order : Balfour's, Ramsay's and Kenmore's battalions first, then Belhaven's troop of horse, followed by Levin's regiment, with a battalion of the Generals ; after those followed the baggage horses being odds of 1200, and last of all the Earle of Annandales troop of horse with Hasting's regiment, which were left behind the baggage, lest the ennemy might detach men about the hill to attack it, or that the country men, feeing it without sufficient guard, might not fall a plundering of it. Having past with the five battalions and the troop of horse, we halted upon a field of corn along the side of the river, both to expect the passage of the baggage, with Hasting's regiment, and the troop of horse, and to distribute a communication to the forces.

While the General ordered Lawder to advance with his 200 fusiliers and the troop of horse which was past some hundreds of paces upon an hill towards the way from whence he expected the enemy might appear, who presently advertised that some partys of them began to discover themselves betwixt us and Blair; whereupon the General, galloping to the ground from whence they were discovered, ordered Colonel Balfour to dispatch quickly the distribution of his ammunition, and to put the men under arms, while, having observed the motion of the ennemy, he would chuse the field of battle. Being come up to the advanced party he saw some small partys of the ennemy, the matter of a short mile, marching slowly along the foot of a hill which lay towards Blair, marching towards us; whereupon he sent orders to Balfour to march up to him in all haste with the foot. But presently upon that order, having discovered some bodies of them marching down an high hill, within a quarter of a mile to the place where he stood, when the gross of their body appeared, fearing that they should take possession of an eminence just above the ground where our forces halted on, of a steep and difficult ascent, full of trees and shrubs, and within a carabin shot of the place whereon we stood, whereby they could undoubtedly force us with their fire in confusion over the river, he galloped back in all haste to the forces, and having made every battalion form by a Quart de Conversion to the right upon the ground they stood, made them march each before his face up the hill, by which means he prevented that inconveniency, and got a ground fair enough to receive the ennemy, but not to attack them, there being, within a short musket shot to it, another eminence before our front, as we stood when we were up the lowest hill, near the river, whereof Dundee had already gott possession before we could be well up, and had his back to a very high hill, which is the ordinary maxim of Highlanders, who never fight against regular forces upon anything of equal terms, without a sure retreat at their back, particularly if their ennemies be provided of horse; and to be sure of their escape, in case of a repulse, they attack bare footed, without any cloathing but their shirts, and a little Highland dowblet, whereby they are certain to outrun any foot, and will not readily engage where horse can follow the chase any distance. Their way of fighting is to divide themselves by clans, the chief or principal man being at their heads, with some distance to distinguish betwixt them. They come on slowly till they be within distance of firing, which, because they keep no rank or file, doth ordinarly little harm. When their fire is over, they throw away their firelocks, and every one drawing a long broad sword, with his targe (such as have them) on his left hand, they fall a running toward the ennemy, who, if he stand firm, they never fail of running with much more speed back again to the hills, which they usually take at their back, except they happen to be surprized by horse or dragoons marching through a plain, or camping negligently ; as the General four days thereafter surprized ten of them at Perth, and Sir Thomas Livingston the ensuing year in Strathspey, as we mall have occasion to touch hereafter.

All our officers and souldiers were strangers to the Highlanders way of fighting and embattailling, which mainly occasioned the consternation many of them were in; which, to remedy for the ensuing year, having taken notice on this occasion that the Highlanders are of such a quick motion, that if a battalion keep up his fire till they be near to make sure of them, they are upon it before our men can come to their second defence, which is the bayonet in the musle of the musket. I say, the General having observed this method of the ennemy, he invented the way to fasten the bayonet so to the musle without, by two rings, that the soldiers may safely keep their fire till they pour it into their breasts, and then have no other motion to make but to push as with a pick.

The General having got up the hill with five battalions and a troop of horse, for Hastings and the other troops were not past as yet, and seeing Dundee master of an eminence so near him, resolved to make the best of that ground, and rather receive the check there in good order, than to put his men out of breath and in disorder, by attacking the ennemy against an hill. Betwixt the height which he had marched up from the river, and the foot of that whereon the ennemy were placed, there was a convenience to imbattail our men in one line, taking the former at our back, tho with a continued ascent from us to them.

The General having got upon the ground which he had remarked, he began to even his line, leaving a little distance betwixt every little battalion, having made two of each, because he was to fight three deep; only, in the midst of the line, he left a greater opening where he placed the two troops of horse (the other being come up just as he had taken his ground with Hastings battalion) of a design when the Highlanders approached, and that the fire of the line should be spent, to make them fall out by the larger intervall, to flank the ennemy on either side, as occasion should offer, not daring to expose them to the ennemy's horse, which was composed all of gentlemen, reformed officers, or such as had deserted of Dundee's regiment out of England, which was the reason he placed them behind the foot till all the fire were over on both sides: He sent also a detachment of firelocks of each battalion to the right hand to fortify Hastings regiment, to whom he was obliged to leave that post. Being come up after he had taken his ground, not willing to make unnecessary motions so near the ennemy, and because the ennemy were so very close upon him, and he always in action giving his ground to every one, they distinguished him, which drew their papping shot over all where he moved, whereby severals were wounded before the engagement, and finding that Balfour had advanced too far his regiment out of the line, observing that the ennemy made no motion to attack as yet, after he had advertised them not to be surprised at the motion, because it was only to bring them in a line with the rest, lest they should be flanked; he made them retire, and recommending the care of the left wing (betwixt which and the right there was a boggy ground, which, on a sudden could not without hazard of bogging be galloped) to the Brigadier Balfour, returned along the face of the line to the right, where finding all ready to receive the ennemy, he made a short speech to some of the battalions which stood nearest him, representing the unquestionable justice of the cause, regarding not only the Protestant interest in Britain, but in all the world, whose loss humanly seemed mainly to depend on the success of his Majesties enterprize, for the defence thereof, as well as of the temporal happiness of their country, confiding in the maintenance of their laws, which confirmed it to them, besides the obligation of honour and conscience, which lay upon them not to betray by a criminal faintheartedness, their masters service, by whom they were entertained, and last of all their own safety ; assuring them that if they kept firm and close they should quickly see their ennemy's take the hills for their refuge : For which reason more than the hopes of pursuing the chase they stript themselves almost naked; but on the other hand, if they happened to give way (as he should not expect) before that rabble of the Highlanders, they might freely conclude few or none of them should escape those naked pursuers far speedier of foot than they; besides that all the men of Athole were in arms ready to strip and knock in the head all runnaways : To avoid, then, those certain ruines, the only visible mean was to Hand to it, like men fighting for their religion and liberty against the invaders of both, which was the true ground of his Majesties enterprize, and not the desire of a crown, as it was of all good men and true Protestant subjects in conjunction with and assistance to him therein, and not the prospect; of advantage by the change.

The ennemys being upon their ground much about the fame time with us, seemed to extend their order beyond our right wing; which the General observing made his line move to the right by the flank, least their design might be to flank, get betwixt him and the pass, which would be a very advantagious post for them, whereby they could cut all communication betwixt us and Perth, from whence we expected six troops of horse and dragoons more, as well as a further supply of provisions, and where they could, by the favour of the Athole men, subsist, and have convenience to joyn as many horse and foot as Dundee's credit in the counties of Angus and Perth could procure in a considerable number, without that we could hinder them but by making a motion which readily might furnish them occasion to attack us with a keen advantage : which motion brought the ennemy, whatever his design might have been, to a stand, and so we lookt upon one another for at least two hours.

The General not willing to attack, for the reasons already alledged, and the Highlanders apparently out of irresolution, which he apprehended to be of design to expect the night, wherein they might happily hope to frighten our men by a sudden motion doun the hill with a loud shout, after their manner, very likely to put new men unaccustomed with an ennemy in a fright and disorder, tho' they could be kept more allert and ready then he could hope for during the whole night; neither durst he venture to pass the river in their presence and so near them, both by reason of the hazard, the souldiers, ordinarily taking such a motion for a subject of apprehension, and the imputation which he had to expect, if he were beat in retiring. He resolved then to stand it out, tho' with great impatience, to see the ennemy come to a resolution, either of attacking or retiring, whereof they had more choice than he; and to provoke them, he ordered the firing of three little leather field-pieces, which he caused carry on horse-back with their carriages, which proved of little use, because the carriages being made too high to be more conveniently carried, broke with the third firing.

The ennemy having a full view of our forces, by reason of the height they possest above us, discerned presently the General, which drew their shot into all places where he stood or walked, whereby severals of our men were wounded before the engagement; and to have the so much nearer aim, they possest themselves of some houses upon the ascent of the height whereon they stood, which the General not willing to suffer, least the ennemy should be emboldned thereby, ordered his brother, commanding his own regiment, before whose front the houses were, to detach a captain with some fire-locks to dislodge them; judging withall that that skirmish might draw on a general engagement, which he earnestly longed for before the night approached. The captain chased the ennemy's detachment to their body with the loss of some of their number; but shortly thereafter, and about half an hour before sunset, they began to move down the hill.

The General had already commanded the officers, commanding battalions, to begin their firing at the distance of 100 paces by platoons, to discourage the approaching Highlanders meeting with continual fire: That part of their forces which stood opposite to Hastings, who had the right of all, before the Generals, Levins and Kenmore's regiments, came down briskly together with their horse, and notwithstanding of a brisk fire, particularly from the General's own battalion, whereby many of the chief gentlemen of the name of Macdonald, who attacked it, were killed, pushed their point, after they had fired their light pieces at some distance,[5] which made little or no execution, with sword in hand, tho' in great confusion, which is their usuall way: Which when the General observed, he called to the Lord Belhaven to march up with the first troop of horse, ordering him to flank to the left hand the ennemy, the fire being then past on all hands, and coming to handy strokes if our men had stood, appointing the second troop to do the same to the right; but scarcely had Belhaven got them without the front of the line, where they had orders to wheel for the flank, tho' their very appearance made the ennemy turn away from the place where they saw the horse coming up, but contrary to orders, they began to pass, not knowing whereat, and presently turned about, as did also Kenmore's and the half of Levin's battalion.

The General observing the horse come to a stand, and firing in confusion, and the foot beginning to fall away from him, thinking happily that the horse would be pricked to follow his example, and in all cases to disengage himself out of the croud of Highlanders which came doun just upon the place where he was calling to the officers of the horse to follow him, spurr'd his horse through the ennemy, (where no body nevertheless followed him, but one of his servants, whose horse was shot in passing,) where he judged, by the way they made for him, tho' alone, that if he had had but fiftie resolute horfe, such as Colchefter's, he had certainly, by all human appearance recovered all, notwithstanding the foot was just flying over all, tho' sooner upon the left, which was not attacked at all, than to the right, because the right of the ennemy had not budged from their ground when their left was engaged. Balfour's regiment did not fire a shot, and but the half of Ramsays made fome little fire. Lieutenant Colonel Lawder was posted advantageously upon the left of all, on a little hill wreathed with trees, with his party of 200 of the choice of our army, but did as little as the rest of that band, whether by his or his mens fault is not well known, for the General would never make search into the failings of that business, because they were a little too generally committed ; resolution and presence of mind in battle being certainly a singular mercy of God, he denyeth and giveth it when and to whom he will, for there are seasons and occasions, that the most firm and stout-hearted do quake and shake for fear: As Solomon saith, 'The wicked flee when none pursueth, but the righteous is bold as a Lyon;' and tho' all sincere christians be not resolute, it is because it is not their vocation, for I dare be bold to affirm that no truly sincere christian, trusting in God for strenth and support, going about his lawfull calling, shall be forsaken of him, whether military, civil, or ecclesiastick ; not that sure victory shall always attend good men, or that they shall always escape with their lives, for experience doth teach the contrary, but that God, upon whom they cast their burdens and care, shall so care for them, that they shall be preserved from shame and confusion, and that they have his promises by whom are the issues against death and innumerable means inconceivable to us, to redress the disorders of our affairs, to support their hope and mind in the greatest of difficulties: As the General confest, that immediately upon this defeat, and as he was marching of the field, he could not cast his thoughts upon any present means to redress his breach, but recommended earnestly unto God to direct; his judgement and mind to fall upon such methods as the success fhould manifest him to be the chief Author thereof, wherein he hath also been heard, as the pursuit of this relation shall demonstrate. But to return to our purpose. Having passed through the croud of the attacking Highlanders, he turned about to see how matters stood, and found that all his left had given way, and got down the hill which was behind our line, ranged a little above the brow thereof, so that in the twinkling of an eye in a manner, our men, as well as the ennemy, were out of sight, being got doun pall mall to the river where our baggage stood.

At which sad spectacle it may be easily judged how he was surprized, to see at first view himself alone upon the field, but looking further to the right he espyed a small heap of red coats, whither galloping, he found it to be a part of the Earle of Levin's regiment, with himself, his Lieutenant Colonel, Major, and most of his officers upon their head, whom the General praised for their stedfastness; but seeing the men in confusion, there being some few of other regiments got among them, prayed the Earle with his officers to see to get them speedily in condition to receive the ennemy, whom he minutely expected, while he galloped further to a part of Hastings, which the Colonel was marching up to their first ground, which he affirmed to have left in pursuit of the ennemy, who, thinking to fall in his flank, he wheeled with his pikes to the right upon them, whereby they leaving him, repaired to the rest of their forces, which they saw among the baggage at the river-side, the plundering whereof gave time to many of our runnaways to get off, and having joined Hastings with the rest of Levins, he dispatched a nephew of his, captain of his regiment, seeing him on horseback, (tho' he had eight wounds with broad swords upon his body) after his runnaways to exhort all officers, whom he could meet with, to keep up their men, and labour to bring them back to joyn him, in which cafe he assured them of advantage.

Mean time seeing the officers could bring their men into no order, and looking every minute for the ennemy's appearing, he visited a garden which was behind, of a design to put them in there in expectation of succour, but presently changed his purpose, considering, if succour failed, as readily would fall out, there was no hope of escaping out of the ennemy's hands by defending an inclosure so far from new relief.

While he was in those irresolutions, in expectation of his nephews return, he brought at last news that all was gone clear away out of all reach, and that such as he had spoke to, noticed him not ; mean time he espyed numbers of men as it were forming themselves along the edge of the wood which was on Balfour's left, and where Lawder had been posted with 200 men, and because he had not as yet been particularly informed of the behaviour of that wing, and it being already after sun-set, he was doubtful whether those men might not be some of his own men, who had retired to the wood upon the Highlanders descent; so, exhorting the officers to labour to get their men in a condition to make at least one discharge if they were attacked, galloped up to the wood to view those men nearer, which having discovered to be ennemy's,[6] he stepped back softly to his men, and bid them have special care to march off very softly, whereby happily the ennemy judging they were resolved to receive them briskly, would have respect; for them and let them retire quietly, the obscurity hindring them of a full view of our number, but that if they would offer to run, they should be sure to have the Highlanders among them ; so, leading them softly down the hill he past the river, where he halted a little to get over all his men, and to observe whether the ennemy would approach the river after him. A little before his retreat the Lord Belhaven with the Earle of Annandales Lieutenant and Cornet[7] and some four or five horsemen came up to us, which served for scouts to discover during the retreat.

The ennemy lost on the field six for our one, the fire to our right having been continued and brisk, whereby not only Dundee, with several gentle men of quality of the countys of Angus and Perth, but also many of the best gentlemen among the Highlanders, particularly of the Macdonalds of the Isles and Glengarie were killed, coming down the hill upon Hastings, the General, and Levin's regiments, which made the best fire and all the execution ; particularly the Generals battalion made great fire, being well exercised thereto by his brother, who, being his lieutenant colonel, commanded the battalion, and was killed on the spot with severals of the old souldiers pikemen, who stood by him after the shot had run away: There were also two captains and five subalterns of that battalion killed, and the other two captains left wounded upon the spot ; for certainly the greatest force of that side was poured upon that battalion, and the reason was that some, who were officers among the ennemy, had carried arms in the regiment abroad, and were of opinion if it were beat that it would facilitate the rest of the work; but there was a great difference betwixt it, when they had known it, and this time, as was also of the other two regiments come out of Holland, which were mostly new levied men, the King having taken away their best and oldest men to recruit the Dutch regiments in England. The reason of the firmity of Levins regiment, was first, that they were not so numerously attacked, and secondly, that he had many more officers proportionable to the number of men than the three Dutch regiments, and very good brisk gentlemen; the same advantage Hasting's had, besides that I prefer the English commonality in my judgment in matter of courage to the Scots. The Brigadier Balfour was killed labouring with a few persons by him to get off, after his regiments had abandoned him. There was a lieutenant colonel of Kenmore's regiment also killed[8], and a captain of Ramsay's with fome more officers, which I do not remember, only that most part of the slaughter and imprisonment of officers and souldiers was in the chasce.

The General having got the small rests of his forces safely over the river, and seeing no disposition, so far as he could discern, of the ennemy to pursue him, he bethought himself which way he had best retire; and notwithstanding of the contrary advice of all the officers who would have him to descend the plain country of Athole to Dunkeld and Perth, he resolved rather to march into the Highlands three or four miles, and then over to Strath Tay and along the foot of the hills, over the Castle of Drummond, where he had a garrifon, to Stirling, whither he resolved to make all the speed possible to fall upon some present measures; but tho' there were who represented to him that those few afrighted men would make no resistance if the ennemy pursued, together with the necessity of his making haste southward, he would never resolve to alter his resolution with those few men till he had conducted them into a place of security, notwithstanding he was very well satisfied of the truth of what they alledged. The reason of the resolutions was, that he apprehended more the pursuit of Dundee (whom he knew not to have been killed) with his horse, than that of the Highlanders, whom he knew to be so greedy of plunder that their general would not get them that night to pursue us ; therefor he resolved to keep the most inaccessible ground for horse, besides that he knew all the men of Athole would be in arms and run the whole night and next day upon the runnaways, therefore resolved to quite altogether the track of that country, and tho' he was pursued, his men would not fight; as well as of the necessity of his haste to Stirling ; he judged it would tend to the disreputation of the service, as of himself in particular, if after he had got off those few men in a body in presence of the ennemy, they should happen by his leaving them to be dispersed and fall into their hands, resolving at the same time never to halt much for such as would not keep up, because of the consequence, both of loosing time, and of the ennemy's, and such of the people of the country through which he must needs march off, as this success would induce to declare for them cutting before him, which they might easily do with hopes, tho they should not be advertised of his rout till next morning: Marching then off, as he had concluded, he met in the obscurity about two miles off the field of battle with Colonel Ramsay, who had kept up the matter of 150 runnaways altogether almost without arms, and knew not in the world how he would best get them off; whom the General having joyn'd into his party, continued his way up a little river, which fell into that which he had crossed before, till he came to some little houses where he saw light, and having got out the man of the house, enquired of him concerning the ground and the way to Strath Tay and the Laird of Weem's lands, who was our friend, his eldest son having been in the action with a company of 100 Highlanders, which he levied for their Majesties service.

The countryman having sufficiently informed him of all his demands, and guessing himself at the situation of the country, by the map, so far that he could not carry him far out of the way, he crossed that second river, and pass through very ill ground over hills and boggs to the Weem; and next morning at the dawning of the day the people of Strath Tay, alarmed with our approach, whom they took for the Highlanders, and fearing for their houses and cattle, did raise a great noise and shout, whereat our men, judging it to be the ennemy, got before them, and began all to break off to the hills, if the General and some officers on horseback had not, with their pistols in hand, threatened them back again ; but the obscurity hindring a full view at any distance, the matter of 100 or more got away, who altogether were knockt in the head and stript, or taken prisoners, and we pursued our march with very little halt all that day, being on a Sunday, the 28th July, discovering the country all along as we marched in uproar, and arrived late in the night at the Castle of Drummond, and next day at Stirling, finding all the county of Perth in arms in favour of the rebels, tho' no considerable body of them together as yet.

NOTES

[1] Perth, or more properly St. John's Toun of Perth. By the eighteen century it simply became more commonly shortened to Perth, although the old name survives in the local football team; St. Johnston FC.

[2] John Murray, eldest son and heir of John Murray, Marquess of Atholl.

[3] Lieutenant Colonel George Lauder of Brigadier Balfour's Regiment.

[4] William Arnot – perhaps a former officer of the Scots Brigade.

[5] By 'light pieces' Mackay is presumably drawing a distinction between small-bored hunting weapons and heavy calibre military muskets.

[6] As discussed in the text these mysterious figures in the trees were Lieutenant Colonel Lauder and his men after all and later that night would make their own escape attempt down the Pass.

[7] Lieutenant William Lockhart of Cleghorn National Archives of Scotland (NAS) PA2/33, f.56-56v *Commissions to the lieutenants of horse.*

[8] John Fergusson of Craidarroch.

Appendix IV

The Battle of Dunkeld

The following is from *The Exact Narrative of the Conflict at Dunkeld, betwixt the Earl of Angus' Regiment, and the Rebels, collected from several Officers of that Regiment, who were Actors in, or Eye-witnesses to, all that's here narrated in reference to these Actions.* [1]

The said regiment being then betwixt seven and eight hundred men, arrived at Dunkeld, on Saturdays night the 17 of August,1689, under the command of Lieutenant Collonel William Cleland, a brave and singularly well accomplished gentleman, with 28 years of age. Immediately they found themselves obliged to ly at their arms, as being in the midst of their enemies. Sunday, at nine in the morning, they began some Retrenchments within the Marquess of Athol's yard-dykes, the old breaches whereof they made up with loose stones, and scaffolded the dykes about. In the afternoon, about 300 men appear'd upon the hills, on the north side of the town, who sent one with a white cloth upon the top of a halbert, with an open unsubscribed paper, in the fashion of a letter, directed to the commanding officer, wherein was written as follows, *We, the gentlemen assembled, being informed that ye intend to burn the town, desire to know whether ye come for peace or war, and do certifie you, that if ye burn any one house, we will destroy you*

The Lieutenant-Collonel Cleland returned answer, in writ, to this purpose:
We are faithful subjects to King William and Queen Mary, and enemies to their enemies; and if you, who send those threats, shall make any hostile appearance, we will burn all that belongs to you, and otherwise chastise you as you deserve.

180

But in the mean time, he caused solemnly proclaim, in the mercat-place, his majesties indemnity, in the hearing of him who brought the foresaid paper;

Munday morning, two troops of horse, and three of dragoons arrived at Dunkeld, under command of the Lord Cardross, who viewed the fields all round, and took six prisoners, hut saw no body of men, they being retired to the woods.

Monday night they had intelligence of a great gathering by the firey cross; and, Tuesday morning, many people appeared on the tops of the hills, and they were said to be in the woods and hills about Dunkeld, more than 1000 men. About eight of the clock, the horse, foot, and dragoons made ready to march out, but a detach'd party was sent before of fourty fusiliers, and fifteen halbertiers, under command of Captain George Monro, and thirty horse with Sir James Agnew, and twenty dragoons with the Lord Cardross his own cornet; after them, followed ensign Lockhart, with thirty halbertiers. The halberts were excellent weapons against the Highlanders' swords and targets, in case they should rush upon the shot, with their accustomed fury. They marched also at a competent distance before the body. One hundred fusiliers were under the command of Captain John Campbel, and Captain Robert Hume, two brave young gentlemen; and upon the first fire with the enemy, Captain Borthwick and Captain Haries, with 200 musquetiers, and pikes, were likewise commanded to advance towards them; the Lieutenant-Collonel having proposed, by method, to get advantage of the enemy in their way of loose and furious fighting. The body followed, having left only 150 foot within the dykes.

The first detached party, after they had marched about two miles, found before them, in a glen, betwixt two and three hundred of the rebels, who fired at a great distance, and shot Cornet Livingston in the leg. The horse retired, and Captain Monro took up their ground, and advanced, fireing upon the rebels to so good purpose, that they began to reel and break, but rallied on the face of the next hill, from whence they were again beat. About that time, the Lieutenant Collonel came up, and ordered Captain Monro to send a serjeant, with six men, to a house on the side of a wood, where he espyed some of the enemies. Upon the Serjeant's approach to the place, about twenty of the rebels appeared against him, but he was quickly seconded by the Captain, who beat them over the hill, and cleared the ground of as many as appeared without the woods; and upon a command sent to him, brought off his men in order. Thereafter, all the horse, foot, and dragoons retired to the town; and that night, the horse and dragoons marched to Perth the Lord Cardross, who commanded them, having received two peremptory orders for that effect. The second was sent to him, upon his answer to the first, by which answer, he told they were engaged with the enemy, and it was necessary he should stay.

In that action, three of Captain Monro's party were wounded, one of which died of his wounds. William Sandilands, a cadet, nephew to the Lord Torphichen, and a very young youth, being of that party, discharged his fusie upon the enemy eleven times. The prisoners taken the next day told us that the rebels lost about thirty men in that action.

After the horse and dragoons were marched, some of the officers and souldiers of the Earl of Angus's Regiment, proposed that they might also march, seeing they were in an open useless place, ill provided of all things, and in the midst of enemies, growing still to greater numbers; the vanguard of Canon's army having appeared before they came off the field. The brave Lieutennant Colonel, and the rest of the gentlemen officers amongst them, used all arguments of honour to perswade them to keep their post; and for their encouragement, and to assure them they would never leave them, they ordered to draw out all their horses to be shot dead. The souldiers then told them they needed not that pledge for their honour, which they never doubted; and seeing they found their stay necessar, they would run all hazards with them.

Wednesday with the mornings light, the rebels appeared, standing in order, covering all the hills about, (for Canon's army joyned the Athole men the night before, and they were repute in all, above 5000 men.) Their baggage marched alongst the hills, towards the west, and the way that leads into Athole, consisting of a train of many more than 1000 horses. Before seven in the morning, their cannon advanced down to the face of a little hill, close upon the town, and 100 men, all armed with back, breast, and head piece, marched straight to enter the town, and a battalion of other foot closs with them. Two troops of horse marched about the town, and posted on the south-west part of it; betwixt the foord of the river and the church, and other two troops posted in the north- east of the town, near the cross, who, in the time of the conflict, shewed much eagerness to encourage and push on the foot.

The Lieutenant Colonel had before possessed some out-posts, with small parties, to whom he pointed out every step for their retreat. Captain William Hay and Ensign Lockhart, were posted on a little hill, and the Ensign was ordered with twenty- eight men, to advance to a stone dyke at the foot of it. They were attacked by the rebels who were in armour, and the foresaid other battalion. And after they had entertained them briskly with their fire for a pretty space, the rebels forced the dyke, and oblig'd them to retire, firing from one little dyke to another, and at length to betake themselves to the house and yard- dykes; in which retreat. Captain Hay had his leg broken, and the whole party came off without any more hurt.

A Lieutenant was posted at the east end of the town with men, who had three advanced sentinels, ordered, upon the rebels closs approach, to fire and retire, which accordingly they did; and the Lieutenant, after burning of some houses, brought in his party.

Lieutenant Stuart was plac'd in a baricado at the cross, with twenty men, who, seeing the other Lieutenant retire, brought his men from that ground, and was killed in the retreat, there being a multitude of the rebels upon them.

Lieutenant Forrester, and Ensign Campbell were at the west end of the town, within some little dykes, with twenty- four men, who fired sharply upon the enemies horse, until great numbers of foot attack'd their dykes, and forc'd them to the church, where were two Lieutenants, and about 100 men.

All the out-posts being forc'd, the rebels advanced most boldly upon the yard- dykes all round, even upon those parts which stood within less than fourty paces from the river, where they crowded in multitudes, without regard to the shot liberally pour'd in their faces, and struck with their swords at the souldiers on the dyk, who, with their pikes and halberts, returned their blows with interest. Others, in great numbers, possest the town houses, out of which, they fired within the dyks, as they did from the hills about: And by two shots at once, one through the head, and another through the liver, the brave Lieutenant Collonel was killed, while he was visiting and exhorting the officers and souldiers at their several posts. He attempted to get into the house, that the souldiers might not be discouraged at the sight of his dead body, but fell by the way. And immediately thereafter, Major Henderson received several wounds, which altogether disabled him, and whereof he died four days after. Captain Caldwal was shot in the breast, and is not like to recover. Captain Borthwick was shot through the arm, going with succours to the church; and Captain Steil got a wound in the shoulder, which he caused pance, and returned again to his post.

The Lieutenant Colonel being dead, and the Major disabled about an hour after the action began, (which was before seven in the morning) the command fell to Captain Monro, who left his own post to Lieutenant Stuart of Livingstoune: And finding the soldiers galled in several places by the enemies shot, from the houses, he sent out small parties of pikemen, with burning faggots upon the points of their pikes, who fired the houses; and where they found keys in the doors, lock't them, and burnt all within; which raised a hideous noise from these wretches in the fire. There was sixteen of them burnt in one house, and the whole houses were burnt down, except three, wherein some of the regiment were advantageously posted. But all the inhabitants of the town, who were not with the enemy, or fled to the fields, were received by the souldiers into the church, and sheltered there.

Notwithstanding all the gallant resistance which these furious rebels met with, they continued their assaults uncessantly, until past eleven of the clock. In all which time, there was continual thundering of shot from both sides, with flames and smoake, and hideous cryes filling the air: And, which was very remarkable, though the houses were burnt all round, yet the smoake of them, and all the shot from both sides, was carried every where outward from the dyks upon the assailants, as if a wind had blown every way from the center within.

At length the rebels, wearied with so many fruitless and expensive assaults, and finding no abatement of the courage or diligence of their adversaries, who treated them with continual shot from all their posts, they gave over, and fell back, and run to the hills in great confusion. Whereupon, they within beat their drums, and flourished their colours, and hollowed after them with all expressions of contempt and provocations to return. Their commanders assay'd to bring them back to a fresh assault, as some prisoners related, but could not prevail; for they answered them, they could fight against men, but it was not fit to fight any more against devils.

The rebels being quite gone, they within began to consider, where their greatest danger appeared in time of the conflict; and for rendring these places more secure, they brought out the seats of the church, with which they made pretty good defences; especially they fortified these places of the dyk which were made up with loose stones, a poor defence against such desperate assailants. They also cut down some trees on a little hill, where the enemy gall'd them under covert. Their powder was almost spent, and their bullets had been spent long before, which they supplyed by the diligence of a good number of men who were imployed, all the time of the action, in cutting lead off the house, and melting the same in little furrows in the ground, and cutting the pieces into sluggs to serve for bullets. They agreed that in case the enemy got over their dyks, they should retire to the house, and if they should find themselves overpower'd there, to burn it, and bury themselves in the ashes.

In this action fifteen men were killed, besides the officers named, and thirty wounded. The account of the enemies loss in uncertain; but they are said to be above 300 slain, amongst who were some persons of note.

That handful of unexperienced men was wonderfully animated to a steadfast resistance against a multitude of obstinat furies. But they gave the glory to God, and praised him, and sung psalms after they had fitted themselves for a new assault. Amongst many who shewed extraordinary courage, some young gentlemen, cadets, deserve a special testimony and remembrance; as William Sandilands, above named; James Pringle of Hultrie; William Stirling of Mallachen; James Johnstoun, a reformed Lieutenant, and several others.

Diverse officers besides those above specified, viz. another Captain John Campbell; Captain Haries; Lieutenant Henry Stuart; Lieutenant Charles Calzell; Lieutenant Oliphant; Lieutenant Thomas Haddo; ensign William Hamilton, and most of all the other officers behaved very worthily, at their several posts, throughout the whole action, and deserve well to be recorded, as men of worth and valour. And the whole souldiers did every thing with such undaunted courage, and so little concern in all the dangers and deaths that surrounded them, and stared them in their faces, that they deserve to be recommended as examples of valour to this and after ages, and to have some marks of honour fixt upon them. And it is expected, his majesty will be graciously pleased to take notice both of officers and souldiers.

Lieutenant John Blackadder's account, written to his brother within two hours of the engagement.2

DUNKELL, Wednesday, Aug. 21, 1689
D.B. – I have taken this first opportunity to shew you I am in good health, because I believe many false reports will, by this time, be come to your ears anent our Ingagement, which was this same day; but for your certain information, the manner and way was this:

On Saturday last we came to this town at night, and camped within some walls between the church, and a house belonging to the M. of Athol. On Sabbath morning, the country people, and Atholmen appeared on the Hills round us in tens and twenties; and about four afternoon a party of 60 or 80 men drew up on a hill above us, and within a little while, sent down a letter to our Lieut. Coll. full of threatenings and boastings, the which he answered as briskly, and after carried up the Indemnity, and proclaimed it in the Messenger's hearing, and so he retired.

Mean time notice had been given to St. Johnstown, [Perth] to the forces there, to come up to our help, and accordingly on Monday morning came Lord Cardros with four troops of dragoons and one troop of horse; upon which, the Lieut. Coll. detatched out the most part of the Regiment, who, with the Horse, went to meet the Enemy, who appeared in several parties, to the number of about 5 or 600 men (ours being about the same number) Some small parties went out and skirmished; but Cardros, after an Hour or two's stay, brought in his men to the Town; our Lieut. Coll. did the like. An hour after, Cardross told the Lieut. Coll. he must needs go back to St. Johnstown, being expressly ordered by Coll.

Ramsay so to do. Our men were mightily discouraged to hear this; but whatever could be said, the Horse would not stay, and it was much for us to keep our men from going along with them whether we would or not, but the Lieut. Coll. compelled them and told them. That tho' every man went away, he resolved to stay himself alone; so we past Tuesday night also in Arms.

This morning about six of the Clock, the enemy appeared on the Hills, and whereas we expected only the enemy we had seen the day before, we saw to the number of 3 or 4000 Men draw up above us, which proved to be the whole force of Coll. Cannon, the which one of the prisoners we took, gave out to be 4000 men, besides the addition of the Countrey. Our Lieut. Coll. making a virtue of necessity, being nothing discouraged, posted the men so as they might most annoy the enemy, planting them behind dykes and ditches, which he caused to be cast up, and in the Church and Steeple, and in Athol's house. When he had done so, the enemy approached very fast, the Highlanders came running on like desperate villains, firing only once, and then came on with sword and target; a troop of the Enemies horse, (brave horse, and all gentlemen) beset one side, on purpose, we think to have cut us off when we fled, which they nothing doubted off. A Party was sent out under the command of Capt. Hay (Park Hay's Son) to keep them up, which fired on them, and then retired, not being able to restrain their great number and fierceness, pressing in upon us to the very cross in the middle of the town, where another party of our men fired on them, and they retired in order. After which, the Highlanders came swarming in on all sides, and gave a desperate assault in four places all at once, first firing their guns, and then running in on us with sword and target. But it pleased God, that they were also bravely repulsed, our men still firing on them, where they came on thickest. In this hot service we continued above three hours, the Lord wonderfully assisting our men with courage, insomuch that old soldiers, that were with us said. They never saw men fight better, for there was not the least sign of fear to be seen in any of them, every one performing his part gallantly. But (which is never enough to be

lamented) our dear and valiant Lieut. Coll. at the beginning of the action going up and down encouraging his men, was shot in the head and immediately died; our Major also received three wounds, so that I fear he will not live.

Notwithstanding all these discouragements, our men fainted not, but fought so, that the Enemy at last found themselves necessitated to flee back on all hands, leaving a number of their dead carkasses behind them, and a great many of them getting into houses to fire upon us, our men went and sett fire to the houses, and burnt and slew many of them. One of the prisoners we have taken, told us. That after they were gone off, their officers would have had them come back, and give us another assault, but they would not hear of it, for they said we were mad and desperate men. Upon their retreating, our men gave a great shout, and threw their caps in the air, and then all joined in offering up praises to God a considerable time for so miraculous a victory. I must really say. The Lord's presence was most visible, strengthening us, so that none of the glory belongs to us, but to His own great name; for we clearly saw. It was not by might, or our power, nor by conduct, (our best officers being killed at first, or disabled) so that we have many things to humble us, and to make us trust and eye him alone, and not his instruments. I pray God help me, not to forget such a great mercy I have met with, not receiving the least hurt, notwithstanding several falling on my right and left hand. This is a true and impartial account of the whole affair, which you may communicate to others in case of misrepresentation; The Enemy retired, as we hear, to the Castle of Blair. We expected still they would assault us again, but word being sent to St. Johnstown at; 12 o'clock, we expect speedy help from thence. This in haste from

Your affectionate Brother,

(Sic Surscribitur) J. BLACKADER.

NOTES

1. Crichton, Andrew *The Life and Diary of Lieut. Col. J. Blackader: Of the Cameronian Regiment* (H.S. Baynes, Edinburgh 1828), pp.42-46.
2. ibid pp.47-49.

Appendix V

Balhaldie's Account of Killiecrankie

The passages below are transcribed from the *Memoirs of Sir Ewen Cameron of Locheil*, by a John Drummond of Balhaldie. Identification of him is uncertain but he was almost certainly a younger son of Alexander Drummond of Balhaldie, Locheil's son-in-law, who served in the campaign. The narrative set out here is not therefore written by an eyewitness, but as he tells us of Killiecrankie: 'I have had occasion to talk with severall gentlemen, and others who lived in that neightbourhood, and who knew the most minute circumstances of that glorious action, and likeways with several of the Chiefs, besides Low-country gentlemen and others who were eye-witnesses to all that passed.'

The manuscript was completed by 1737, but not published until the Maitland Club did so in Edinburgh in 1842:

> In this posture were King James his affairs about the middle of July 1689, when the Lord Murray, son to the Marquess of Atholl, so often mentioned, arrived in Atholl; where he gave out that he was determined to joyn Dundee in his late Majesty's service with all the power he was able to raise, and soon got together a body of 1200 good men. With these, he pretended he would defend his country, till the Highland army should be in a condition to march. But Stewart of Ballachan, a dependant on the family of Atholl, began very early to entertain suspicious thoughts of his intentions; and haveing specifyed the reasons of his jealousys to the Viscount of Dundee, he, by his orders, putt himself and a party of his followers into the Castle of Blair, a strong house, and one of the seats of the family of Atholl, and well scituated to keep open the communication

between the army and the people of that country, who declared in favours of King James. The Lord Murray, who knew the importance of the place, haveing, upon his arrivall, summoned the Governour to open the gates, was answered, that seeing he had garrisoned the house by his General's orders for the King's service, he was resolved to keep it till he was commanded to give it up.

Enraged to be refused access to his own house, and that too by one of his own vassalls, he wrote very instant letters to General M'Kay, who was then in the South, to march with all heast to his assistance, and reduce the castle; shewing, at the same time, of what use and importance it would be to their designs. M'Kay immediatly upon this drew together his army, consisting of six or seven regiments of foot, and two new-levyed troops of English horse, and marched straight into Atholl.

Dundee, having had repeated information of M 'Kay's advance, and knowing well that if the castle was reduced, it would cutt off all inteligence betwixt the Northern and Western Highlands, besides that he justly putt the highest value upon the loyalty and courage of the Athollmen, he resolved by all means to prevent it; and made such haste with the Clans that he had about him, amounting to about eighteen hundred men in all, that he arrived before the enemy; haveing left orders for the rest of his army to follow him with all speed, though the day appointed for their rendezvouze was not yet come.

Locheill had non then but his Lochaber men with him, and they did not exceed 240; but upon the first allarm had dispatched his eldest son John and severall other messengers into the adjacent countrys of Morvine, Swynart, Ardnamurchan, and other places, through which the Camerons are dispersed, to bring them up with all hast. But Dundee, being every moment advertized of the quick advance of the enemy, he was affraid there might be a necessity of engageing them before Locheill could arrive, if he stayed in Lochaber till these men joyned him. Unwilling, therefore, to want the advice and assistance of a person who had given so many repeated proofs of his great abilitys in manageing of Highlanders, he sent express upon express, commanding him to follow with the men he had about him, and to leave the care of the rest to his son. While his Lordship waited for Locheill, who came to him before he entered Atholl, he dispatched Major William Graham and Captain Ramsay to the Lord Murray, (who had not vouchsafed to send any return to the letters he had formerly wrote to him,) with orders to represent to his Lordship the honours and advantages he might procure to himself and his family, if he would heartily joyn him in King James his service. That it would be ane easy matter to reduce all Scotland, inclinable of itself to throw off the present yoak; that if they succeeded in the first attempt, it should be made known to the King that it was owing to him onely, but that if he refused so glorious ane opportunity of exerting his loyalty to his late kind and indulgent master, who had, even dureing the short time that he exercised the Royal authority, so highly distinguished that family by the honourable and beneficiall imployments which he had heaped upon his father; he begged him to considder how much such a monstrous peice of ingratitude would reflect upon his own and his father's honour.

But his Lordship was deaffe to all arguments, and would not so much as see the messengers, nor return them ane answer; but they had wisely taken care to inform his men of the import of their commission, which was every way agreeable to their inclinations. They were soon convinced, from the treatment of these gentlemen, that his Lordship had been all the while imposeing on them, and therefore, in order to discover his reall intentions, they addressed him all in a full body, and prayed him either to joyn with my Lord Dundee in King James his service, or otherwayes they threatned instantly to leave him. But his Lordship thought it not proper to give them any other return, but a command to waite his orders; and they being, on the other hand, already determined how to proceed, without further ceremony, run to the river of Tumble which was near them, filled their bonnets with water, and drank King James his health with many loud huzzas and acclamations, and so deserted him in a full body.

Dundee was, in the meantime, on a quick march to Atholl, but before he entered that country, Major-General Cannon overtook him with three hundred new-raised, naked, undisciplined Irishmen; which had this bad effect, that the Clans, who had been made believe they were to be supported by a powerfull army from Ireland, with arms, ammunition, and all other provisions, saw themselves miserably dissappoynted; but they were still further discouraged, when they heard that the ships that King James had sent over with great plenty of meale, beefe, butter, cheese, and other necessarys, were taken by English ships in the Isle of Mull, where General Cannon had loytered so long, that the enemy had information of their arrival.

But the brave Lord Dundee was not to be discouraged by accidents of this nature. He had gained so upon the affections of his small army, that, though half starved, they marched forward as chearefully as if they had not felt the least effects of want. He arrived attthe Castle of Blair upon the 27th day of July, and had intelligence that M'Kay with his army had already entered the Pass of Gillychranky. 'This was a narrow path att the foot of a steep, rugged mountain, with a precipice and river below, and a high hill on the opposite side, where three men with great difficulty could walk abreast. It is several miles in length, and though the late Duke of Atholl has been att the trouble of making it passable by coaches and carriages, yet to this day, ane army might be stopt in its march by a few resolute men posted at the mouth or issue of it, and other convenient places; nor is there any other way to march ane army into Atholl from the South but by this pass or defile.

Dundee, before he proceeded further, haveing thought it proper to have the advice of his councill, called all his principall officers together, and laid the case before them according to the information he had received; and the question was, whether they should continue beside the Castle of Blair, the preservation whereof was the occasion of their sudden march, untill their troops arrived, which behooved to be within a few days, the very nixt, or that succeeding it, being the day on which their general rendezvouze was appointed, or whether they should march directly forward and fight the enemy?

The old officers, who had been bred to the command of regular troops, were unanimously of the first oppinion, alleadgeing that it was neither prudent nor cautious to risk ane engadgement against ane army of disci plined men that exceeded theirs in number by more than a half: That as the reputation and success of their arms depended upon the first battle, so they thought it was wise to attend the arivall of their men, and to try their courage by some light skirmishes before they adventured on a general action: That by this means, they would in a manner secure a victory which would not only give ane eclat to their arms, but likeways intimidate the King's enemys, and raise the spirits of his friends, who with impatience waited the event of their first attempt That the Highlanders, though hardy and brave, were but raw undisciplined troops, who had never seen blood; besides that, they had been wasted and spent by want of provisions, discouraged by their late disappointments, and the remains of their strength exhausted and drained off by their last long, quick, and fatigueing march, deprived not onely of the comforts, but even of the common necessarys of life: That they had, indeed, performed wounders in Montrose his wars; but then, as they had not laboured under the above inconveniencys, so att first they had onely to doe with militia, who were in every respect inferior to themselves; but att present, they were to fight a numerous, well-disciplined body of regular troops, conducted by ane old, experienced General, and encouraged and heartned by plenty and aboundance: And that though the Highlanders might be their equalls, which was even a kind of presumption to imagine, yet that it would be next to madness to fancy them their supperiors in any one quality that belonged to a souldier. That, therefore, it was their oppinion, that since the General had already accomplished his design by covering the Castle of Blair from the seige wherewith it was threatned, they ought by all means not onely to attend the arivall of their men, but also to give them time to recover their strength and spirits by necessary rest; and that, in the meantime, it were proper to awake and rouze up their courage by some brisk attacks and light skirmishes, wherein especial care ought to be taken that they should allways have the advantage.

Such was the oppinion of these gentlemen; and it seemed supported by so many strong reasons, that it for some time occasioned a general silence: But, att last, Alexander Macdonald of Glengary, a gentleman of no small reputation, took the opportunity of declareing his sentiments in that debate …[1]

Glengary differed in oppinion from the officers whom I have mentioned. He represented that though the Highland army had suffered much by the want of provisions, and from the fatigue they had been putt to, yet these hardships did not affect them in the same manner that they commonly did souldiers who are bred in ane easyer and more plentifull course of life: That the Generall would find them both ready and able to engage, and perhaps defeat ane equal number of the enemy's best troops: That as nothing delighted them more then hardy and adventurous exploits, so it was his oppinion that they should march immediatly, and endeavour to prevent the enemy's getting through the pass: That, if they could be there in time, it would be ane easy matter to stop their advanceing into the country till they were able to give them battle: That, supposeing them already clear of the Pass, yet to waite there till they were attacked by M'Kay would so discourage their men, that they would soon grow of no value, and lose that spirite and resolution which commonly accompanys agressors: And that, finally, his advice was allways to keep the army in sight of the enemy, and to post them in such strong ground, as might not onely be a defence to them from sudden at tacks, but also enable them to make quick salleys, and engage partys of them in brisk skirmishes, as often as opportunity offered.

The Chiefs in generall subscribed to this oppinion; but Dundee, haveing observed that Locheill was all this while silent, refused to declare his oppinion till the other gave his: 'For,' said he, 'he has not onely done great things himself, but has had so much experience, that he cannot miss to make a right judgement of the matter, and, therefore, his shall determine min!' Locheill answered, that his Lordship much overrated the small things he had done, for they were but little tumultuous sallys and skirmishes, without any order or conduct, and that the success he had was rather owing to the intrepidity and courage of his men than to any thing in himself; and that, therefore, no example could be taken from them. That the reason he had not spoke was, that he had already determined himself to submitt to his Lordship's conduct, which was so exactly adapted to the genius of the Highlanders, that he needed no advice; but that, since he had commanded him to give his oppinion, it was in one word 'To fight immediatly, for our men,' said he, ' are in heart; they are so far from being afraid of their enemy, that they are eager and keen to engage them, least they escape their hands, as they have so often done. Though we have few men, they are good, and I can venture to assure your Lordship that not one of them will faill yow. It is better to fight att the disadvantage of even one to three, than to delay it till M'Kay's dragoons and cavalry have time to joyn him. To pretend to stop them in the Pass is a vain project, for they have undoubtedly gott through it ere now, and to march up to them and not immediatly to fight, is to expose ourselves to the want of provisions, seeing we can spare no men for forageing; besides, we will discover that, even in our oun oppinion, we are unequall to the enemy, which would be of dangerous consequence among Highlanders. If the enemy shall be allowed time to march up and offer to attack us, and we retreat, it will be still worse. If your Lordship thinks proper to delay fighting, and wait the arrivall of our men, my oppinion is, that we immediatly retreat again to the mountains and meet them; for I will not promise upon the event, if we are not the aggressors. But be assured, my Lord, that if once we are fairly engaged, we will either lose our army, or carry a compleat victorey. Our men love allways to be in action.

Your Lordship never heard them complain either of hunger or fatigue while they were in chace of their enemy, which att all times were equall to us in number. Employ them in hasty and desperat enterprizes, and yow will oblige them; and I have still observed, that when I fought under the greatest disadvantage of numbers, I had still the compleatest victoreys. Let us take this occasion to shew our zeall and courage in the cause of our King and countrey, and that we dare to attack ane army of Fanaticks and Rebells att the odds of near two to one. Their great superiority in number will give a necessary reputation to our victorey; and not only fright them from meddling with a people conducted by such a General, and animated by such a cause, but it will incourage the whole kingdome to declare in our favours.'

Ane advice so hardy and resolute could not miss to please the generous Dundee. His looks seemed to brighten with ane air of delight and satisfaction all the while Locheill was a-speaking. He told his councill that they had heard his sentiments from the mouth of a person who had formed his judgement upon infallible proofs drawn from a long experience, and ane intimate acquaintance with the persons and subject he spoke of. Not one in the companey offering to contradict their General, it was unanimously agreed to fight.

When the news of this vigorous resolution spread through the army, nothing was heard but acclamations of joy, which exceedingly pleased their gallant General; but, before the councill broke up, Locheill begged to be heard for a few words: ' My Lord,' said he, 'I have just now declared, in presence of this honourable company, that I was resolved to give ane implicite obedience to all your Lordship's commands; but, I humbly beg leave, in name of these gentlemen, to give the word of command for this one time. It is the voice of your councill, and their orders are, that yow doe not engage personally. Your Lordship's bussiness is to have ane eye on all parts, and to issue out your commands as yow shall think proper; it is ours to execute them with prompitude and courage. On your Lordship depends the fate not onely of this little brave army, but also of our King and country. If your Lordship deny us this reasonable demand, for my oun part, I declare that neither I, nor any I am concerned in, shall draw a sword on this important occasion, whatever construction shall be putt upon the matter!'

Locheill was seconded in this by the whole councill; but Dundee begged leave to be heard in his turn: ' Gentlemen,' said he, ' as I am absolutely convinced, and have had repeated proofs of your zeale for the King's service, and of your affection to me, as his General and your friend, so I am fully sensible that my engageing personaly this day may be of some loss if I shall chance to be killed; but I beg leave of yow, however, to allow me to give one *Shear-darg'* (that is, one harvest-day's work) to the King, my master, that I may have ane opportunity of convincing the brave Clans that I can hazard my life in that service as freely as the meanest of them. Ye know their temper, Gentlemen, and if they doe not think I have personal courage enough, they will not esteem me hereafter, nor obey my commands with cheerfulness. Allow me this single favour, and I here promise, upon my honour, never again to risk my person while I have that of commanding you.'

The Councill, finding him inflexible, broke up, and the army marched directly towards the Pass of Killychranky, which M'Kay had gott clear of some short time before. Att the mouth of the Pass, there is a large plain which extends itself along the banks of the river, on the one side; and on the other rises a rugged, uneven, but not very high mountain.

M'Kay still drew up his troops, as they issued out of that narrow defile, on the forsaid plain; and that he might be capable to flank Dundee on both sides, in case of ane attack; he ordered his battle in one line, without any reserves, and drew up his field-batallions three men deep onely, which made a very long front; for, as I have said already, his army consisted of no less than 3500 foot, and two troops of horse.

Haveing thus formed his lines, he commanded his troops, that were much fatigued with the quick march they had been obliged to make, to prevent being stopt in the Pass, to sitt down upon the ground in the same order they stood, that they might be somewhat refreshed.

Dundee keept the higher ground, and when his advanced guards came in view of the plain, they could discover no enemy; but still as they came nearer they observed them to start to their feet, regiment by regiment, and waite the attack in the order above described. But Dundee never halted till he was within a musquet-shot of them, and posted his army upon the brow of the hill opposite to them; whence, having observed distinctly their order, he was necessitated to change the disposition of his battle, and inlarge his intervals, that he might not be too much out-winged. But before he could effect this, the enemy began to play upon him with some field-peices they had brought with them for the seige they intended, and then their whole army fired upon them in platoons, which run along from line to line for the whole time Dundee took up in disposing of his troops; which he performed in the following order:

Sir John M'Lean, then a youth of about eighteen years of age, with whose character I shall hereafter take ane opportunity to entertain the reader, was posted with his battalion on the right; on his left the Irishmen I have mentioned under the command of Collonell Pearson [Purcell]; nixt them the Tutor of Clanranald, with his battalion. Glengary, with his men, were placed nixt to Clanranald's; the few horses he had were posted in the centre, and consisted of Low-country gentlemen, and some remains of Dundee's old troop, not exceeding fourty in all, and these very lean and ill-keept. Nixt them was Locheill; and Sir Donald's battalion on the left of all. Though there were great intervals betwixt the battalions, and a large void space left in the centre, yet Dundee could not possibly streatch his line so as to equall that of the enemy; and, wanting men to fill up the voyd in the centre, Locheill, who was posted nixt the horse, was not onely obliged to fight M'Kay's own regiment, which stood directly opposite to him, but also had his flank exposed to the fire of Leven's battalion, which they had not men to engage, whereby he thereafter suffered much. But, what was hardest of all, he had none of his Clan with him but 240, and even 60 of these were sent as Dundee's advanced guard, to take possession of a house from which he justly apprehended the enemy might gall them, if they putt men into it. But there was no helping the matter. Each Clan, whither small or great, had a regiment assigned them, and that, too, by Locheil's own advice, who attended the Generall while he was makeing his disposition. The designe was to keep up the spirite of emulation in poynt of bravery; for, as the Highlanders putt the highest value upon the honour of their familys or Clans, and the renoun and glory acquired by military actions, so the emulation between Clan and Clan inspires them with a certain generous contempt of danger, gives vigour to their hands, and keeness to their courage.

The afternoon was well advanced before Dundee had gott his army formed into the order I have described. The continual fire of the enemy from the lower ground covered them, by a thick cloud of smoake, from the view of the Highlanders, whereof severals dropping from time to time, and many being wounded, they grew impatient for action. But the sun then shineing full in their faces, the Generall would not allow; them to engage till it was nearer its decline.

Locheill, as well to divert as to incourage them, fell upon this stratagem. He commanded his men, who, as I have said, were posted in the centre, to make a great shout, which being seconded by those who stood on their right and left, ran quickly through the whole army, and was returned by some of the enemy; but the noise of the cannon and musquets, with the prodigious echoeing of the adjacent hills and rocks, in which there are several caverns and hollow places, made the Highlanders fancy that their shouts were much brisker and louder than that of the enemy, and Locheill cryed out, ' Gentlemen, take courage. The day is our own. I am the oldest commander in the army, and have allways observed something ominous and fatall in such a dead, hollow, and feeble noise as the enemy made in their shouting. Ours was brisk, lively, and strong, and shews that we have courage, vigour, and strength. Theirs was low, lifeless, and dead, and prognosticates that they are all doomed to dye by our hands this very night!' Though this circumstance may appear triffleing to ane inadvertant reader, yet it is not to be imagined how quickly these words spread through the army, and how wounderfully they were incouraged and animated by them.

The sun being near its close, Dundee gave orders for the attack, and commanded, that so soon as the M 'Leans began to move from the right, that the whole body should, att the same instant of time, advance upon the enemy. It is incredible with what intrepidity the Highlanders endured the enemy's fire; and though it grew more terrible upon their nearer approach, yet they, with a wounderfull resolution, keept up their own, as they were commanded, till they came up to their very bosoms, and, then poureing it in upon them all att once, like one great clap of thounder, they threw away their guns, and fell in pell-mell among the thickest of them with their broad-swords. After this the noise seemed hushed; and the fire ceaseing on both sides, nothing was heard for some few moments but the sullen and hollow clashes of broad-swords, with the dismall groans and crys of dyeing and wounded men.

Dundee himself was in the centre with the horse, which were then commanded by Sir William Wallace of Craigie. The gallant Earl of Dumfermline had formerly that charge, but that very morning, Sir William having presented a commission from King James, that noble Earl calmly resigned, much to the dissatisfaction of Dundee; and from this small incident, it is affirmed, flowed the mine and disappointment of that undertaking. When they had advanced to the foot of the hill, on which they were drawn up, Sir William Wallace, either his courage faileing him, or some unknown accident interposeing, instead of marching forward after his Generall, ordered the horse to wheele about to the left, which not onely occasioned a halt, but putt them into confusion. Dundee, in the mean time, intent upon the action, and carryed on by the impetuosity of his courage, advanced towards the enemy's horse, which were posted about their artillery in the centre, without observeing what passed behind, untill he was just entering into the smoak. The brave Earl of Dumfermline, and sixteen gentlemen more, not regarding the unaccountable orders of their Collonell, followed their Generall, and observed him, as he was entering into the smoake, turn his horse towards the right, and raiseing himself upon his stirrops, make signes by waveing his hatt over his head for the rest to come up. The enemy's horse made but little resistance. They were routed and warmly pursued by those few gentlemen; and as to Wallace and those with him, they did not appear till after the action was over.

The Highlanders had ane absolute and compleat victorey. The pursute was so warm that few of the enemy escaped; nor was it cheap bought to the victors, for they lossed very near a third of their number, which did not ammount fully to two thousand men before they engaged.

It was formerly observed that Dundee was so far out-numbered by M'Kay, that he was obliged to streatch his front as near equall to his enemy's as possibly he could, in order to prevent being flanked; but this he could not effectuat so; but still there was a large voyd space in the centre, opposite to which the battalion commanded by the Earl of Leven was posted; and which, there being none to attack, remained still enteare: besides, on M'Kay's right there was another battalion conducted by Collonell Hastings that outstreatched Dundee's lines so far on the left, that there was onely half of it assaulted and cutt off, and the other stood still on the field of battle. The sixteen gentlemen I have mentioned returning from the pursute of the enemy's horse, were much surprised to find these men standing entire, and upon the very ground where they were first posted. The brave Earl of Dumfermling proposed to gather about fifty or sixty Highlanders, whom they observed straggleing through the field of battle looking after their dead friends, and to attack them. Though none of the companey could speak Gaulick, (as the Highlanders call their language,) yet Mr Drummond of Balhaldys, being son-in-law to Locheill, and haveing some acquaintance among them, made a shift to get so many of them together, that they adventured to march against Hastings' half battalion. But that of Leven's, which stood att some distance, observeing this motion, advanced to their assistance; and the Highlanders, whereof many were rather followers of the army than souldiers refuseing to engage, the gentlemen were obliged to retreat, and on their way discovered the body of their noble General, who was just breathing out his last. The fatall shott, that occasioned his death, was about two hand's-breadth within his armour, on the lower part of his left side; from which the gentlemen concluded, that he had received it while he raised himself upon his stirrops, and streatched his body in order to hasten up his horse, as I have related. Observeing still some small remains of life, they halted about the body to carry it off, but Leven's battalion advanceing in the interim, fired smartly upon them, and wownded Mr Haliburton of Pitcurr so mortally that he dyed within two days thereafter. He was a gentleman of that resolution that he dissembled it for the time, and retired with the rest ...[2]

When the Earl of Dunfermline, who had then his horse shott under him, and the other gentlemen, had gott themselves out of the reatch of the enemy's shott, and poured out a flood of tears on the hearse of their great General,[3] they discovering some Highlanders that had returned from the pursute, again employed Mr Drummond to gather as many of them as he could, in order to attack these men. He having prevailed with about sixty of them to follow him, met, as he returned, some of the Chiefs, with a few of their men, who likeways joyned him; and, marching all in a body towards the enemy, they found them possessed of a gentleman's house that was near the field of battle, from which it was in vain to attempt to dislodge them. About the middle of the night, the army returned from the pursute, but the enemy took the opportunity of retreating in the dark, and as they were marching through the Pass, the Atholl men, whom I have mentioned, keeping still in a body, attacked them, killed some, and made all the rest prisoners; so that of the troops that M'Kay brought with him the sixth man did not escape. No less than eighteen hundred of them were computed to fall upon the field of battle.

When day returned, the Highlanders went and took a view of the field of battle, where the dreadfull effects of their fury appeared in many horrible figures. The enemy lay in heaps allmost in the order they were posted; but so disfigured with wounds, and so hashed and mangled, that even the victors could not look upon the amazeing proofs of their own agility and strength without surprise and horrour. Many had their heads divided into two halves by one blow; others had their sculls cutt off above the eares by a back-strock, like a night-cap. Their thick buffe-belts were not sufficient to defend their shoulders from such deep gashes as allmost disclosed their entrails. Several picks, small swords, and the like weapons, were cutt quite through, and some that had scull-capes had them so beat into their brains that they died upon the spott.

The Highlanders, as I have said, payed dear enough for their victory; but it was remarked that few or none of them were killed after they drew their swords, and that the greatest part of them fell within a few paces of their enemy when they received the last fire, before they themselves discharged; after which, their loss was inconsiderable.

Locheill lost in this action one hundred and twenty of his men, which was just one half of his number, and was occasioned by a furious fire that he received in the flank from Leven's battallion, which, as the reader has been told, had no enemy to engage. His post was against M'Kay's own regiment, which he routed and destroyed in a manner that few of them ever returned to their colours. So keen was he that day, that he spoke to his men one by one, and tooke their several engagements either to conquer or dye. He was then past the sixty-third year of his age, but strong, healthfull, and vigorous. His men obeyed him so readily, when he commanded them to march, that he was not able to keep pace with them; but, leaveing them to the protection of God, he satt down by the way, and deliberatly pulling off his shoes that pinched him, had the agility to gett up with them just as they drew their swords.

The Highlanders had been so fatigued by that day's work and the proceeding marches, that after the pursute was over, they were unwilling to return to the field of battle till they were somewhat recovered by a little rest, and it was with no small difficulty that Locheill prevailed, in the end, with their Chiefs to lead them back. By this it appears how unjustly the Earl of Balcarrass (though otherways ane impartial author) has charged them with looseing the fruits of so important a victory by their unseasonable avarice. His Lordship alleadges, that so soone as they came among the enemy's baggage, they stopt and allowed M'Kay and several other eminent persons to escape, while they were employed in riffleing it; and that if the troops that keept the field had beheaved as they ought to have done, they might have fallen upon them, and changed the fate of the day. But as I have had occasion to talk with severall gentlemen, and others who lived in that neightbourhood, and who knew the most minute circumstances of that glorious action, and likeways with several of the Chiefs, besides Low-country gentlemen and others who were eye-witnesses to all that passed, so from their con curring accounts of it, I can assure my readers, that the Highlanders pursued so far, that they could not distinguish friends from foes before they gave over, though the rout began about the setting of the sun: That they were so excessively fatigued, that they inclined to rest themselves there during the dead of the night: That it was midnight ere they returned, which gave opportunity to these troops to attempt their escape, as I have related: And that they neither saw the enemy's bag gage nor the field of battle, till the sun was some hours up nixt morning. And what is a further proof of that Lord's mistake it is universally agreed, that the Earl of Leven, though not attacked, and generally all those that had horses, fled so early, that some of them rode thirty miles that night; and M'Kay, as soon as he saw his troops broken, went off with a few horses in such time, that, notwithstanding of the badness of the road, he sleept that night in the Castle of Weems in Kaynoch; so that, unless several partys had been posted beforehand in proper places, it was impossible to prevent their escape.

That noble author is likeways guilty of another mistake, in chargeing the loss of the brave Viscount of Dundee upon the cowardice of Sir Donald Macdonald's men. I have already informed the reader of the circumstances of that tragical event, from the relation of severalls of the sixteen gentlemen who accompanyed him in the last moments of his life; and shall now give ane account of the behaviour of these Macdonalds, from as good authority.

Sir Donald and his battalion were posted on the left of the Highland army, and had the misfortune to have their flank exposed to the fire of Hastings' regiment; and Sir Donald, observing several of his men to fall, and that there were some houses and dykes opportunely scituated to cover his men from the fire, while the army was a forming. He commanded them to sitt down, in which posture they continued till orders were given to engage. But the aid-du-camp who carried these orders not haveing courage enough to pass through the intervall betwixt them and Locheil's men, where the enemy's fire was very hott, he called out to such of them as were nearest, that the Generall wanted them, and they not understanding the orders, and their being entangled among dykes and houses, occasioned some confusion, but they quickly recovered themselves, and charged with so much bravery that they cutt off the regiment that was assigned them.[4] Now, if the reader will reflect on the extent of Dundee's front, occasioned by the great intervals that were left between the battalions, and that Sir Donald was posted on the extremity of the left wing, he will not imagine it probable that Dundee, who charged in the centre, would make signs, att so great a distance, for Sir Donald to advance, who could not possibly perceive him. The truth seems to be, that the Earle of Balcarrass, who then was a prisoner of state in the Castle of Edinburgh, hearing that Dundee was shott as he was makeing signs for his people to come up, and not haveing ane opportunity of conversing with any of them I have mentioned, mistook the matter, and charged the misfortune of his death on the wrong persons; which 1 am convinced he would have rectifyed, if he had given us another edition of his Memoirs ...[5]

Besides the death of Pitcur, which I have already related, the Laird of Largo, a young gentleman of about twenty-four years of age, of great hopes, and Chieftane of a branch of the M'Donalds of Kyntyre, [MacDonald of Lairgie] was also killed in the heat of the action, with several gentlemen of the same family. There like ways fell att the same time a brother of Glengary's, five near relations of Sir Donald M'Donald, several gentlemen of the McLeans, and a multitude of others whom it were tedious to recount.

But the death of Gilbert Ramsay was attended with such remarkable circumstances that they deserve to be related. He was a young gentle man bred to the law, which, haveing studyed att Leyden with great application, he, about the same time that the King left England, past his tryalls, and was admitted Advocate with the general applause of that learned Faculty. The confusions that followed made him quitt the bar, where it was expected he would soone become eminent, and joyn my Lord Dundee, whom he attended in quality of a volunteer, with great cheerfullness. After that General had made his disposition, and while they waited his orders to engage, the gallant Earl of Dunfennline calling for some spirits, and, filling a dram with his own hand, drank 'A health to the King, and success to his arms.' And when it came in course to Mr Ramsay, betook the glass in his hand, and addressing himself to his Lordship, 'I assure you, my Lord,' said he, 'that this day we shall have a glorious victory over the King's enemys; but I shall not have the pleasure of seeing it.' And, haveing thus spoke, he pledged the health, and drank his glass.

The gentlemen who were nixt him observeing ane unusewal flush and disorder in his countenance, which they had not formerly taken notice of, inquired seriously into the reasons of his expressing himself so. He answered frankly, that he had a dream that morning, immediately before he awaked, wherein not only the action itself, with everything that was to happen remarkable about it, but allso the order of the troops on both sides was fully represented to him; and that there was not a person of any note to fall there but he saw their wounds bleeding: That every circumstance that had hitherto happened was a confirmation of what he saw before in his sleep; and that he was now fully convinced that the remaining part would come to pass in the same manner. The Lord Dunfermline, and the gentlemen on both hands, joyned their endeavours to prevaill with him not to engage, but he was obstinate, and said that he was determined to acquitt himself of a duty which he thought indispensibly incumbent on him, seeing his Majesty was deserted by those who ought by their offices to have served him; adding, that he could meet death without the least apprehension, and that he had related his dream meerly on account of its novelty. Soon after this, the army began to move, and Mr Ramsay, being one of these sixteen that followed

my Lord Dundee, fell by Mr Drummond's right hand, where he was first posted.

I have been the more particular in discribing this action in all its circumstances, because I have observed that none who have wrote of these times have, either out of partiality, or for want of information, been pleased to favour the world with a full and genuine relation of it.

But the greatest proof of the importance of it is the general consternation wherewith all those of the contrary party were seized, upon the first news of M'Kay's defeat. The Duke of Hamilton, Commissioner for the Parliament, which then satt att Edinburgh, and the rest of the Ministry, were struck with such a panick, that some of them were for retireing into England; others into the Western Shires of Scotland, where all the people, almost to a man, befriended them; nor knew they whither to abandone the Government, or to stay a few days untill they saw what use my Lord Dundee would make of his victory. They knew the rapidity of his motions, and were convinced that he would allow them no time to deliberat. On this account, it was debated, whether such of the nobility and gentry as were confyned for adhering to their old master, should be immediately sett att liberty or more closely shutt up; and though the last was determined on, yet the greatest Revolutioners among them made private and frequent visits to these prisoners, excuseing what was past, from a fatall necessity of the times, which obliged them to give a seeming complyance, but protesting that they allways wished well to King James, as they should soon have occasion to show, when my Lord Dundee advanced.

But the news of that great man's death quickly dissipated all their fears, and the short-lived loyalty of these politicians shortly thereafter was changed into ane affected biggotry, and ill-nature against all who differed from them in opinion; so true it was, what Dr Pitcairn said of him in the forementioned verses:

'*Te moriente, novos accepit Scotia cives, Accepitque novos, te moriente deos*' [New people fill the land, now thou art gone, New gods the temples, and new kings the throne']

The nixt morning after the battle, the Highland army had more the air of the shattered remains of broken troops than of conquerours, for here it was litterally true, that 'The vanquished triumphed, and the victors mourned.' The death of their brave Generall, and the loss of so many of their friends, were inexhaustible fountains of grief and sorrow. They closed the last scene of this mournfull tragedy in obsequys of their lamented Generall and of the other Gentlemen who fell with him, and interred them in the church of Blair of Atholl with a real funeral solemnity, there not being present one single person who did not participate in the general affliction.

General Canon, who was the oldest officer there, took upon him the command of that melancholy army; and the third day after the battle, which was the same on which the rendezvouze had been appointed by the Lord Dundee, they were joyned by five hundred of Locheil's men, conducted by his son John and his cousine Glendissery, two hundred of the Stewarts of Appine, a party of M'Gregors, commanded by McGrigor of Roroe, two hundred and fifty of the M'Phersons, as many of the M 'Donalds of the Breas of Lochaber and Glencoe, and the whole men of Atholl; and haveing marched the day following to the Brea of Mar, they were likeways joyned by the people of that country, and by the Farquarsons, Frazers, with the Gordons of Strathdown and Glenlivet; so that the army amounted now to five thousand brave men. Besides these, the Northern Shires were all in arms, and the greatest part of the Low-country gentry, through all parts of the kingdome, were ready to joyn them, and expected their advance with impatience; and it was generally computed that, before they arrived at the Borders of England, they would be forty thousand men strong at least; so general was the inclination at that time to have restored King James. But so soon as Dundee's death was generally known, the scene changed, and all those mighty preparations, and that universall spirit of Jacobitism, vanished into nothing.

The first thing the new General attempted miscarried, for want of conduct; for, haveing detached a party of Struan Robertson's men, and some of those he had from the Brea of Mar, to Perth, with orders to seize a considerable quantity of meale and other provisions which the enemy had left there, they loytered so long after they had executed their orders, that M'Kay had intelligence of their being in those parts, and of the bad order they keept; and marching against them with a strong body of horse and dragoons, surprized and defeated them. It is true their loss did not exceed thirty men, and that they made good their retreat to the mountains, notwithstanding they were warmly pursued by a regiment of horse for many miles; yet it not onely exposed their want of conduct, but also showed that they were not invincible, as their late behaviour att the battle of Kilychranky made many people fondly believe they were.

M'Kay had so well accquanted himself with the abilitys and characters of their general officers, that he now boldly adventured to march against them with inferior numbers, though he had often fled from Dundee when he was att least equally strong; and advanced within a few miles of them. The neighbourhood of the enemy makeing it necessary for them to advise how they were to proceed, a councill of war was held in the old castle of Auchindown, where the first thing that fell under debate was, whither the Low-country officers, who acted as volunteers without any command, had a tittle to sitt and vote ? And a second question was started, whether or not they should fight M'Kay, whose strength consisted chiefly in horse, immediatly; or, if they should, in consequence of the commands they there received from King James, march to Kintyre and the Western Shires in order to suppress them ?

Locheill and the Chiefs argued strenuously against these officers haveing votes in their councill, for these reasons: 1st, They were unacquainted with the Highland discipline, customes, and manner of fighting, which, differing widely from what they were bred to among regular troops, might make their votes of pernicious consequence: 2dly, As it was unreasonable that simple Captains and subalterns, who brought no accessions of strength to the army but their own persons, should have equall powers with those that actually had regiments, or att least very considerable bodys of good men; so these officers being supernumerary to the Highland Chiefs, it was in their power to carry matters as they pleased, in prejudice of those who had the actual command. However, they agreed that the advice of these gentlemen should be demanded before any question of importance should be determined. As to the second poynt, Locheill, who took upon him to speak first, as being the oldest Chief and of most experience of any there, was of opinion, that, seeing they acted by King James his authority, his commands were not to be disputed; but that seeing his Majesty could not att that distance rightly understand the present scituation of his affairs here, he declared that they ought immediately to fight M'Kay, and then march Westward: That he saw no reason to delay fighting; they had the marrow of the High lands about them, flushed with victory, and eager for a new opportunity of exerting their valour, and of revenging the death of their late brave General, and of so many of their friends: That if they expected the Northern Shires and Lowland gentry to joyn them, they must doe something to incourage them, and to establish the reputation of their new General: That though the enemy had more horse, yet the late cowardly flight of those att Kilychranky had removed all the fears that the Highlanders had formerly of them; and that, for his part, he was so little apprehensive of them, that he was willing to fight all they had with his own Clan, assisted by the three hundred horse that had of late joyned them; and, in a word, if they lossed this opportunity, when M'Kay had no more than equall numbers, and began a cowardly retreat, when it was in their power to serve the King effectually, and gain honour to themselves, they would not onely loose their friends, their reputation, and their army, which would dayly diminish, but they would even become the jest and diversion of the kingdome.

Notwithstanding of what was said by Locheill, who was vigorously supported by the other Chiefs, it was carried in the councill of war, not onely that the Lowland officers should vote, but that they should march through Aberdeenshire, and over the Carnamount, without fighting the enemy. It will be hard to assign any other reason for this ridiculous march, excepting that of increasing their army by the conjunction of their Northern friends; but the event showed that they mistook their measures, for this retreat proved so fatall to their affairs, that the army became dispirited, and dayly diminished, when they saw every thing goe cross to their inclinations, and M'Kay's reputation encreased so, that the Government was in no further apprehensions of danger from that quarter.

Locheill, seeing the King's orders neglected, and that nothing was to be expected but fatigue from their ill-concerted measures, retired to Lochaber, in order to repose himself; and left the command of his men to his son, who continued with them dureing that inglorious campaign. Sir Donald [M'Donald of Sleat] and several others Mowed the same example, and left the care of their men to their nearest relations.

General Canon's army was now so reduced, that he was obliged to betake himself to the mountains; and so marched round the skirts of the Highlands, while M'Kay keept the plains below, every day in sight of each other, exchanging bravadoes to fight, but the one durst as little goe up to the high-ground, as the other descend to the low; so that they were in mutual fear of each other.

Thus they continued for the space of a month, till Canon had intelligence that the Cameronian regiment, so called from their following one Cameron, ane extravagant Fanatick Preacher, amounting to 1200 men, and commanded by Lieutenant- Collonel Cleland, had taken possession of Dunkell, with a designe to destroy the country of Atholl. To prevent this, he resolved to dislodge them, and might have easily effected it, had he used a little policy, and sent a small party of five or six hundred men to have trained them out of the town, where they were strongly fortifyed, and keept the army att a short distance, as he could easily have done, without the enemy's getting any intelligence, the people thereabouts being all his friends. But he, without regard to good policy, marched his army, which was now dwindled away to about three thousand men, in a full body to their trenches, beat the enemy's out-guards, and entering the town in the very face of their fire, without any thing to cover them, brock through all opposition, and rushed in upon such of them as were posted in the lesser houses, where they putt all they found to the sword without any mercy. Never was there, on any occasion, more resolution and less conduct shown than in this; and so surprizeing was their boldness, that they stood naked in the open streets exposed to the enemy's fire, and killed them in the windows, till they cleared the town of them, and drove them into the Marquess of Athol's house, which, being a strong place, they were not to be beaten from that post so easily. So little did their General reflect on what he was to doe, that though he had several cannons and field-pieces which had been taken from the enemy, yet when he came to apply them, he had not so many balls as he had guns. However, the bravery of his men, in a great measure, supplyed his defect in conduct; and had he had patience to have stood to the attack, he would infallibly have carried his poynt, and covered his weakness by the happy effects of a bold temerity; for, besides the loss of their two commanding officers, Cleland and Fullartoun[6], both brave men, who, with many others, were killed; notwithstanding of the strength of their post, their ammunition was all spent to a shott, and they upon the very poynt of surrendering att discretion, when the General commanded his men, even against their own inclinations, to retire.

Many of the Highlanders were wounded, but not above eighteen or twenty of them killed, which looked like a miracle; but the true reason was, that the enemy's shott somewhat resembled thunder, in this, that it had more noise than effect; for, observeing that the Highlanders putt their guns to their eye, and that they seldome mist their mark, they had not courage to expose themselves, but shott att random, whereby they did little execution. There were above three hundred of them killed, and a great many more wounded; but the greatest part of this slaughter was of those who were slain att first in the little and less tenible houses of the toun.

By this weak conduct, Canon suffered so extreamly in his reputation, and his men were so dispirited by his misimploying their valour, that, the winter now approaching, they dropt away, and he in the end obliged to retreat to Lochaber, where the remainder were dismissed, excepting the few Irishmen whom I have mentioned, and the Lowland officers, who were dispersed into such quarters as the country afforded. Nor did the Low-country gentlemen entertain, after this, the least hopes of success, unless they gott a General that was capable to conduct them. Several of them had proceeded so far, that they knew not how to re treat; and Mr Drummond of Balhaldys, who, from the beginning of the war, had kept close with them, haveing stole privately, after the affair of Dunkell, into his oun country, was, by a Letter from the Councill of the 20th December, thereafter commanded to attend their pleasure again [st] the 14th of the nixt month; which, in common prudence, obliged him and many others to make their submissions by accepting of the benifite of the indemnity, till King James his affairs should be better conducted, and in a more promiseing posture.

NOTES
[1] At this point Balhaldie interrupted the narrative to launch into a long-winded and tedious digression anent Glengarry, his antecedents, history, character and appearance.
[2] Another panegyric then follows, this time on the subject of Pitcurr.
[3] As they had failed to recover the body of their general at this point, this assertion must be taken as hyperbole.
[4] Stirring as it sounds there must be some doubt as to this. The regiment they are said to have

'cut off' was evidently not Hastings'; while Balhaldie claims that Locheil's people dished Mackay's, despite being so badly shot up. As discussed in the text it seems more likely that it may have been Sir Alexander Maclean's Regiment [unmentioned by Balhaldie] and Sleat's men who gave the regiment its quietus, not Locheil's.

[5]   Then follows another very lengthy panegyric, this time of Dundee, before moving on to the fate of lesser actors.

[6]   This is an error, John Fullartoun did not join the regiment until after Dunkeld, when he was promoted from the Earl of Leven's Regiment to replace Cleland as lieutenant colonel (he was later killed at Steinkirk in 1692 which may be the source of the confusion). The second field officer to die at Dunkeld was actually Major John Henderson.

Appendix VI

The Siege of Edinburgh Castle

Amidst all the excitement of Killiecrankie and Dunkeld it is easy to forget the four-month siege of Edinburgh Castle which lasted from 13 March to 14 June. The text below is transcribed from *The Siege of the Castle of Edinburgh 1689*, an eighteenth-century pamphlet reprinted by the Bannatyne Club in Edinburgh in 1828. Beyond the initials W.R. the author is unknown but he was evidently a member of the garrison and it has been conjectured was a Catholic chaplain:

> The Convention being assembled, the first thing resolved on was, that the Governour should be ordered in ther name to render up the Castle, and that he, with the officers of his profession, should withdraw themselves. Two members of the Convention came to intimate to him this order, bearing that he was to give his answear immediatly, and to obey the order within twenty-four hours. He asked time to give his answer, and thes deputed members returned without granting him time.
>
> The same day, the Earle of Dumfermleing (who had the Governour's sister to wyfe) came and told him that he foresaw the King's enemies would be masters in the Convention; and that he was resolved to leave it and retire himselfe. And after some measures concerted betwixt them for his Majesties service, he returned home to the North, where he ordinarily resided. The Governour having given him a writing, wherby he entreated all his friends, and commanded all his vassalls, to joyne and obey his brother-in-law, in all occasions he should judge proper for the King's service, and keeping the country under his obedience. He lykewise gave him ane order to Master Innes, his Master of Horses, to deliver

to the Earle of Dumfermling all the horses he should have neid of; which order Mr Innes obeyed, and followed the Earle, in company with the Earle of Dundie, togither with about thirtie other gentlemen of the Duke of Gordon's vassals.

After this, the Duke had notice, by severall billets sent him, that the Convention was resolved to set a pryce upon his head, if he refused to obey them; and the nixt day tuo Earles came deputed from it to the Castle, to know the Governour's last answer concerning the delyvery of it.

He thought it best for his Majesties service to enter upon terms of agriement with them, and drew up some articles to be presented to them; and amongst others, a generall indemnity for himselfe and his friends, both Papists and Protestants, with liberty to goe where they pleased, without being called in question for what was past; and that all those who would go beyond seas should have pasports. The deputies carryed thes articles to the Convention, and shortly returned to the Castle to know who were the friends the Governour spoke of in his articles; who told he should name them when the Convention had signed ther consent to his proposalls. After severall messages betwixt the Convention and the Castle, the Duke named all the clans of the Highlands, without specifying who were his friends or foes. This proposal did so offend one of the deputies, that he became very angry; and being returned to the Convention, would scarcely give accompt of his negociation to the president and others of the assembly.

Those very clans thereafter obtained more than the Duke desyred for them, though they had done a great daile of prejudyce to the kingdom in their marches and countermarches, which shews how little the Convention understood their bussiness, and yet they durst forfeit their King.

The Duke desired the message might be put in writing, and time allowed to advise; which being denied, his Grace sent the following answer to the Convention:

March 15. 1 am willing to comply with the commission I received by the Earls of Lothian and Tweeddale, as to my removal from the Castle of Edinburgh: though I cannot do it as a Papist, that being dangerous, and I not convicted; for I hope being in employment without taking the test (contrary to an Act of Parliament), is no conviction of Popery. I received, not long ago, a letter from the then Prince of Orange, desiring that I would leave the Castle of Edinburgh; which I promised to do, but expected certain reasonable time to be first granted to myself and garrison. I hope I have not merited so ill of my country, as that I may not be trusted with the castle, until a return come to this letter, which I expect every hour. But if that cannot be granted, barely on my promising not to molest or harm any person, especially those of this illustrious assembly, I proffer hostages, or bail to the value of £20,000 Sterling, for my peaceable deportment: Otherwise I expect, before my removal,

I. A general indemnity for myself and friends, both Protestant and Papist, as also absolute security for our lives and fortunes in time coming; with assurance that the same shall be ratified in the next ensuing Parliament.

II. A security for all Protestants of the garrison, who incline to stay in it, to continue in their employments; and for those who shall go out with me, either Protestants or Papists, to go beyond seas, or remain within the kingdom, as our occasion shall lead us.

III. That the garrison be completely paid off all bygone arrears, and have liberty to dispose of their goods within the castle as they please.

To which the Duke had this return:

The meeting of the Estates having considered the paper given in, and subscribed by the Duke of Gordon, in answer to their order do declare.

It is not the mind of this meeting, that the Duke, his officiating as governor of the castle, or of any other employment, or his quitting of his command at this time, shall import any acknowledgement or conviction against him, or those under him, of his or their being Papists.

Incontinently after, the Viscount of Dundie, did, by Cockburne younger of Lanton, a gentleman of quality and merit, advertize the Duke, that the Convention were instantly to give him a solemne and formall sumonds, by the heraulds with ther coats of armes : And the same hour came tuo heraulds, tuo pursevants, and tuo trumpeters sounding ther trumpets, and approaching to the walls, read with a loud voyce the summonds, by which the Governour is ordained, with all other Papists in the garrison, to remove themselves

It is also resolved, that the meeting of the Estates will not allow the Duke his keeping the government of the castle, either upon promise, bail, or hostages, for his peaceable deportment, until he get a return of the letter written by him to the then Prince of Orange.

It is likewise resolved, that the indemnity offered by the meeting of Estates, shall only extend to those belonging to the garrison, and their servants, either Protestants or Papists; and the persons who are to have the benefit of the said indemnity shall be expressly named, if the Duke desire it; and that the indemnity to be granted by this meeting shall contain a clause, that it shall be ratified in the next Parliament.

As to the last article of the paper, that those of the garrison who please to retire with the Duke, shall have liberty either to go out of the kingdom or stay in it, as they think fit; and shall have liberty to dispose of their goods, and have safe conduct granted to them for that effect, the same being desired before the dissolution of the meeting of the Estates; but that they may not take out with them any arms, ammunition, or store, but what they shall instruct properly to belong to them. And,

Lastly, it is agreed, that the officers and soldiers of the garrison shall have payment of their bygone arrears; but refuse to give them assurance of their being continued in employment.

It had been moved, and agreed to in the Convention, that the Duke should have safe conduct to come there in person, but he went not; and refused to give up the castle upon the terms offered; however, he sent a letter to the Viscount of Dundee to be communicated to the Convention, in which he condescended to resign his command to the Earl of Airly, his father-in-law, but the overture was rejected, thence immediatly, upon paine of treason. At the same tyme was read a proclamation, discharging the subjects to convers with or assist the Duke, or any under his command, that should remaine in the garison after that proclamation, whether Papists or Protestants; and promising a reward of sex months' pay, with ane indemnitie, to the Protestants in garrison, on condition they sould seaze the Duke and Papists persons, and delyver them up with the Castle into the hands of the Convention. The Duke spoke to the heraulds, and bid them tell the Convention from him, that he keept the Castle by commission from ther common master, and that he was resolved to defend it to the last extreamitie. In end, he gave some guinies to the heraulds to drink the King's good health, and all honest men's in the Convention, which they promised to doe; and he advysed them, in drollery, not to proclame men traittors to the State with the King's coats on ther backs; or at least they might turne them.

After the heraulds were gone, the Duke called the garrison togither, and caused the Ensigne publickly read the summonds to them, and then told them, they saw the danger they were to run; that for his own part, he would not be threatned from his duty to God and his Prince, and wes resolved to keep the Castle for his Majestie's service; that those who were not willing to hazard themselves with him might goe where they pleased, and have ther full arrears payed them, which he did. Wherupon Will Cahoune and Andrew Ford, gunniers, went away, having refused to obey in generall all ther superiour officers, though they were content to swear obedience to the Duke's commands; which was not accepted of, because of the bad example it might give. And the day following, John Auchmouty lietennant of the company, Arthur Forbess master gunnier, John Scot chirurgeon, John Crichton and Thomas Hume Serjeants, Alexander Kelman and John Cahoune corporalls, Oliver St Clair sutler, tuo drummers, and betwixt sixty and seavinty private centinells, left the garrison, notwithstanding ther oath few dayes befoir. They being gone, the Governour caused shut all the gates of the Castle, and disposed all things for defence.

The same day a gentleman out of Ireland came to the Castle, pretending to bring a letter from his Majestie, and assurances from the Duke of Tyreconnell to the Governour, that if he could keep the Castle six weeks, he should have ane army of 20,000 men at his command, when the Governour saw the letter, he found it was not directed to himselfe, bot to the Chancellour, and in his absence to the Archbishop, and in his absence to another; whereupon he made scrouple to open it. Bot one less scroupulous standing by, opened and read it, but saw no orders at all in it concerning the Castle. The gentleman who brought it was asked, if his Majestie was in Ireland when he came from thence, and he answered he was not. Then the Governour sent him with the letter to the Earle of Balcarras and the Viscount of Dundie.

Dureing thes transactions, John Gordon of Edintore was frequently employed to advertize friends of the circumstances of the garrison, and what necessaries were wanting, and especially Sir James Grant of Davey, advocat, whose predecessors had still followed the familly of Huntly in the King's service, during the civill warr in King Charles the first tyme, and shared with the same in sufferings on that accompt. Thir two gentlemen made it ther work to supply the Castle from tyme to tyme with those things they were advertised it stood most in need of; and though they did all was in ther power, yet any provisions came into the Castle during the siege were very inconsiderable. Francis Gairdin of Midstrath, John Innes, Henry Gordon, Andrew Ross, gentlemen, with some others, came into the Castle to remaine for its defence. And Sir James Grant, finding ane English lawyer, and afterwards Captain William M'lntosh of Borlum, goeing for Ireland, he gave instructions to each of them, representing exactly the condition of the Castle, and reasons why it could not be maintained longer than the beginning of June.

The garrison at that tyme consisted of the Grovernour, the liuetennant governour, the ensigne, four Serjeants, of whom one was sick, and about six score centinells, but without cannoniers and enginier, or chirurgeon, or drogues, or carpenter, or money. The garrison was formerly divyded into three squadrons, viz. The Governour's, the liuetennant's, and the ensigne's; but now the Duke cast them into two divisions, and one was commanded by the ensigne, and the other by Mr Gardin [of Midstrath, under his Grace]. The principle posts were the high guard house, the low guard, and sally port. One entire squade mounted each night, consisting of the captaine of the guard, tuo Serjeants, tuo corporalls, and about 40 centinells, besides the gentlemen voluntiers. Ther wer 8 centinell posts in the day tyme, and 17 by night.

March 16. The Duke sent a line to the Earle of Tweedale, entreating him to call at the garrison, hopeing what he had to communicate to him should not be disagrieable; but he came not.

The 17th day of March, one of the garrison deserted.

The 18th, the Convention made place guards about the Castle, to hinder the entry of any provisions, and to intercept any person that should come forth of it with any message. The same day the Governour sent out his horses with his coachman, who was apprehended and imprisoned.

The Governour went and visited the magazine of the Castle, and found only 8 score barrells of powder, in very ill order, and many of them not full; the generall or master of the artillery having removed all the rest, as is said above, and many of his company taking service under the enemies, (for himselfe did shortlie afterwards,) made known to them the small quantity of ammunition left in the Castle, with which it could no longer hold out.

This day the Cameronians, to the number of about 7000, lately come to Edinburgh to take the guarding of the Convention, drew up in the publick great streets of the city. Thes Cameronians (so called from one Cameron, a preacher, or famous ringleader among them) are the worst kynd of Presbyterians, who confyne the church to a few of the western shyres of the kingdome of Scotland; disclaime all Kings (save King Jesus) who will not worship God after ther way; think it ther duty to murder all who are out of the state of grace, that is, not of ther communion; in a word, who take away the second table of the Decalogue, upon pretence of keeping the first; and who are only for sacrifice, but for no mercy at all.

The same day Donald M'Donald, and tuo gentlemen of the name of Grant, came into the Castle, and brought a letter to the Governour, shewing ther were severall conspiracies forming against him, and that the King had wrote a letter to the Convention, which was read, bot no regaird had to it.

The day following, the Governour, with a telescope, perceaved some horsemen appearing on the north side of the toun, and drawing towards the castle. It was the Viscount of Dundie, who, seing the convention had resolved to renunce all alledgiance to their lawfull soveraigne, and laid asyde all kind of respect for him; he abandoned ther assemblie, and comeing to the foot of the rock, the Governour spoke to him from the top of the wall, and then went out and discoursed with him. Hee told what had passed in the convention at the receaving of the King's letter, and the small impression it made upon the members of that assembly. The Governour askit a sight of the letter; but Dundie had no copy, and the Governour never saw it. Then Dundie parted from the Governour and returned to his own pairty of about thirty or fourty horse, and went away with them towards his own dwelling beside Dundie. After that tyme, the Governour never receaved any letters from him.

March 19. The Duke having procured safe conduct for our ensign, sent him out this day with the following instructions:

I. You are to advise with Sir James Grant and Sir Thomas Gordon, my ordinary counsellor at law, and any other lawyer they shall think fit to call, how the officers and others in garrison can be secured in law, as to their lives and fortunes

II. It being altogether dangerous for me and my garrison to remove out of the castle, whilst the town is so crowded with vast numbers of strangers, who have already taken possession of posts formerly guarded by the town of Edinburgh, I desire the posts may be returned to the town, and the strangers removed.

III. Since so much aversion was expressed against some of the Highland clans being comprehended within the number of my friends, I am content to restrict it to twenty Protestants and twenty Papists, who are, or have been, in public employment; and this, besides those within the garrison.

IV. Since he was absolutely refused, that such Protestants as might incline to stay in the Castle, should be secured in their employments, I desire that such of them as are still here, shall have six months pay, besides what shall be due to them, for defraying their charges to any place, off or within the kingdom, whither their occasions shall lead them.

V. That after the place is given up, the Lieutenant-Governor may have the use of his lodgings for eight or ten days, for clearing accounts with the garrison; and that my servants and others may have a competent time for dispatching affairs within the Castle.

VI. That the officers and others may have liberty for themselves and servants to carry their swords within the town, and make use of horses and ordinary travelling arms in the country; and so long as I shall stay within the kingdom, that they may have their abode in any place of it, according to their interest and convenience.

VII. That my officers and soldiers may have the disposal of the stores, or a competent gratuity on that head.

VIII. That I may have a pass to wait on his Majesty any time within three months, to give him reason for putting this place into the Estates hands, and to return safely.

IX. That I have a guard of forty horse, of my own chusing, to attend me home; and that I may keep them together while I am in the kingdom: the like being granted to my grandfather at the pacification of 1645 or 1646. This, with the first and last articles of my former propositions, which were granted. The Ensign returned with this answer:

March 19. The meeting of the Estates having considered the instructions given in and subscribed by the Duke of Gordon to Ensign Winchester, annent the surrender of the Castle of Edinburgh, they do agree to the following articles.

I. That the Duke's officiating in the government of the Castle of Edinburgh, or in any other employment, or his quitting of his command at this time, shall not import any acknowledgement or conviction against him, or any person under his command, of their being papists; but that the Duke, and those persons that are at present in the garrison with him, and their servants, as well Papists as Protestants, shall have a full indemnity from the Estates for any thing done by them at any time against the laws of the kingdom; and that the same indemnity shall contain the names of ilk ane of the said persons, if they desire the same; and a clause, that it shall be ratified in the next Parliament.

II. The Estates do allow that Mr Winchester do consult Sir James Grant and Mr Thomas Gordon, or any other lawyers they shall please to call, annent the security to be given to the Duke and his officers, soldiers, and others within the garrison, as to their lives and fortunes; the same being always done in presence of one of the members of the meeting.

III. That the Duke and those of the garrison that shall please to retire with him, shall have full liberty to go out of the kingdom, or to stay in it : and to dispose of their goods, which they shall insist to belong to themselves, not being arms or ammunition, as they shall think fit; and they shall have safe conduct for that effect, the same being desired before the dissolution of the meeting of the Estates.

IV. That all the officers and soldiers of the garrison shall have punctual payment of their bygone arrears; and the Lieutenant-Governor shall have a secure place with a guard appointed for him to stay in the town for eight days after the surrender, for clearing accounts with the garrison; and that the Duke's servants, not exceeding three at a time, shall be allowed the liberty to go up to the castle and return as they please, for the said space of eight days, for carrying away their goods and dispatching their affairs in the Castle.

V. That the Duke, and those who are presently with him in the garrison, shall be allowed, during their abode in the town of Edinburgh, to carry their swords, and to keep their horses and ordinary arms, as any of the rest of the lieges are allowed to do by law.

VI. That the Duke shall have the guard of forty horsemen, to be named and commanded as the Estates shall be pleased to order; who shall be maintained upon the public charge, and shall have orders to carry the Duke home to the place of his ordinary residence in the country, and immediately to return; the Duke finding caution, that the said guard shall not be any way hindered or molested in their return.

VII. The estates do agree to give a gratification to the officers and soldiers in the garrison, according to the condition they shall find the stores in, at the time of surrendering the Castle.

The Cameronians had now blocked up the Castle, and begun a small entrenchment in widow Livingston's yard, westward, very near the Castle; and taken up for posts the Weigh-house, the West Port, and St Cuthbert's Church.

This night another of our men deserted.

March 21. The Ensign (having safe conduct) was this day again sent to manage the treaty with the Convention; and brought back an account, that they agreed that the forty horse attend his Grace for fourteen days, to go home, and the Duke to name them, including his servants; but that they disperse within twenty-four hours after his homegoing. That they meet him on the other side of the Burnt Island Ferry, whether the Estates would conduct him. That they shall not join the Lord Dundee, &c. and the Duke to find surety for that effect. That, at the surrender of the Castle, the avenues thereof be guarded with the town guards, together with such of the Earl of Levin's Regiment as he shall appoint. That Gordons of Auchintoule and Glasturin be indemnified for acting in public employments; and five priests, now in prison, to be named by the Duke, to have passes, they finding caution to remove out of the kingdom within twenty days. That the commissionate officers carry their ordinary fire-arms, beside their swords; and the soldiers to be paid for their fire-arms by the Estates, &c.

Sometyme after this, the Governour desyreing speach of some without. Captain Lawder, who commanded the blockade, was sent to him to know what his pleasure was. By him, he sent a lyne to the magistrates of the toun, intimating his desire to continow a good understanding with them; and that the Captaine sould show the convention, he desired a safe conduct to be granted for Mr Winchester, Ensigne of the Castle, a young gentleman of wit and courage, which being granted, he sent him to propose some articles of treaty with the Convention; and with him he writes a letter to the President Duke Hamiltoun, in these termes:

May it please your Grace,

The singular prooftes your Grace and the States have bein pleased to give me of your kindness, would highten (if possible) the concerne I have alwayes had for the good of my country and countrymen Permit me, then, [most humbly,] to lay before your Grace and the States, the imminent danger to which this poor kingdom is exposed, to become very soon the theatre of the most bloody and irreconceallable warre that hes bein in Europe this age, if not prevented by extraordinary prudence. Permitt me likewise to represent, that of all the ancient nobilitie and gentry of which this illustrious assembly is composed, perhaps ther is not one whose selfe or predicessors hes not receaved reiterated marks of his Majestie's or ancestours bounties and clemency. Should we then, for the misfortunes of a four years reigne, forget the benefites we have receaved from one hundreth and ten Kings and Queins. For my oun pairt, it's known to severalls of the Estates, and particularly to your Grace, the severe usage I have had thes three years from the court, yet, I wold lay doun my lyfe to procure a good imderstanding between his Majestie and his subjects, as I most sincerely and affectionatly offer my endeavours for procureing it. And if the Estates sall think fit I shall wait on his Majestie, who is now in Ireland. I hope, as all Scotland will most dutifully assert the just prerogatives of the crowne, the King will be pleased to setle the property, religion, and liberties of the subject on such sure foundations, that they shall never be shaken by the avarice and ambition of evill ministers. May it please your Grace, I thought myselfe bound in conscience to represent to you and the Estates what this paper containes; and it is with much respect that I am

your Grace's most obedient and most humble servant.

The Duke desired this letter might be recorded by the Convention, but it was refused; and not finding any rationall correspondence from them to his proposalls, he breaks of all farder negotiation with them, and makes bonfires in the Castle for the King's arrivall in Ireland, dischargeing all the cannons thryce, in token of rejoyceing on that accompt.

[About this time the Cameronians had broken ground a little southward of their other trench. We beat a parley; and a cessation for some time was agreed to which gave an opportunity to our men to cast up a work at the sally port, to secure them from the enemies' small shot, to which they had been greatly exposed.]

The 25th March, the Cameronians were relieved by General Major Mackayes men, sent from England, being three regiments, twelve companyes in each regiment. The Cameronians had the thanks of the Estates, and a publick act passed acknowledging their good service.

With Mackay came cannons, provisions, armes, and ammunition, and he caused furnish store of packs of wooll, to make his approaches in order to the siege of the Castle. He had formerly served in the King's army, and had a pension of his Majestie before the Prince of Orange's coming to England; but some months before, he declared to the King that he could serve him no longer, wherupon his pension was stopped; yet thes of his clan or trybe had given good proofe of ther loyalty during the troubles of the Covenant. He had bein formerly the Duke of Gordon's friend, and therefoir the Duke wrote to him, shortly after his arryveall, proposeing a conference with him, to try if he could induce him to returne to his Prince's alledgeance. To which Mackay answered, that he could not accept of that conference without tuo privy coucellours were present at it. The Governour replyed, he would discourse with him alone only, and that he might judge his party did not confide in him, since they would have him accompanyed with tuo witnesses.

[John Gordon having been sent out of the garrison to bring in a surgeon and carpenter (for as yet we had neither) one Thomas, an English surgeon, did undertake; but approaching the Castle, in order to be received at the sally port, his courage failed him, and so he returned back to the town.]

The penult of March, the Governour being advertised that the enemies were casting up ground on the west side of the Castle, came with officers in the night tyme upon the rampart that lookt that way; and by the light of some squibs throwne perceaved ther approach: wherfore he made place the cannon in battery, and discharge upon the works to destroy them, which had good effect. He continued fireing upon them the nights following, which retarded ther labour; but this continuall fire did consume much of his ammunition. The Castle was so ill furnished of things necessary, that the Governour was oblidged to send out seaven men under Mr Gardin's command to make some provisions; upon which a party of the besiegers deserted their posts in the trenches, and Mr Gardin returned safe with his men, bringing with them some loads of straw, wherof ther was need, to charge the cannon; wherfore the besiegers would thenceforth perniitt no kind of provisions to pass near the Castle into the city.

[A parley was beat to send in some packs of cards, but denied. They now began to play upon us with bombs they had brought from Stirling Castle, but we received no great damage by them.]

Upon the 3d of Apryll some of the besiegers were perceaved to be lodged about the old towre of Cottis on the west; and severall great guus were fired upon them, which beat doun ane old wall, and did execution. About this tyme, John Gordon brought in a brewar, and tuo Irish gentlemen, and lykewise one John M'Pherson, son to Kylyhuntlie, one of the Duke's vassalls in Badenoch, a very smart, ingenuous, and darring young man, who rendered good and faithful service in this siege. [As we perceived them coming, we fired warmly upon the besiegers' guards at the west port, and freed them from that post. Sir George Lockhart, Lord President of the Session, having been barbarously assassinated on Easter Sunday, by one Cheesly of Dalry, a parley was this day beat by the besiegers, for a cessation during his interment in the Greyfriar's church, and readily granted.]

6th of Apryll. The besiegers had now, with the losse of men, finished a battery at the Castle of Collops, ane old ruined tower south of the garison, and planted thereon two cannon, 18 pounders; but in a few hours they were both dismounted. Captaine Dumbarr fired tuo of the seaventein bombs upon the besiegers' battery, but without success.

[This day we had an account that John Gordon (who had been sent out with letters) was made prisoner, but that he had dropt the letters he had in custody, and so they fell not into the enemy's hands. His Grace caused cut a part of the bridge at the entry to the garrison.]

11th day. On Mr Scott went in publickly to the garrison in this maner; he brought the besiegers' advanced centinell along the Castle-hill with him upon pretence of speaking to a gentleman in garison about important bussiness, and to returne immediatly. When they were come near the Castle gate, Mr Scott called for the Ensigne, and before they tuo had exchanged many words, he bid the centinell fairweell, and was receaved in at the gate. The centinell was invited to follow him because of his danger in returning, but the poor fellow, being drunk, went to his post, where he was immediatly seazed, and hang'd tuo dayes after.

[A carpenter having undertaken to serve in the garison this day, we perceived him coming with five Irishmen, and put ourselves in a posture to secure them, in case any of the besiegers appeared; but the carpenter, treacherously or timorously, went back, and delivered himself prisoner, discovering those who had engaged him: upon which some were secured and others fled.]

The same day the garrison heard a great noise in the toun, mixt with the sound of trumpets, and thought the heralds were coming with a new summonds to the Governour to render the Castle; but afterwards it was found to be on the accompt of the proclamation of the Prince of Orange, in quality of King of Scotland.

Some persons, who have no good will to the Governour, took occasion to blame him for not fyreing upon the toun, att the tyme of this proclamation, but it is easy with reason to refute this objection, though envy and malice will still be barking:

1st. Neather the Governour, nor officers of the Castle, knew certainely before, what was the ground of this solemnity.

2do. The place of the toun, at the cross, where the proclamation was made, was out of sight of the Castle, and covered from it by the Tolbooth, or common prison; and a great many other buildings stand in a right lyne betwixt the Castle and the Cross, so that the cannon bullets could not touch any person about the cross.

3rd. The Governour's duty being to defend the Castle the King had entrusted to him, he could not judge it prudent to consume to no purpose the powder, wherof he had so small quantity.

4to. Although he had known what wes the occassion of the solemnity, he might have judged he could not be blamed in following the example of Generall Ruthven, who had formerly defended the Castle of Edinburgh, dureing the Rebellion against Charles the First, and was made Earle of Forth and Brentford for his good and faithfull service. He sustained the siege a whole year against the toune, and yet did not fyre upon the buildings, nor upon the Parliament House, dureing the siege; and his conduct in this was approved severall years afterwards by the Duke of Lawderdale, then High Commissioner for the King in Scotland.

5to. His fyreing on the toun could not hinder the proclamation, much less the occassion of it, and it might have done prejudice to those who were no less sorry at it than he was; for the rable had threatned from the beginning of ther commotion, that if the Popish Duke, should fire on the city, during ther insolencies against Papists, they should leave non of that profession alyve in and about the toun; which was a very easy matter for them to execute : And the pillaging of ther goods and houses, and insolencies, upon the persons of those that had misfortune to fall in ther way, gave too much ground to beleeve they would have made good their threatnings upon such a provocation.

Soe that those who blame the Duke of Gordon for not fyreing on the toun at this occassion, would be puzled to assigne any rationall motive that might have oblidged him so to do, or exeemed him from the censures of prudent men if he had done it : All they could alledge would be, that he should have showen his just indignation and horrour at the Convention's procedure in prejudice of his Soveraigne; but could that demonstration of his displeasure have brought any advantage to his prince's cause or affaires; or could any judicious person have thought it of such weight, as to be put in the ballance with the prejudice and trouble, many of the King's weil-wishers would have sustained; and might not the Convention justly have flouted at him with the poet's words, *vana sine viribus ira*.

[The passage by the sally port, that we had formerly made use of for sending out and receiving intelligence, being now closely blocked up by the besiegers, we shut up the entry, and filled it with earth; and we had by this time discovered a new passage, more safe, from the gate of the Castle over the north loch. When any person was to come in to us (of which we generally got exact information, sometime before, by a sign in a window of the city from Mrs Ann Smith, grandchild to Dr. Atkins, late Lord Bishop of Galloway), or went out, we sent a party of six men, commanded by a gentleman, to conduct them over the loch; and when got in safe to the garrison, we gave the signal to Mrs Smith, by firing a musket off the half-moon,]

About the 20th of Apryll, Mr Smith, the Duke's chirurgeon at Gordon Castle, being sent for by his Grace, came into the Castle of Edinburgh to the great comfort of the garrisone, being a man weill skilled in surgery, and both very loyall and courageous.'

The 29th, Henry Gordon having being sent out for intelligence, returned after two dayes with Liuetennant James Hay, John Macky, and one Launders ane Irishman; having by reason of the darknes of the night, lost other three of their company, who had designed to serve in the garrison. The besiegers drained the Loch on the north side of the Castle and toun, to divert the springs from the wells in the Castle; but their designe took no effect.

The 9th of May, the Castle fired some great gims upon a hous near the enemies battery, having discovered soldiers in it; and, artillery we were informed killed severalls in it. The enemies began to cast up a battery northward of the garrison, at the Multrasie-hill.

[This was the day they had appointed for a public thanksgiving; but we could perceive no great demonstrations of joy amongst them by bells or bonfires.]

The 11th of May, William Urquhart came into the garison and went out againe for some necessaries, and returned after four dayes with John Falconer, bringing with them, by Sir James Grant his moyen, a rope for mounting the cannon, which came very seasonably, for they had been necessitate to make use of the well rope; so ill was the garrison provydit of things necessary for its defence.

Some days after, John Gordon obtained his liberty, there being no proof against him, and returned to the garrison with three Irishmen and Mr Smith (the Duke's surgeon), to the great comfort of all therein; for though providence had hitherto protected our men from wounds, they did not fancy themselves invulnerable; and many of them had sickened by this time. They informed that the beseigers' great bombs were arryved from England, and that ther shells weighed above a hunder weight. That Sir James Grant above mentioned, was made close prisoner, for corresponding with the castle. The said W^{ll}. Urquhart was killed with Ensigne Winchester afterwards, at the water of Boyn in Ireland, in their Prince's service.

While the enemies carried on ther works and ther approaches, the Governour beat doun the parapets, which were but tuo foot high, that he might pnt his batteries in security against the enemies cannon. And having no cannoniers, he choysed twelve of the most vigorous of the soldiers to be employed in the service of the cannon, imder the direction of Captaine Dumbar, who knew most of artillery of any in the Castle.

All the artillery the Castle had, was a peice of 42 pound ball, one of 36 pound, four of 24 pound, one of 18, and tuo of 12; all these of brass, and besides them, severall of iron, of 24, of 16, of 12 pound balls, but not much worth. Ther were lykewise some litle feeld peices, and a morter peice of 14 inches of calibre, and 15 bombs.

The Castle was not in a condition to make a sally, by reason of the small number of soldiers, a part of whom had no inclination for the service, and would have laid hold on that occasion to desert; and those that were faithfull happening to be killed, the Governour would have been left to the discretion of mutiniers, who, finding themselves the stronger party, would have undoubtedly betrayed him.

About this tyme the Governour receaved letters from the Earle of Dumfermling, who was in the north with the Viscount of Dundie, showeing they had about 100 gentlemen on horse with them; and that at St Johnstone, they had surprysed, and seazed the Lairds of Blair and Pollock, with some other officers of the enemies, while they were making their levies; and had got also some litle money in hands of the collector of the publick impositiones; and were, with the prissoners and the horses they took, returned againe to the mountaines, where they had neid of some orders from the Governour; who gave a returne to the Earle of Dumfermline's letters, and satisfied all his desires, to the end they might be in a condition to send releefe to the Castle before the first of June, judgeing he could hold out no longer without he got succours. He gave the same advertisement to the rest of his friends who adhered to the King's interest, and all this with advyce and concurrance of the Lieutennent Goveruour.

The 17th of May the Governour caused sound the wells, and found the high well only 10 foot deep, and the other wells were dry.

May 18. This night Mr Macpherson and one of the Duke's footmen were sent out. 'We now kept no men at the high guard house, which had been hitherto our main guard; for all were posted at the sally port and low guard.

On Sunday 19th, the enemy haveing got their new artillery planted, about 10 a'clock at night they began to fyre upon the Castle with their great bombs, from a battery they had raised from the west corner of the toun wall. They had planted tuo morter peices, and threw the bombs in pairs; but all of them went over the Castle, or fell short of it at the West Port, not without dammage to the houses of the toun; or splite upon the top of the wall of the Castle, where ther was a centinell, who brought some fragments of it to his comrades. [I cannot say whose work the besiegers were about, but they never failed to ply it hard on the Lord's day : upon which one of our Highlanders observed, that, though he was apt to forget the days of the week, yet he well knew Sunday, by some mischief or other, begun or hotly carried on by our reformers.

Upon ther fireing, the Castle gave them several! great guns pointed to ther bomb battery, but without success, the morter peices standing very low, and not requyreiug ports, wherupon the garrison thought best to spaire ther powder on that occassion.

The Governour ordered all in the garrison to remove ther lodgings to the vaults, and took himselfe to one lykewise; and about the same tyme he became sickly, and continued so for some days : Notwithstanding wherof, the same night, when the besiegers began to play with their bombs, he went with Captaine Dumbar and others to the sally port, where he discoursed over the wall with one of the enemies centinells, but could learne little from him. [However, som of our men would daily divert themselves in drolling the besiegers; and there were amongst them those that seemed to favour the King's interest, and would often begin discourses to that purpose, in Irish, with some of the Highlanders, but frequently were interrupted by their commanders.]

20th May. About one a'clock in the morning, when they had ceased from fireing ther bombs, ther fell much snow, which, notwithstanding the season of the year, did ly a great part of the day tuo foot high. The soldiers gathered the snow, and put it into vessells, which served them for water, tho very unwholsome, for fear the wells would faile. [Thus nature seemed to suffer at this unnatural bombarding of his Majesty's fort with his own bombs, and by his natural subjects too.

This day they fired no bombs by reason of the storm.

This night Mr Macpherson and the Duke's servant returned.

21st May. About 10 a'clock at night the besiegers fell to work againe with ther bombs, and continued till after 12 a'clock, having fired about 16. One of them ruined the stair of the church; another falling on the rock at the back of the lower guard hous, tumbled doun whole on the soldiers upon duty, and one Duncan Grant thinking the danger past, went near to look to it. It broke beside him, but he sustained no more prejudice by it save a litle of his hearing for 24 houres.

After this the soldiers became better acquainted with the bombs, and could judge by ther elevation wherabouts they would fall: Some of them did break in the aire, others were smothered in the earth, wherewith the parapets were only backt, six of which they digged for and found whole. The Governour appointed a centinell on the Hauke hill, to give notice so soon as he saw the mortar peice fyred, and before the bomb was at its elevation, the word, viz. a bomb, would be thorough the garison, one takeing it instantly from another, so that every one might be on his guard before it fell.

22d May. Some of the besiegers from the Castle hill, the West Port, and other advanced posts, as also from the windows in the toun, fired upon the soldiers in the garrison, which provocked them to fyre at the besiegers, when they perceaved them in the streets; killing a centinell at the Castle hill, and casually wounding some persons not concerned. The Duke had alwise given strict orders not to fyre towards any part of the toun, but only at the batteries, trenches, and guards, without the toun, wherby the Castle was block up; and at such as were perceaved going to or comeing from the said batteries, guards, or trenches. Yet contrary to his knowledge, these his orders were sometymes transgressed, especially meetting with provocatione of fyreing from the streets and windows of the town.

By this tyme ther was much timber work in the Castle brocken by the bombs, and many of the soldiers being halfe naked, it fell out very seasonably, to be fire[wood.] The Governour had caused gather the splinters of the bombs to returne upon the besiegers in caice of ane assault.

23 May. A gunner's wife falling in labour, the Governour caused beat a parley to send in a midwyfe, which was refused; [but the gentlemen authorised to treat, proposed to send the woman out, to be taken care of. But this being so nearly related to the known jest of one, who finding himself too near a warm fire, proposed to remove the chimney, we did not suspect them to be in earnest. However, the poor woman was safely brought to bed.]

The Governour having observed a work cast up the mght befoir on the street about the weigh hous, proposed a parley to speak about the removall of it. The besiegers pretend it was done by the tounsmen to secure them from shott. His Grace demonstrated, that any defence ther could not save the toun, though it were sex story high, and declaired he knew not of any fireing that way; and promised, that upon removeing ther work, ther should be no ground of complaint thenceforth upon that head; otherwayes, not knowing the designe in it, he would be oblidged, in defence of the garrison, to fire at any work were cast up within the reach of his cannon; so that by ther fault the toun might suffer against his inclination. But the besiegers were so little concerned for the toun, that they would not condescend to demolish it, nor permitt the toune major to speake with the Duke, though he was seen comeing up the Castle hill for that purpose. After they had gone and returned severall tymes, and nothing concluded on, ther were people perceaved throwing it doun, and ther was no further trouble about it.

Whilst the Duke and ther officers were treating about this at the Castle gate, the besiegers fyred thrie bombs towards the low guard at the same gate; wherupon a gentleman in garrison said to some without, I judge we are in greater danger by your faith (broken by fyreing under parley) than by your works, (alluding to the work cast up, then under debate.) Att this parley, they told the Duke they had ane engineer could throw 100 bombs at once upon the garrison. Wherunto he replyed. He should be very glad it were put in practice, for at that rate he should be soon rid of them.

This night they fyred about 20 bombs, some falling within the court, and one within the great magazine; two upon a brasse gun, which only broke her wheele.

[About eleven this night a soldier's wife in garrison was sent out.]

24th May. The besiegers began first to fire their bombs in the day time, when they were the more dangerous, because not so easily perceaved as in the night. About 8 a'clock at night, a bomb split in the low halfe moon, amongst the soldiers, rankt in order to be releeved, but without any hurt.

[This night the soldier's wife returned.]

25th day. They had now got the elevation of the Castle exactly, and severall bombs were throwne into the place, which defaced most of the upper roumes, as also the church, magazine, &c., and severall small armes were broken.

[This afternoon we discovered a fleet of Dutch doggers making up the Frith, and concluded they were chased by the French fleet, but it proved a mistake. About eleven at night Henry Gordon was sent out.]

Sunday 26th day. The besiegers having finished their new battery northwards of the Castle, began early this morning to fire with three cannon (two of them 24-pounders) upon the pallace and gun-ports of the high halfe moon. They beat down the balcony of the top of the wall: Most of the balls split in pieces; nor were they sparing of ther bombes on the Lord's day, especially in tyme of divyne service, as much bent to doe ill, as the Scribes and Pharisees were to hinder the doeing good on the Sabbath. But the church in the garrison being ruin'd by the bombes, the soldiers heard sermon in a vault, [under the room which was the powder magazine before the siege.]

27th day. They fyred briskly both from the north and south batteries with ther cannon, but threw no bombes; and the garrison burned very litle powder in exchange, designed to save some barrells for the solemnity of the 29th.

About this tyme the Governour had communicated to him the contents of a letter, from a persone worthy of credit, from Ireland, which deprived him of all hopes of succours from thence; att which he was so much the more surprysed that the French fleet had beat that of England at Bantry Bay; which victory made the King's friends in Scotland hope for a speedy supply.

28th May. Tuo bombs fell thorow the leads, and split in the store-house, where thrie or four soldiers were receaving ther allowance off drink, but did no other damage, save the losse of the ale, which oblidged the garrison to drink water for some dayes, till more ale was brewed. The same afternoon, a bomb haveing fallen into the roume where the publick records were keipt, occassioned the beatting of a parley in the garrison. And the Duke sent a letter to the Lord Ross, giveing him ane accompt of the accident that had happened, threatning losse to the kingdome in generall, and desyred to speak with his lordship about the matter. The Lord Ross would not come, but a Captaine was sent from Duke Hamilton, to whom the Governour proposed the removeing of the records to another roume, at the sight of some commissionated by the Estates. He told the Captaine lykewise, that he was to put out the royall flag, but hoped nobody would be surprysed at it, being only on accompt of the solemnity enjoyned that day, by a standing Act of Parliament, for the restoration of the royall lyne after Cromwell's usurpation.

Immiediatly after the captaine wes gone for the 2d tyme about the matter of the records, the enemy fyred tuo cannons from the north batterie. The Duke a litle befoir had caused draw out the ball from most of the great guns, and had fired them with powder only for the solemnity. But upon the unexpected breaking of the parley, the balls were put in again and discharged at the besiegers batteries: So the publick records of the nation lay still where they were, att the wilfull hazard of the besiegers bombes, notwithstanding all ther pretensions for the publick good.

[This night Henry Gordon returned, and brought an account, that one of the besiegers mortar-pieces had split; and that the great leaders in the Reformation, upon appearance of the Dutch doggers, got together horses, attendants, arms, &c., and made vast preparations, as if they had been to fly to, or for the King's host.]

29th May. The garrison observed the solemnity of the day with bonfyres and some fyre works; when the besiegers threw bombes, the Castle returned them squibs, and chearfully drank a health to the King, Queen, and Prince of Walles, in a mortifyeing liquor. The besiegers with their bombes aymed cheifely at the bonfires of the Castle, which seemed to them a publick upbraiding of their disloyalty. But at other occassions they aymed at the pallace, which gave occassion to the Govemour to say, they medled too litle with the walls, if they resolved to take the Castle by assault, and too much with the lodgings, if they intended to get and keep it long upon capitulation.

[Lieutenant Hay, being under some indisposition, had leave to go out this night; and the soldiers wife, (who had been sent out a few days before, and returned) was to have gone after him upon some message from the Duke; but she deferred her journey on pretence she was afraid of the bombs, of which they fired many this night.

May 30. This night the soldiers wife was again ordered out, but would not stir, pretending the night was too clear.]

May 31. About one a'clock in the morning, some of thes on the low guard heard the besiegers at work on the south syde of the Castlehill, and shortly after they could perceave ground broken at a small distance from the low halfe moon: Upon which it was resolved to send out a party of fourtein men to beat the enemy from it. But a debate happening betwixt the gentlemen of the tuo squades, each pretending a right to be of the party, the Governour discharged the intended sally.

This night, Mr Ross went out, and with him Ochterlonie's wife (who was [ordered] out tuo severall nights before, but both tymes deferred to goe, upon frivolous excuse). And at the same tyme one Joannet Cunniughame went upon some message from the Ensigne; and as the soldiers were bussied in seing them over the North Loch, one Robison a serjeant, a Papist, and Irishman borne, who had bein Serjeant in the King's service, had refused to serve under the Prince of Orange, and begged through all England to be quit of that service, and had come into the Castle on hazard of his lyfe; one Paterson, a corporall; one Ochterlouny, the woman's husband that was sent out, and tuo centinells, deserted. She had got 12 or 14. crounes to bring in drogues for the use of the garrison, who now perceaved she had bein accessory to the treachery, and that her delayes from one night to another, on frivolous pretences, were only to watch ane opportunity till the deserters sould have the low guard; (for the souldiers changed posts every tyme they mounted,) and, consequently, all advantages of ane escape : For the corporall had altered the muster roll of centinells, to get the knaves packt together for ther game, and they could easily get over the wall wher ther post was, [and Robison had the custody of the key of the wicket of the outer gate, and actually carried it with him.]

This desertion did much discourage the garrison; for, besides the discovering of the secreit passages, correspondence, and weaknesses, it proved a great stumbling block to those who understood litle, or had but a superficiall concerne in the cause or Governour. Wherfore, immediatly after the desertion, one Runcyman, the Governour's footman, was dispatcht to the toun, to give all correspondents notice, that they might abscond, and had orders to returne by the North Loch passage, against tuo or thrie nixt afternoon.

The 1. June, about four in the afternoon, he was perceaved returning that way with his sword drawen; and the garison having planted some great gunes towards the besiegers guards, did with them and small shot fyre so warmely, that they thought it most fit to let the footman returne safe into the Castle. He gave account that he had bein arrested the night before be the besiegers' guards, and before he could get liberty, centinells were planted at the lodgings of Mistress Ann Smith, (grand chyld to the late Dr Atkins Bishop of Galloway), who corresponded with the garrison by signes, from a window looking towards it from the city; that Mr Hay was seazed in his chamber, in the meane tyme he was there to advertise him of the danger bot the footman passed for Mr Hay's servant, and escaped under that pretext; that the Governour's letters, and others from the garrison, were in the enemyes hands, bot most of them were written obscurely, and had fained or no subscriptions.

The footman returning safe to the Castle in sight of the enemies, [and they fancying he had some extraordinary message in charge,] did so picque them, that they fired incessantly from four to 8 a'clock; and in that space did throw upwards of fourty bombs into the garrison. The gentlemen of the garrison had delayed ther dinner, expecting the footman's returne; and after his arryveall, the cloath being laid in a closet one pair of stairs up in the pallace, (where most of them had dyetted hitherto,) it was by meer accident removed to a vault; and before dinner was weell begun, a bomb burst in the closet, and tore to peices everything therin. Another burst in the kitchen among the servants, without hurting any. One split on the top of the pallace, and broke the firelock in a centinell's hand, but himselfe suffered noe dammage; and another, falling through the leads into the roumes of the pallace, broke a door; and John Stewart of Bogs, a very stout and honest gentleman of the Duke's family, was sore wounded in the face, and lost ane eye by the splinter of it.

Before this, ther had bein no creature wounded in the garrison with all the enemyes cannons and bombs, save only a cow of the Liuetennant Governour's by a musquet shot, which was great part of the fresh provision they had dureing the siege, whatever report went abroad about it.

The besiegers set up a flag of orange colour on their north battery as a signe of joy, conceaved, from the notice given them by the late deserters of the weak condition of the garison.[1]

The Convention seazed all those in toun, who had keept correspondence with, and given intelligence of the garrison; men and women; the Lady Largo; Mistres Ogilvy; Joannet Cunninghame; but they were most cruelly bent against Mistres Smith and Mr Hay. This deprivall of correspondence with the toun did discourage the garrison extreamly.

Att releeving the guards at night, the Govemour spoke to the tuo squades severally to this purpose: That his enemyes must acknowledge he had imdertaken the defence of this place, and declared for the King, when all Brittaine seemed to have abandoned his interest; and had done so, only upon a principle of conscience and loyalty : And as conscience determined him then to one act of justice, so it oblidged him now to study the preservation of all those in garrison, which he reckoned another; and then addit, Gentlemen, let me assure you, I doe not use to breake promises to you; if we be not releeved in a competent tyme, I will capitulate, and every one of you shall have as good termes as myselfe.

[The whole garrison unanimously declared their abhorrence of the desertion, though they could not be ill pleased to get rid of the company of rogues and cowards; and that they were firmly resolved to live and die with his Grace in defence of this place, for his Majesty's service.

There were now some alterations made in posting our men. The main guard was kept at the sally-port; and six centinells, commanded by a gentleman, were posted a little eastward. At the low guard we had two gentlemen, with a serjeant, corporal, gunner, and nine soldiers; one part of which were posted in the lower half moon, and the other in Crichton's yard; besides five centinels, commanded by a gentleman, at the portcullis].

The beseigers discharged all further treating but by the white flag. About eleven at night Mr Ross returned safe, notwithstanding the search made for him upon the deserters' information. As he came towards the North Loch he perceaved a small party of the besiegers, on the other syde, advancing towards the garrison to intercept him (the nights being then neir the shortest at the summer solstice, and the twilight continueing all night); but tuo of the garrison appearing on Wallace Tower, they retired to ther guards.

[We beat a parley, and his Grace seemed to entreat for favour to Robison and the other deserters, as if they had been sent out by order, and occasionally fallen into the besiegers hands, on purpose to procure them the harder measure; but it took no effect. And now they discharged all further treating except by the white flag.]

2d of June. Sunday, [between 11 and 12] at night, the garrison wes allarmed, some hundreds of the besiegers being discovered in the corn feilds very near the Castle northwards; and upon misinformation of a boy in the garrison, that they had begun ane assault, the drums beate, upon which all the soldiers not upon guard ran towards the sally-port halfe naked, with ther armes, but without any command. Mr Gardine, being captaine of the guard, sent to advertise the Duke that ther was no danger: Bot he was abroad before the messenger arrived; and such was his care of the garrison, that he could not be perswaded for some tyme to returne to his lodging.

The souldiers that were not upon duty, were ordered to attend in a vault until farther orders. The Lieuetennant-Governor took a halbert, and with the Ensigne went the rounds till morning; and Mr Gardine used such dilligence, that he wes not above halfe ane hour togither from any post; and the very women appeared at the walls to defend them. The garrison fired very warmely on thes men of the besiegers with great and small shot, and they quickly retired.

3d day. Airly in the morning, they were perceaved to have brocken ground, where the garison first discovered them; yet stayed not to make any lodgement; and ther disorder could be conjectured by the great number of faggots which lay scattered, as if they had been sowen, along the corn feilds, where they had marched, or rather run away.

The same day the besiegers took up a post on north syde of the Castlehill, to obstruct all communication betwixt the garrison and its friends in the toun; and the garrison dismounted both ther cannon on the south battery; and the 4th day, shot grenades out of a hand morter peice at ther new post, on the north syde of the Castle-hill. The Lieutennant-Governour proposed to send out a party of sex men to beat them from it, but the Duke had all along declared his aversione of hazarding any of the few men he had, except upon more urgent occassions.

The garrison dismounted one of the besiegers' great guns on the north battery. They kept a guard betwixt a wall, within pistol shott of the new post; had broken ground in 13 or 14 places round the garrison, and fired this day 24 bombs and many cannon. [The same day Captain Dunbar dismounted three of their cannon.]

5th day. The garrison perceaved some of the besiegers posted behind a wall near the West Church; and fyred severall great guns upon them, which made a large breach in the wall; wherupon they fled, and as was thought, left severalls dead and wounded. Therafter they were perceaved throwing up earth at the back of the West Church, (one of ther posts,) and the garrison called to them to make the hole large, supposing they had not a few to bury in it.

This day they threw no bombs.

6th day. [At this time we had taken notice of a more than ordinary concourse of people coming from the west, and flattered ourselves with hopes that his Majesty had landed some forces there, and the rebells were running upon the noise; but this only augmented the number of our disappointments.] They threw one bomb into the garrison, about tuo a'clock in the morning, [which was matter of conjecture to us,] and the garrison fired severall cannon upon their guards at the West Church, and at the back of the toun, near the North Loch, which did execution; as also, whilst the Governour wes at denner, some great guns were fyred, without his knowledge, upon ther guards at the West Port.

7th day. [Colin Sutherland] a private centinell in the garrison, after a tedious sickness, dyed, and 8th day was buryed, with thrie volleys of small shott.

9th day. Now the garrison had no maner of information from the toun, and [our provisions being very near spent, and great part of the garrison sickly,] were longing much for intelligence. But the besiegers, having understood from our deserters, the particular places by which our men got safe out and into the Castle, and having accordingly posted guards to interrupt them, it was reckoned a very difficult task. However severall gentlemen and others offered to adventure out; and one John Grant being pitched upon, was conveyed over the wall opposite to the West Port. He promised to informe himselfe dilligently if ther were any hopes of releefe for the Castle, and to give a signe at a place agried upon, a mile distant, in caice ther were any hopes; and if ther were none, he sould give another different signe, and should retire himselfe to the north of Scotland, least he might be apprehended.

10th day. [Mr Grant gave us on this day a sign from the Long Gate that he was got safe out, and would return the next day.]

The garrison observed the solemnity of the day for the birth of the Prince of Wales; and a litle after midnight,' the besiegers began again to play with ther bombes, haveing remained peaceable neighbours from the 4th day, save one they fired on the sixth.

The same night Mr Gardine, with six men, sallyed out without the Duke's order, and chaced ther enemies from ther posts on the Castle-hill.

11th day. John Grant appeared at the place appointed, and gave the signall, by which the Governour and the officers understood ther was no hopes of succours. Therfore not haveing receaved any letter from tlie King, or any that appeared for his Majestie, except that from Tyrconnell, when the garrison was first blocked up, and that not directed to him, nor any order at all in it regarding the Castle; and the messenger (probably out of his own head,) said only, that within sex weeks Tyrconnell would send releefe; and it was now thrie months since that promise, which, in reality, was never made : for when Tyrconnell went to St Germans, after the battell at the Boyn Water in Ireland, he denyed to the Duke of Gordon himselfe that ever he promised any such thing, nor wes he truely in a condition to send him such forces as could releeve him. And it was about a month afterwards that only 500 Irish, instead of the pretended 20,000 landed in the Highlands, of whom the garrison knew nothing at this tyme, they not being yet embarqued at Knockfergus.

2do. Att the conference with the Viscount of Dundie, the Duke did not condescend how long he could keep out the Castle, tho its said Dundie promised releife within 20 days; and now after thrie months, nether he nor others who stood for the King were in a condition to give any releife at all.

3rd. The soldiers deserting so frequently, leaping over the walls; and the last deserters having given information to the enemies of the condition of the Castle, and of its scarcity of provisions and ammunition, which made them set up the Orange flag, and stop all correspondence from friends in the toun.

4th. There were more as twenty men sick in the garrison, and ther number was daylie encreassing, and scarse fourty healthfull to doe duty. From the first tyme the besiegers began to play with their bombs, there were not men sufficient upon duty to releeve the night centinells, so that some were best able to endure hardship, stood from 10 at night to tuo or thrie in the morning; and besides ther were often men constantly employed in ditching, scoureing, raiseing, or removing batteries, as was thought neidfull.

5th. The water of the garrison was very bad, and a great part of the cause of so many sick men, which in short tyme would have disabled the rest, reduced to drink therof for want of better liquor.

6th. There were not victualls for 10 days, save bread and salt herrings.

7th. The ammunitions were near spent.

8th. All other things necessary were wanting; no coalls nor wood, save the wrack of buildings brocken doun by the bombes.

Upon thes considerations it was judged fitt to beat a parIey, in order to capitulate. About 6 a'clock the white flag was put out, and Major Somervell, with another of the besiegers officers, came to the draw-bridge befoir the Castle gate, but made some scrouple to advance further. So the Duke stood at one end of the bridge with the Lieuetennant-Governour, and Major Somervell with ther officers at the other.

The first thing proposed was as to the person with whom the Governour might safely treate, and who could give security for performance of articles. Duke Hamilton, commissioner for the Parliament (made up) of the Convention, or of the Convention transfigured into a Parliament, after the example of England) wes named. But the Governour desired to sie his commission, he not being oblidged to know of that transfiguration. So the Major went for further instructions, and in a short tyme returned with Major-General Lanier, the Lord Colchester ane English nobleman, and Collonell Balfour. Then the exchange of hostages was under consideratione. They demanded the Lieuetennant-Governour, and ofiered Major Somervell, which the Duke would not condescend to, but offered Mr Gairdin for a gentleman of lyke quality and fortune.

Whilst this was under debate, came a message from Duke Hamilton, nether to give nor to take hostages, but to treat without that formality. So the treaty ended this night, and lykewise the cessation; for incontinently the besiegers fyred thrie great guns on the Castle, which answered them with as many, and afterwards ther was warm fireing on both sides.

12th day. This morning the treatty began againe [and before they entered upon any terms of surrender, the besiegers went for further instructions upon preliminaries]. But John Grant, takeing the opportunity of the cessation, came imprudently, contrary to his instructions, into the garrison, which made the Governour think he had gott some good newes since the tyme he gave the signall; but upon examination he could say no more than that ther were noe hopes of releeflfe.

Major-Generall Lanier, knowing of his entry, and pretending it was a breach of the treaty, declared he would break off the same unless he were delivered up to him, which the Governour refused; and the treaty was brocken off, which made those of the garrison understand they should have but a very bad composition with the enemies.

Major Sommervell insisted, that the Duke ought to meet Sir John Lanier halfe way betwixt the tovn and castle; but the gentlemen in garrison opposed it; and somewhat too hotly reflecting on the treachery of ther centinells. Major Somervell said, that Lanier would not break his word for sex tymes the value of the castle; and the Ensigne of the garrison replyed, that he had brocken his word, and oath too, to a much better man than any upon the place (viz. the King), [and, for any thing he knew, for a less reward].

Then the major threatning man and child with the sword in caice the treaty held not, Mr Gairdin replyed, that ther men must have greater courage, and those of the garrison less, befoir it came to that. Severall other tairt expressions were used, and then they parted; and shortly therafter one of ther Ensignes came up and discharged any further treating. Then they condemned Lieuetennant Hay and Joannet Cunniughame to be put to death, for corresponding with the Castle, and haveing bein in the same.

The Governour, with Captaine Dumbar, proposed to Collonell Winram Lieuetennant-Governour, to Mr Winchester Ensigne, and Mr Gairdin Volunteer, a means to eschew the cruelty of the enemyes; which was, to put themselves on head of thes soldiers in the garrison, who were vigorous and had courage to hazard; and, in the night tyme, to force ther passage to the sea side, not tuo myles distant, and ther to seaze some boat, and get over to the other side. For the example of Sir William Kirkaldy of Grange was not of so old date as it could not be remembered. This gentleman was Governour of the Castle of Edinburgh for Queen Mary, after her rebellious subjects had forced her to renunce the government, and threatned her with death and infamy, while they keept her prissoner in the Castle of Lochleven; and, having bravely defended it for the space of 33 days, against the continuall battery of 30 brass cannons, and frequent assaults of the besiegers, was at last forced to render the same and themselves to the mercy of ther enemyes, and of Queen Elizabeth of England, who willed Grange, his brother, and two citizens of Edinburgh, to be publickly hanged on the mercat place. However, that proposall of the Duke's to escape by the sea seemed too dangerous, and not to be put in practice unless the enemies refused to grant the safety of lyves.

About eight a'clock at night, the Govemour having called the garrison togither, told them, that according to his promise, he had begun a treaty of capitulation, which was unexpectedly brocken of; and desired, if any man's heart failled him, he might declare it, and he should have liberty to be gone: He put them in mynd how fyve rogues had lately deserted (last of May), and gone over the walls, when they might have had patent gates, and how infamous they were even with the enemy.

Therupon all the garrison unanimously declaired ther resolutions of liveing upon bread and water with his Grace. Then he added. Perhaps some may be ashamed to own ther fears before a company of resolute men; but if soe, let any man who hes ane inclination to leave the garrison tell me in private, and I will find out a passage for him; and, gentlemen, for you that will live with me, I shall be ready to dy with you, if it come to that, you may take my word on't; which was answered with huzzas.

The besiegers had, ever since the treaty was brocken of, fyred smartly on the garrison from all ther batteries and posts about it; and about eleven at night a body of them were perceaved advanceing towards it on the north syde of the Castle-hill; and when they were come near the ditch, thos from the Castle fired on them so smartly as that they were forced to a disorderly retreat. Their officers were heard calling out, Advance, dogs; and the garrison mocked them, saying, Ye dogs, will not you obey your officers? Then they were perceaved rolling packs of wool up the Castle-hill, with intention to place a battery midway betwixt the toun and Castle; and the garrison directed their shot to that place. All upon duty behaved themselves with great courage. Ther were but 19 men, commanders and commanded, upon the low guard, and they would have no reinforcement; and so litle was their fear of the enemies bombes, that they still returned them great and small shot while those machines of terrour were flyeing above their heads, and sung aloud at all posts, When the King shall enjoy his oun againe. Mr Gardine was Captaine of the guard this night; Henry Gordon commandit a post in the low halfe moon; John Falconer another at the centinell's box near the low guard-house; a Serjeant and corporall within Creichton's yeard, and John [James] Gordon of Edintore at the portcullice. The mutuall fireing continued from 12 a'clock at night till past tuo a'clock in the morning, and one of the gunners of the Castle was killed by a musquet shott throw a gun-port.

13th day. The garrison fired warmly at the besiegers' men posted behind the wool packs on the Castle-hill, till about sex a'clock, that they relented to menadge ther powder, having spent last night and the morneing 12 or 13 barrells of powder; at which rate in sex dayes they would not have had one barrell remaining.

One of the Governour's cooks was shot thorow the body, but yet not mortally wounded. The Governour, though indisposed, omitted not to visit the posts with all solicitude, and to observe what the enemies had done; and found ther lodgments advanced on the Castle- hill. Coll. Winram said to him, It were fitt to write a line to desire the enemies to renew the treaty. He answered, the nixt session of the Convention was to be expected, and that he would not beginne againe to treat till John Grant, who had been the occassion of the intermission, should be gone out of the Castle, least he should be oblidged to delyver him up. A short tyme after, the Governour is advertised that he was gone, and Collonell Winram renewes the instance of writing, and offers to carry the letter. The Governour writes to Major-Generall Lanier; and Collonell Winram gives the letter to Captaine Moody, who commanded the besiegers' guards, and desired to speak with the Governour. He, after some difficulty, condescends, and the Captaine brings with him the Lord Colchester, at which the Governour was surprysed, finding them employ a stranger, wher they had so many countreymen.

To them he gave the articles, which were drawn up the day before, with consent of all the officers, in the following termes.

The Duke of Gordon hath so much respect for all the Princes of King James the Sexth's line, as not to make conditions with any of them for his own particular interes : so he renders himselfe entirely on King William's discretion.

Ito. That Collonell Winram, Lieutennant-Governour of the Castle, shall submitt himselfe to King William's pleasure, his lyfe being secured; and all the rest of the garison shall have ther lyves, libertyes, and fortunes secured; and lykewise passports shall be granted to those who will take oaths not to bear armes against the present government.

2do. The garrison shall be allowed to march out with ther swords and bagage belonging properly to themselves.

3to. That all the gentlemen, voluntiers, servants, and others within the garrison, shall have the same capitulation with the rest of the garrison.

4to. That all maner of persons shall have the benefite of the first article, who have keept correspondence with the Castle, and who have not been in armes; and being at present in Edinburgh, or in the same county, shall be indemnifyed, and have the benefite of this capitulation.

5to. That sick soldiers shall have liberty to dispose of themselves as they shall thinke best, they behaveing themselves as becometh.

6to. That all officers, gentlemen, servants, and others, shall have the same benefite which other lieges have, they living peaceably.

7to. A considerable post within the Castle shall be immediatly, after security is granted to the garrison for the above written articles, put in possession of the forces imder Major-General Lanier.

That the garrison should march out with drmns beating, and displayed banners, which is ane ordinary article in capitulation, the Duke thought not fit to require it; that being only used in countries where the soldiers of the capitulating garrison may march with a guard of thier enemies to another garrison of ther own Prince; which could not hold in this caice. And, besides, it had happened in former tymes at the surrendering of this Castle, that the garrison therof marching doun the streits in that maner, the rable insulted over them, and this occasions slaughter and effusion of blood, which was to be evited.

He professed a particular respect for King James the Sext of Scotland and First of England, because of the particular affection that King had for his family. For although the Kings before and after him had still lookt upon it as the most faithfull and steadable friend to the Crovm, yet the affection King James had towards it was more than ordinary, and most endearing. For finding the reformers of religion too imperial and impertinent pedagogues for a King, he made use of the Marquis of Huntly to keep them within some bounds, whose power and following could help much to counterpoise theirs; and whose zeale for the royall interest would spare nether lyfe nor fortune to obey his commands, which were intimate to him by private letters, written with the King's own hand in a most oblidging straine.

About thrie a'clock in the afternoon, the Lord Colchester returnes to the Castle gate, where the Duke and the Lieutennant-Governor received him. He rendered to the Governour the articles he had received from him in the morning, and at the same tyme delyvered to him other articles drawen up by Major-Generall Lanier, which were very disadvantageous, and by which he would have the Governour and Lieuetennant-Governour to remaine prissoners of

241

warr. Colchester went away after he had given these new articles to the Governour; and within a short tyme therafter returned, and brought word, that all the volunteers and soldiers of the garrison should not losse a penny, and might retire themselves to any place of the kingdome they pleased; that the Lieuetennant-Governour sould have lyfe and fortune safe; and as to the Governour, since he would make no conditions for himselfe, he sould remaine prissoner of warr at the discretion of the Prince of Orange.

The garrison had difficulty to part with the Castle upon any terms, much like one who losses a suite at law by the sentence of the supreame judicatory : Although the evidences and grounds of the sentence convince all unconcerned persons of the justice therof, yet he cannot hinder himselfe from regrateing the losse of what he wes desireous and hopefull to retaine; so, these stout and loyall gentlemen and soldiers found the surrender of ther Castle very unpleasant to ther spirits, and ther frettings and regrates gave occassion to some of the Duke of Gordon's enemies, to blame him for the surrender of it; and not knowing why he would not make any conditions for himselfe, to suspect his loyalty. But all impartial and equitable persons will easily justify him, if they consider, that although he and his garrison might have for a short tyme keept in their lyves with water instead of drink, and coarse oatmeale for bread, and old salt herrings for all kynd of kitchin; and even therof they had no quantity to last long; yet not having powder for 8 dayes of so hott service as the last day, wherin they spent betwixt 12 and 13 barrels; and not having men sufficient to furnish all the posts, nor sure of the fidelity of a great part of thes they had; when that powder should have bein spent, which the enemies nearer approaches and constant fireing would have made be very soon, they might have remained incapable to hinder the besiegers from comeing over ther walls, and ther persons and lyves had been at the dis- poseall of ther mercy.

Common prudence, therfoire, not allowing the Governour to let matters come to this extremity, he thought fitt to accept of the conditions brought by the Lord Colchester, and so all acts of hostility ceassed.

The garrison having now a frie comunication with the besiegers' forces, these acknowledged to have sustained a considerable loss the night preceiding, and that many of ther men had deserted upon that accompt.

About 10 a'clock at night, Major Somervell marched with 200 men into the Castle, and had all the posts therin delyvered to him, except the high guard hall, and great court, which those of the garrison keept. Afterwards, the Governour haveing drawen them up in the court, he told them that he must oun they had served him faithfully, and he knew not wherin he had been unkynd to them; but, if he had wronged any, he desired them to speak, and they should have reparation; and entreated them not to make any disturbance with the other soldiers now come into the garrison, for they were too few to conquer, and too many to be made a sacrifice. He gave each of the centinells some money to bear their charges home. This night Captaine Dumbar, Mr Scot, and some others who had more particularly incurred the displeasure of the rable, went privatlie to the toun.

14 June. Three full months after the siege began, the garrison marched out, but not in a body, that they might be the less noticed; yet some of them were very ill treated by the rable; and Major-General Lanier took possession of the gates of the Castle, which the Duke of Gordon had keept, in obedience to his lawful Soveraigne, after all Great Brittaine had renunced it, save a few that appeared for him with the Viscount of Dundie.

NOTES
[1] whilst the besiegers were at the height of their fury, we perceived a large clout, of an orange colour, mounted on their north battery ; and rationally concluded it to be the frolic of some young spark- errant, who had procured an old petticoat from his lady mistress, and kept in view to inspire him with courage to commence hero for her sake ; rather than any emblem of terror to us, or right on the besiegers' side.

Bibliography

Considerable attention has been paid in recent years to what is termed the 'Highland Problem' in the seventeenth century, and the work of Bruce Lenman, David Stevenson and Paul Hopkins is pre-eminent in this field. The latter in particular, in his *Glencoe and the end of the Highland War* (John Donald 1989) successfully weaves both that 'problem' and the wider political issues into a greater whole and provides essential reading. John Prebble's classic account of *Glencoe* is highly readable, but his conclusions are questionable.

Almack, Edward, *The history of the Second dragoons: 'Royal Scots greys'* (London. 1908)

Atholl, John, Duke of, *Chronicles of the Atholl and Tullibardine Families* (Edinburgh, 1908)

Balcarres, Colin, Earl of, *Memoirs touching the Revolution in Scotland*, ed. Lord Lindsay (Bannatyne Club, Edinburgh, 1841)

Balhaldie, J. Drummond of, *Memoirs of Sir Ewen Cameron of Locheil* (1842)

Burnet, G., *A History of his own time* (6 vols. Oxford, 1833)

Cannon, Richard, *Historical Record of the Royal Regiment of Scots Dragoons* (Longman, Orme & C. London, 1840)

Chiefs of Grant, The, *Sir Wm Fraser* (3 vols. Edinburgh, 1883)

Crichton, Andrew, *The Life and Diary of Lieut. Col. J. Blackader: Of the Cameronian Regiment* (H.S. Baynes, Edinburgh 1828)

Dalton, Charles, *The Scots Army 1661-1688* (William Brown, Edinburgh, 1909)

Dalton, Charles, *English Army Lists and Commission Registers 1660-1714* (6 vols. London 1892-1904)

Fergusson, J. *Papers Illustrating the History of the Scots Brigade in the Service of the United Netherlands* (Scottish History Society, Edinburgh 1898)

The Graemid, ed Rev, A.D. Murdoch (Scottish History Society, Edinburgh 1888)

Grant, James *The Old Scots Navy from 1689 to 1710* (Navy Records Society, London 1914)

Highland Papers Vol IV (Scottish History Society 3rd Series, Edinburgh 1934)

Hopkins, Paul, *Glencoe and the End of the Highland War* (John Donald, Edinburgh 1986)

Innes, M.(ed.), *The Black Book of Taymouth* (Bannatyne Club, Edinburgh 1855)

Lawson, C.C.P. *History of the Uniforms of the British Army* (Kaye Ward, London 1969)

Lenman, Bruce, *The Jacobite Clans of the Great Glen 1650-1784* (Methuen, London 1884)

Livingstone, Thomas, *A true and real account of the defeat of General Buchan and Brigadeer Cannon, their High-land Army, at the Battel of Crombdell upon the 1st of May; 1690. In a Letter from Sir Thomas Livingstone to General Mackay* (Edinburgh, 1690)

Mackay, H., *Memoirs of the War carried on in Scotland and Ireland 1689-1691* (1833)

Mackay, William, *Urquhart and Glenmoriston; a Highland Parish in the Olden Time* (Northern Counties Press, Inverness 1914)

Minute Book of the Managers of the New Mills Cloth Manufactory (Scottish History Society, Edinburgh, 1903)

Prebble, John, *Glencoe; the story of the Massacre* (Secker and Waeburg, London, 1966)

Register of the Privy Council of Scotland. 3rd Series, Vol. 14 (1689-1689)

Scott, C.L. *The Armies and Uniforms of the Monmouth Rebellion* (Partizan, Leigh on Sea, 2008)

Shaw, Lachlan, *History of the Province of Moray* (New Edition Thomas D. Morrison, Glasgow, 1882).

Stevenson, Dr. David, *Alasdair MacColla and the Highland Problem in the Seventeenth Century.* (John Donald, Edinburgh 1980)

Stewart,of Garth, David, *Sketches of the Highlanders of Scotland* (Edinburgh 1822)

Terry, Charles Sandford, *The Pentland Rising and Rullion Green* (Maclehose & Son, Glasgow 1905)

Terry, Charles Sandford *John Graham of Claverhouse, Viscount Dundee* (London 1905)

Tomasson, Katherine and Buist, Francis *Battles of the '45* (Batsford, London 1962)

Walton, Clifford; *History of the British Standing Army 1660-1700* (Harrison and Sons, London 1894)

Articles

Dr. Paul Hopkins: *Loup Hill. 16th May 1689: The First "Battle" of Dundee's Jacobite War.* Kintyre Antiquarian and Natural History Magazine 1998 no.18 June 1998 and no.19 July 1998

Stevenson and Caldwell *Leather Guns and other Light Artillery in mid-17th Century Scotland*, Proceedings of the Society of Antiquaries of Scotland 108

C.V. Wedgewood, *"Anglo Scottish Relations 1603-1640"* Transactions of the Royal Historical Society 4th Series vol.xxxii (1950)

Index